Modern Japan's Place in Worl

Masayuki Yamauchi • Yuichi Hosoya
Editors

Modern Japan's Place in World History

From Meiji to Reiwa

 Springer

Editors
Masayuki Yamauchi
Institute for Global Affairs
Musashino University
Tokyo, Japan

Yuichi Hosoya
Faculty of Law
Keio University
Tokyo, Japan

Translated by
Keith Krulak
Washington, DC, USA

ISBN 978-981-19-9595-8   ISBN 978-981-19-9593-4   (eBook)
https://doi.org/10.1007/978-981-19-9593-4

Translation from the Japanese language edition: "Nihon Kingendaishi Kōgi - Seikō to Shippai no Rekishi ni Manabu" by Masayuki Yamauchi and Yuichi Hosoya, © Masayuki Yamauchi, Yuichi Hosoya 2019. Published by CHUOKORON-SHINSHA. INC. All Rights Reserved.

Cover image: The Portsmouth Peace Treaty, Japanese and Russian delegations in discussion
© The Mainichi Newspapers

This Springer imprint is published by the registered company Springer Nature Singapore Pte Ltd.
The registered company address is: 152 Beach Road, #21-01/04 Gateway East, Singapore 189721, Singapore

Introduction

History as an "Enormously Rich Resource"

Political leaders are lonely people. Where can they possibly turn when they must make difficult decisions? Will their decisions turn out to be the best in that situation? Might there be any other options? Being human, political leaders naturally are beset by such uncertainties and hardships. We all have uncertainties, worries, and regrets because we cannot predict the future. And so, what should those in positions of responsibility rely on when they are pressed to make important political decisions?

Professor Ernest R. May, of Harvard University's Department of History, took note of decision makers who, when confronting challenges, gleaned lessons from history by referencing past examples. As he put it, "Potentially, history is an enormously rich resource for people who govern." And yet, "such people usually draw upon this resource haphazardly or thoughtlessly." Meanwhile, "[b]y and large, those of us professionally occupied in teaching and writing history have put out little effort to help them" (May 2004).

May wrote these words in 1973, nearly half a century ago, recounting the misfortunes caused by failing to learn "lessons from the past." Little has changed since then, I think: many political leaders, perhaps too busy with the many tasks before them, make no effort to utilize the "enormously rich resource" of history; historians, too, still "put out little effort to help them." Politicians and historians share a mutual disinterest. They live out their respective lives, each according to their own rationale, enclosed in their own cocoons.

Is the ongoing neglect of such an enormously rich resource really alright? Wouldn't better policies be made by using this rich resource? What a waste it is to turn a blind eye to this enormously rich resource when it is right in front of us.

In fact, there is an example of a history book that brought politicians and historians together by a quirk of fate, thereby saving a country from crisis.

It was the Cuban Missile Crisis of 1962.

A History Book That Changed World History

Young US President John F. Kennedy was advancing preparations for war in order to stop the emplacement of Soviet nuclear missiles in Cuba. War was inevitable, it was believed; it was too late to turn back.

To help inform his decision-making, Kennedy turned to Barbara W. Tuchman's *The Guns of August*, a history book published that January. He finished it in a sitting during a stretch of days harried by nonstop challenges. In her book, Tuchman faithfully describes the process by which, following a series of mistakes and miscalculations, Europe's leaders dove headlong into World War I, a war none of them wanted, as though stumbling and falling from a mountain path (Tuchman 2004).

Indeed, I wonder if we aren't in a similar situation now ourselves. Nuclear war with the Soviets isn't inevitable; we could avoid it through the power of our political decisions, couldn't we? Likely thinking along such lines, Kennedy reconsidered the existing policies that had been deemed irreversible and made a bold policy shift toward dialogue with Soviet Premier Nikita Khrushchev, thereby avoiding a war.

It is generally believed that there are no "what-ifs" in history. Yet, the world might have experienced a nuclear war if Kennedy had not read Tuchman's book then. This was a case of one history book that changed the fate of world history. Kennedy, it is said, gave a copy of the book as a gift to British Prime Minister Harold Macmillan during his visit to the United States in February 1962. It probably left a deep impression on Kennedy, influencing him as no book had before.

On the other hand, it does not mean that politicians have always learned so much from the lessons of history. Thus, Professor May wrote the following:

> Men and women making decisions under conditions of high uncertainty necessarily envision the future partly in terms of what they believe to have in the past. Their understanding of the present is shaped by what they think to have gone on before. Often, their knowledge of what in fact occurred earlier is shallow and faulty, and deficiencies in information breed greater deficiencies and reasoning. (May ibid.)

Professor May's harsh words suggest that there is a danger of political leaders misusing history. To put it another way, he is sounding the alarm about the dangers of politicians who misuse history owing to biased knowledge about past precedents as well as those who will not learn the lessons of history from the enormously rich resource. We must be mindful of the reality that, even when we learn something from past precedents, there are many conflicting and contradictory examples and lessons. We must seek, above all, a sense of balance and a broad scope for deciding among various examples comprehensively, rather than arbitrarily invoking past examples that appeal to us. It is easier said than done. Dealing with history demands prudence and caution.

In this volume that you hold in your hands, we have studied the modern history of Japan since the Meiji period. This history is the path chosen by Japanese politicians, a road not straight or simple, one of any number of possibilities with complex dynamics at work. The crucial thing is, first, to study this previous path they took without any preconceptions and to learn what kind of choices they made.

So, have we become any wiser? Have we gained keener foresight? As we write new history going forward, it will be indispensable to revisit history repeatedly, confirm the path our predecessors have walked thus far, and to understand their options and the difficulties of their decisions.

This book is based on a series of lectures that a group called "Study History, Consider the Future" conducted at the Liberal Democratic Party's (LDP) headquarters from December 2015 to July 2018. The contents of those lectures were then compiled and edited into a small paperback book. The group had been established on October 29, 2015, at a ceremony to commemorate the 60th anniversary of the LDP's founding.

We have focused on two important new trends in this study of modern Japanese history. First, we are all aware of the importance of placing modern Japanese history within a broader global perspective. Modern Japan had been deeply integrated in international society. Even as it was influenced by the international political currents of the time, Japan had also affected the course of modern global history. If the Russo-Japanese War had not happened or had Japan not attacked Pearl Harbor, surely the outlook of the world we would have seen would be radically different. As you shall read, the interaction between Japanese history and global history has generally been at the heart of the arguments in each chapter of this book.

Second, historical research should be liberated from exceedingly ideological orientations both in the right wing and in the left wing that we have seen among Japanese historians. Even granting that some sort of link between the historical past and current political tides is inevitable, our historical interpretations should not be biased by these political ideologies, as we have frequently seen them in historical research in postwar Japan.

The group was set up with LDP Secretary-General Tanigaki Sadakazu as chair, LDP Policy Research Council Chairwoman Inada Tomomi as vice-chair, Upper House Diet member Nakasone Hirofumi as director, and Lower House Diet member Tanahashi Yasufumi as executive secretary.[1] We held the first session on December 22, with Masayuki Yamauchi (professor emeritus of the University of Tokyo) and me (Yuichi Hosoya) acting as advisors; former Cabinet Office Administrative Vice Minister Matsumoto Takashi and sociologist Furuichi Noritoshi attended as observers. Meetings continued over the following 3 years, and the chairmanship passed to LDP Vice President Kōmura Masahiko and then on to LDP Executive Acting Secretary-General Shimomura Hakubun. This book reached publication based on the notes and conclusions of these meetings. Throughout this process, we received a great deal of assistance, especially from Mr. Fukutomi Ken'ichi of the LDP Headquarters staff. We would like to take this opportunity to offer all of them our sincere thanks.

It is our great hope that we might contribute to a deeper and broader historical understanding in Japan through this book, which uses the most advanced, up-to-date

---

[1] All positions are as of the time of the meetings.

academic research. We would be deeply gratified if even one of our readers were to take part in this richly stimulating intellectual activity.

Bibliography: For Further Reading

May, Ernest R. Shindō, Eiichi (trans). 2004. *Rekishi no kyōkun: amerika gaikō wa dō tsukurareta ka* (Lessons from History: How was American Diplomacy Made?). Tokyo: Iwanami Gendai Bunko. [Originally published as: May, Ernest R. 1973. *"Lessons" of the Past: the Use and Misuse of History in American Foreign Policy.* New York: Oxford University Press.]

Tuchman, Barbara W. Yamamuro, Mariya (trans). 2004. *Hachigatsu no hōsei. jōgekan* (Gunfire in August [Two volumes]). Chikuma Gakugei Bunko. [Originally published as: Tuchman, Barbara W. 1962. *The Guns of August.* New York: Random House Publishers.]

Faculty of Law, Keio University   Yuichi Hosoya
Tokyo, Japan

Translation Notes

Except for the editors and author's own name as book editors or chapter authors, the names of Japanese, Chinese and Korean individuals are in traditional order, with family name followed by given name. In the text, Japanese names have macrons to indicate long vowels; common place names, such as Tokyo, Osaka, and Kyoto, do not. Chinese names are in pinyin, except for a few widely known to English readers in alternate romanizations, i.e.: Chiang Kai-shek (pinyin: Jiang Jieshi), Sun Yat-sen (Sun Yixian), and the delegates to Paris Peace Conference. Similarly, Chinese place names are in modern pinyin (e.g.: Beijing not "Peking"; Lüshun not "Port Arthur"; Guangdong not "Canton"), though the Yangtze River (pinyin: Chiang Jiang) as well as references to Mukden (also known as Fengtian, present-day Shenyang) and Japan's Kwantung (Kantō) Army (named after its garrison location, Guandong, or Kantō in Japanese) are retained for greater familiarity for the English reader.

Footnotes are comments by the translator intended to provide additional background to the English reader.

Acknowledgments

The original Japanese edition of this book was published in 2019 by Chukoshinsho (Chuokoron-Shinsha, Inc.), thanks to the total dedication of the publishing editor Mr. Ono Kazuo. We are also very grateful to Mr. Keith Krulak, who spent numerous hours translating the Japanese text into English, frequently referring to original or primary sources to get to the core meaning of the text. We would also like to thank the external advisors who tirelessly advised on this English edition, as well as Mr. Anthony Head, the copyeditor who polished the English expressions, and all the people related to this English edition, for their assistance. Above all, we are especially grateful to Ms. Kawakami Juno, senior editor at Springer, without whom this English translation could not have been published.

We were very fortunate to have leading historians in Japan as contributors to this volume. They have published excellent works on Japan's place in the world in the Japanese language, which cannot easily be read by non-Japanese readers. Therefore, we are delighted that the fruits of all their historical studies can now be shared with this English translation. We firmly believe that this book will contribute to the canon of academic research on modern Japanese history.

Masayuki Yamauchi
Yuichi Hosoya

Contents

Editors and Contributors

About the Editors

Masayuki Yamauchi (山内 昌之) (Afterword) Specially appointed professor affiliated with the Musashino University Institute for Global Affairs, visiting professor at the Mohammed V University in Morocco, and professor emeritus of the University of Tokyo. Born in Sapporo in 1947, he completed a doctoral course at the Hokkaido University Graduate School of Humanities and Human Sciences, but obtained his Doctor of Philosophy degree from the University of Tokyo. Awarded the Medal with Purple Ribbon and Shiba Ryotaro Prize, he is the author of many award-winning books, including *The Dream of Sultan Galiev: The Islamic World and the Russian Revolution* (Suntory Prize for Social Sciences and Humanities); *Radical History* (Yoshino Sakuzō Prize); *The Dying Leviathan: Perestroika and the Nationalities Question in Soviet Central Asia* (Mainichi Publication Cultural Prize); and *The Iwanami Encyclopedia of Islam* (co-editor; Mainichi Publication Cultural Prize).

Yuichi Hosoya (細谷 雄一) (Introduction, Chapter 3) Professor of International Politics of the Faculty of Law at Keio University. Born in Chiba Prefecture in 1971, he studied international politics at Rikkyo (BA), Birmingham (MIS), and Keio (Ph. D.). He was a visiting professor and Japan Chair (2009–2010) at Sciences-Po in Paris (Institut d'Études Politiques), a visiting fellow (Fulbright Fellow, 2008–2009) at Princeton University, and Visiting Fellow at Downing College, the University of Cambridge (2021-2022). His research interests include the postwar international history, British diplomatic history, Japanese foreign and security policy, and contemporary East Asian international politics. His most recent publications include *Security Politics: Legislation for a New Security Environment* (Tokyo: JPIC, 2019); *History, Memory & Politics in Postwar Japan* (Co-editor, Lynne Rienner: Boulder, 2020); and "Japan's Security Policy in East Asia," in Yul Sohn and T.J. Pempel (eds.), *Japan and Asia's Contested Order: The Interplay of Security, Economics, and Identity* (Palgrave, 2018).

About the Contributors

Yoshinobu Higurashi (日暮 吉延) (Chapter 10) Professor of the Faculty of Law at Teikyo University. Born in Tokyo in 1962, he received his Doctor of Philosophy (Political Science) degree from the Graduate School of Political Science at Gakushuin University. He is the author of several books, including *The Tokyo Trial and International Relations: Power and Norms in International Politics* (Yoshida Shigeru Prize); *The Tokyo Trial* (Suntory Prize for Social Sciences and Humanities) [published in English as *The Tokyo Trial: War Criminals and Japan's Postwar International Relations*]; and *Records of War Crime Tribunals: Mainly Related to the Tokyo Trials* (supervising editor).

Masaya Inoue (井上 正也) (Chapter 12) Professor of the Faculty of Law at Keio University. Born in Osaka Prefecture in 1979, he received his Doctor of Philosophy (Political Science) degree from the Graduate School of Law and Politics at Kobe University. He is the author of *A Political History of Sino-Japanese Normalization* (Yoshida Shigeru Prize and the Suntory Prize for Social Sciences and Humanities) and *The Biography of Fukuda Takeo: In Search of Prosperity and Stability in Postwar Japan (co-author)*, among other works.

Shin Kawashima (川島 真) (Chapter 5) Professor of the Graduate School of Arts and Sciences at the University of Tokyo. Born in Tokyo in 1968, he received his Doctor of Philosophy (Literature) degree from the Graduate School of Humanities and Sociology at the University of Tokyo. He is the author of *The Formation of Modern Chinese Diplomacy* (Suntory Prize for Social Sciences and Humanities); *Series on China's Modern History (Vol. 2): Groping for a Modern State: 1894-1912*; *China in the 21st Century*; *Frontier of China*; and other works.

Kan Kimura (木村 幹) (Chapter 11) Professor of the Graduate School of International Cooperation Studies at Kobe University. Born in Osaka Prefecture in 1966, he obtained his Doctor of Philosophy (Law) degree from the Graduate School of Law at Kyoto University. He is the author of *Korean Nationalism as a Small Nation* (Asia-Pacific Award Special Prize); *The Establishment of the Authoritarian System in South Korea* (Suntory Prize for Social Sciences and Humanities); and *The Burden of the Past: Problems of Historical Perception in Japan-Korea Relations* [in English].

Michihiko Kobayashi (小林 道彦) (Chapter 6) Professor emeritus of the University of Kitakyushu. Born in Saitama Prefecture in 1956, he completed the doctoral course of the Chuo University Graduate School of Humanities, but he obtained his Doctor of Philosophy (Law) degree from Kyoto University. He is the author of several works, including *Japan's Continental Policy, 1895-1914: Katsura Tarō and Gotō Shinpei*; *The Collapse of Party Cabinets and the Manchurian Incident: 1918-1932* (Yoshida Shigeru Prize); *Kodama Gentarō: Can You See Port Arthur from There?;* and *Beyond the Historical Awareness of Japan-China Relations* (co-editor; Ōhira Masayoshi Memorial Special Prize).

Ken Kotani (小谷 賢) (Chapter 7) Professor of the College of Risk Management at Nihon University. Born in Kyoto Prefecture in 1973, he obtained his Doctor of Philosophy (Human and Environmental Studies) degree from the Graduate School of Human and Environmental Studies at Kyoto University. He has written several books, including *British Intelligence and Diplomacy: What is Intelligence?*; *Japanese Military Intelligence: Why is Intelligence Not Used?* (Yamamoto Shichihei Prize) [published in English as *Japanese Intelligence in World War II*]; *Mossad: A Sixty-Year History of Covert Maneuvering and Struggle*; *Intelligence: How Should the State and its Institutions Collect Information*; and *The World History of Intelligence: from World War II to the Snowden Affair*.

Ayako Kusunoki (楠 綾子) (Chapter 9) Professor of the International Research Center for Japan Studies. Born in Kobe in 1973, she obtained her Doctor of Philosophy (Political Science) degree from the School of Law at Kobe University. She has authored *Yoshida Shigeru and the Making of Japan's Postwar Security Policy: the Interaction of Ideas for Peace and Stability between the United States and Japan, 1943-1952* and *History of Modern Japanese Politics, Vol. 1: From Occupation to Independence, 1945-1952*, among other writings.

Atsushi Moriyama (森山 優) (Chapter 8) Professor of the School of International Relations at the University of Shizuoka. Born in Fukuoka City in 1962, he obtained his Doctor of Philosophy (Literature) degree from the School of Letters at Kyushu University. He is the author of *The Political Process of Japan's Decision-making for the US-Japan War*; *Why Japan Decided to Enter the War with the US*; and *Intelligence War before the Japan-US War, 1941*.

Hiroshi Nakanishi (中西 寛) (Chapter 13) Professor of the Graduate School of Law at Kyoto University. Born in Osaka Prefecture in 1962, he received a Master of Law degree at the Graduate School of Law at Kyoto University. He has authored several works, including *What Is International Politics? People and Order in the Global Community* (Yomiuri Yoshino Sakuzō Prize); *Beyond the Historical Awareness of Japan-China Relations* (co-editor; Ōhira Masayoshi Memorial Special Prize); *International Political Science* (co-author); and *Kōsaka Masataka and Postwar Japan* (co-editor).

Sōchi Naraoka (奈良岡 聰智) (Chapter 4) Professor of the Graduate School of Law at Kyoto University. Born in Aomori Prefecture in 1975, he received his Doctor of Philosophy (Law) degree from the Graduate School of Law at Kyoto University. He is the author of several books, including *Katō Takaaki and Party Politics: The Road to a Two-Party System* (Yoshida Shigeru Prize) and *What is the Historical Meaning of the 21 Demands? World War I and the Origin of Sino-Japanese Conflict* (Suntory Prize for Social Sciences and Humanities; Asia-Pacific Award Grand Prize).

Takashi Okamoto (岡本 隆司) (Chapter 2) Professor of the Faculty of Letters at Kyoto Prefectural University. Born in Kyoto in 1965, he obtained his Doctor of Philosophy (Literature) degree from the Graduate School of Letters at Kyoto University. He has authored several works, including *China and the Maritime Customs System in Modern Times* (Ōhira Masayoshi Memorial Prize); *Between Dependency and Sovereignty: Early Modern Qing-Korean Relations and the Destiny of East Asia* (Suntory Prize for Social Sciences and Humanities); and *The Birth of China: International Relations and the Formation of a Nation in Modern East Asia* (Asia-Pacific Award Special Prize).

Kazuhiro Takii (瀧井 一博) (Chapter 1) Professor of the International Research Center for Japanese Studies. Born in Fukuoka Prefecture in 1967, he obtained his Doctor of Law degree from the Graduate School of Law at Kyoto University. He is the author of *The German* Staatswissenschaft *and the Meiji Constitutional System*; *The Meiji Constitution in the History of Civilization* (Jirō Osaragi Prize for Commentary and Kadokawa Culture Promotion Foundation Prize) [published in English as *The Meiji Constitution: The Japanese Experience of the West and the Shaping of the Modern State*]; and *Itō Hirobumi* (Suntory Prize for Social Sciences and Humanities) [published in English as *Ito Hirobumi, Japan's First Prime Minister and Father of the Meiji Constitution*], among other works.

Chapter 1
The Meiji Restoration as a Constitutional Revolution

Kazuhiro Takii

Abstract This chapter considers developments in Japan's parliamentary and constitutional systems from the beginning of the Meiji period in 1868. It assesses the significance of the Iwakura Mission to the West and how this influenced public discourse on the need for Japan to transform itself into a constitutional state. It also explains why Itō Hirobumi is typically regarded as the father of the Meiji Constitution (although Inoue Kowashi drafted it), and deems the newly established constitutional system of world significance.

The Meiji Restoration in World History

A century and a half has passed since the Meiji period started in 1868. Events marking the 150th anniversary of the Meiji Restoration were held throughout Japan.

These events wound up being, more often than not, regional promotional projects tied to efforts to revitalize the countryside that were full of nostalgia for tales of national successes, as implied in the central government's slogan "learn from the spirit of Meiji, reaffirm the strengths of Japan" (referenced in measures related to *Meiji 150* promoted by the Cabinet Office and interagency meetings). Japanese look back on the Meiji period as a national adolescence, a time bursting with ambitions and youthful ardor. A glorious period when the remote island nation, left behind by global events, opened itself to outside interaction and set off at an unremitting gallop aiming for the clouds above the hill,[1] rising up to become one of the foremost nations of the world.

Still, something rings false about waxing nostalgic over bygone glories of the Meiji period at a time when Japan's adolescence is long past and its society faces an unprecedented era featuring a declining birthrate, a graying of the population, and low economic growth. The government-initiated *Meiji 150* anniversary events

---

[1] Alluding to author/historian Shiba Ryōtarō's work of that name. See Chap. 13.

K. Takii
International Research Center for Japanese Studies, Nishikyo-ku, Kyoto, Japan

© The Author(s) 2023
M. Yamauchi, Y. Hosoya (eds.), *Modern Japan's Place in World History*,
https://doi.org/10.1007/978-981-19-9593-4_1

1

lacked enthusiasm. And as I mentioned, local authorities staged a great show of activity, busy with a series of projects to showcase their local history of the transformation from the end of the Tokugawa period to the Restoration. Someone should probably check to see whether, in the pursuit of tourism promotion, the discussion of history was impacted by immoderate attempts to downplay any negative aspects.

In any case, it seems rather unlikely that we should end up sketching out an isolated, inward-looking history that focuses on the level of citizens or regional society from the generous amount of contemplation we had about the Meiji period. For Japan, which successfully caught up to the West long ago and now seems to be at a turning point in a historic period of stagnation, I believe that it is vitally more important to make an objective history of its modernization period beginning with the Meiji Restoration and to link it to other histories around the world to create a useful resource of knowledge.

My background is legal history; in particular, I have researched the formation and transformation of modern Japan's legal system with the Meiji Constitution at its core. Here, after outlining the process of the creation and adoption of a constitutional system of government that led to the enactment of the Meiji Constitution, I would like to propose what significance the history of the Meiji Constitution holds in world history. Constitutional system in the nineteenth century typically meant a parliamentary system guaranteeing the political participation of its citizens. Below, I use the terms constitutional and parliamentary systems interchangeably.

Public Discourse: The Precondition for Introducing a Constitutional System

As is commonly known, the introduction of a parliamentary system in Japan was put forward in the Oath of Five Articles (Charter Oath) issued March 14, 1868 (Keiō 4): "Deliberative assemblies shall be widely established and all matters decided by open discussion."[2] Initially, the draft document read "council of feudal lords shall be established." The redaction of "council of feudal lords (rekkō kaigi)" to be replaced simply with "assemblies (kaigi)" appears, from our perspective today, to hold some sort of deep significance. It implies a path toward building a new state, not a federation of feudal lords comprising their separate domains as they were, but a unified state led by the emperor as sovereign ruler. This alteration of terms for the assembly, then, permits the later establishment of an organ representing the people that participates in politics under the lead of a sovereign monarch, the emperor.

The leaders of the Meiji Restoration shared this general course of action. Iwakura Tomomi, for instance, made a recommendation in January 1869 (Meiji 2) for

---

[2]English text from MacLaren, Walter W., 1979. Japanese government documents (of the Meiji period), Bethesda, MD: University Publications of America. As cited in *Wikipedia*.

political reform consisting of four items—build a system of government, cultivate reverence for the emperor, establish a legislative assembly, and relocate the capital. In particular, he advocated founding solid institutions that would preserve the state even if the future did not provide Japan with a benevolent ruler and wise ministers, and as time passed, argued for the creation of an assembly body. So long as an arrangement was established where the emperor would adopt laws and policies based on the proceedings of public discussion in the assembly body, Iwakura anticipated it would mean that the state structure would be stable and resilient, so that is why he called for the introduction of a parliamentary system (Iwakura 1968, p. 685 *ad passim*). His notion was for the legislative assembly to be the core pillar of the national government, providing a unifying force in the system.

Iwakura's call for government to be based on public discourse, which went beyond the differing viewpoints at the end of the Tokugawa period, has recently attracted a great deal of interest and scrutiny once again. The assessments have been mixed (Mitani 2017; Nara 2018). Yet, the belief that the people's representatives should take part in politics, unconstrained by the old class system, came about in this period, and by extension, the notion that Japan should adopt a parliamentary system became self-evident. Nevertheless, it was not all smooth sailing; they had not planned to introduce a parliamentary system with representatives of the people right at the start. It required over two decades to achieve—the inauguration of the Imperial Diet was in 1890 (Meiji 23). Keeping that in mind, first let us look at the early indications of constitutional government in the first year of Meiji.

The Meiji leaders issued several documents on various forms of government that they wrote building off of the Charter Oath. This is when they settled upon the separation of powers (legislative, executive, and judicial) and decided to set up a system with a legislative assembly. A new regional organization of "*fu/han/ken*" (urban and rural prefectures and domains) was created to select members to the legislative assembly; in practice, it was dominated by the feudal domains of the old system. The *Kōgisho*, the first Meiji-period assembly, was established in January 1869 and held its first meeting the following April. Made up of members primarily sent by the various domains, it aimed to be a legislative body, "its primary business being the making of laws" (*Kōgisho*'s draft rules).

This assembly held its last meeting in the July of that year. The smooth deliberative proceedings encountered obstacles, as some members called for a rapid replacement of the old ways with the new, such as the discussion on banning Christianity and western clothes, or the controversy over the proposal Mori Arinori put forward to abolish the wearing of swords. It was premature to set up a parliamentary system for law-making in a form such as the *Kōgisho*. In its place, the bureaucratic reforms of August 1870 established a Syūgiin, merely a government advisory body, not a legislative organ, with a reduced role in the system for deliberation. Once the traditional feudal domains were replaced with new prefectures in August 1871, the Syūgiin existed in name only because its members had been selected by the now-abolished domains.

The legislative advisory body function was carried over to the newly established Left Chamber (*Sain*). A revised administrative ordinance in January 1872 expanded the Left Chamber's power as a legislative deliberative organ—"as a rule, this body shall deliberate on the regulations and laws generally to be issued"—but its constituent members were appointed and dismissed by the administrative organ, the Central Chamber (*Seiin*). This meant temporarily abandoning the idea of the deliberative organ being a representative institution.

So, you could regard the replacement of the feudal domains with new prefectures as a setback for institutionalizing a system for public discourse and public opinion. It did not mean, however, the complete defeat of that concept. Rather, the Meiji leadership continued to search for a proper form of parliamentary government that would be more representative of the people.

The turning point came with the Iwakura Mission. The leaders of the government who got the opportunity to examine Western civilization in its true form for themselves ultimately returned home, after many twists and turns, with a belief for civilizing Japan. It is worth noting that the two key members of the Mission, Ōkubo Toshimichi and Kido Takayoshi, both offered their own written opinions on adopting a constitutional system after their return. Let us examine their opinions next.

The Iwakura Mission and Constitution Considerations: Kido Takayoshi and Ōkubo Toshimichi

Ōkubo and Kido returned home in May and July of 1873 (Meiji 6), ahead of the mission. The two hurried back to Japan after having received news that the caretaker government was involved with radical reforms, resulting in conflict within the administration. Both men considered ways of rebuilding the state as they later came to grips with a significant challenge: the rift in the government caused by the debate over whether to send a punitive military expedition to Korea (*Seikanron*). Faced with this difficult situation, the two of them, by chance, called for the introduction of a constitutional system.

First was Kido. Shortly after his return and without delay, he submitted his opinion regarding a constitution in writing to the imperial court and released something in the same vein to the public in October. The gist of his argument was as follows.

"The urgent task for us today," Kido stated, "is to add more clauses to the Oath in Five Articles, expanding it into the rules of government" (Kido 2003, p. 123). Kido insisted that the pressing matter before the country was to flesh out the Charter Oath and thereby settle on a constitution ("rules of government"). The key to the country's fate, he reasoned, lay in what form the constitution would have.

So, what sort of constitution was suited to Japan in Kido's opinion? In a word, an "autocratic" constitution. As Japan was still a country where civilization had yet to spread widely, Kido explained, the government was obligated to properly guide its citizens gradually to a more civilized state of being by means of the emperor's decisive measures, executed by public officials in the government. What he regarded as the nation's foremost task was the forceful leadership of the emperor and, under him, a government that serves him; he was endorsing a sort of tyranny of the public officials.

We may find his praise of autocracy dreadful. But it contained a deep conviction backed up by the Iwakura Mission's experiences in the West. Although he called it autocracy, he said it must be carried out based on the people's consent. Even speaking about the emperor, he asked rhetorically, "How could the whole country be the private property of one family?" In other words, even though Kido called his concept autocratic, precisely because it was a constitution, its purpose was not to guarantee the tyranny of the monarch, but rather to promote the unity of the people and respect their will. Constitutional government's main objective is precisely the rule of politicians by the will of the people. Accordingly, even as he argued for an autocratic constitution, what Kido was focused on for the future was a constitutional monarchy in which the monarch shares sovereignty with his subjects. He made this point clear in his writings: "Although I speak today of an autocratic constitution, it is only until that time popular discussion occurs, which is the basis for constitution of shared sovereignty, which, in turn, is necessary as the foundation for the people's welfare" (Kido 2003, p. 128). In other words, Kido's plan for enacting a constitution envisions a steady evolution from autocracy to shared sovereignty, anticipating the creation of a citizenry able to shoulder the responsibility of the nation. This was a view he held in common with Ōkubo.

Ōkubo gave Itō Hirobumi, who had been ordered to examine systems of government, a written opinion stating his views on constitutional forms of government in November 1873 (Meiji 6). You could say it was a report of accomplishments in which Ōkubo summarized in careful detail what he came to realize about Western civilization while serving as the Iwakura Mission's deputy; in that sense, it was similar to Kido's report. He began by acknowledging the many varieties of national systems in the West. There are many systems of government in the world, from monarchies to democracies and everything in between. Each had its own historical background, and so it was not possible to determine unconditionally which one was the best. A country's political structure is intrinsically molded and accretes naturally under given conditions, the country's culture and national traits. Consequently, he asserted, any reforms must ultimately conform with the country's "land, customs, manners, and spirit of the age"; one should not thoughtlessly copy another country's institutions.

The issue was to establish a national system suited to Japan's circumstances and political features. Ōkubo, too, considered the formation of a national foundation as the urgent task: "our business, first and foremost, is the rather important and urgent discussion of our national polity." And what had to be done first for that purpose, was "to determine the laws of the nation," i.e. to enact a constitution.

So, as you can see, Ōkubo and Kido shared a broad approach for creating a constitution. Yet, we can identify a gap between the two men just by glancing at the substance of their proposed constitutions. In contrast to Kido's push for a monarchic autocracy, Ōkubo promoted shared sovereignty. As he laid out in his writings, "By having the constitution be a system of shared sovereignty, I believe we establish the monarch's rights above and limit the people's rights below, an arrangement that is completely fair and just" (Ōkubo 2014, p. 186).

So, Kido argued for an autocratic constitution and Ōkubo advocated a constitution where the monarch shares sovereignty with his subjects. But they both shared a structure of a similar quality, assigning the people a political role in that framework. "Can we make a government that excludes the people?" Ōkubo asked rhetorically in his written opinion. This was an ideal he held in common with Kido. As we saw earlier, the true nature of Kido's argument in favor of an autocratic constitution was that it envisioned delegating power to the autocrat temporarily to realize the popular will. Their objective might be characterized as a national political self-awareness to hasten the enlightenment of the people.

Their conceptions concerning the process for achieving this objective were not very far apart. As Ōkubo wrote, "We should not arbitrarily imitate the countries in Europe with their systems for shared sovereignty between the sovereign and his subjects. Our country has a body of law naturally arising from its unbroken imperial line. Its people have their own degree of civilization. We must establish a legal charter only after due examination and consideration of the merits for our country" (Ōkubo 2014, p. 188). It means that Ōkubo and Kido shared a historicist understanding of a constitution: that imperial rule would be shaped by Japan's unique traits and characteristics. The historical school of jurisprudence that the men learned from their experiences in Europe was something that guided their "arguments favoring a gradual process for constitutional enactment" (Talks with Itō Hirobumi in Ōkubo 2014, p. 206).

Kido and Ōkubo did not live to see the establishment of the constitutional system for Japan. The man who, through great efforts, was able to realize their last wishes was Itō Hirobumi. Let us next look at how he enacted the Meiji Constitution.

Itō Hirobumi and Enacting the Meiji Constitution

As previously mentioned, the nation's task since the end of the Tokugawa shogunate had been to establish an organ for public debate (a legislative assembly), after forming a system of government that fostered public discourse and public opinion. The leaders in the Meiji government were keenly aware of this. The journey to making Japan a constitutional state commenced with bureaucrat-driven reforms.

After leaving the government in the wake of the political upheaval in 1873 touched off, Itagaki Taisuke and other influential men now out of power launched and led the Freedom and People's Rights Movement, which evolved into a campaign to establish the national assembly. The push for a constitution, coming from both the bureaucracy and the public, elicited negative and positive reactions until it finally resulted in the promulgation of the Constitution of the Empire of Japan (the Meiji Constitution) on February 11, 1889.

What clearly had a fateful impact on the way to establishing the Meiji Constitution was the political crisis of 1881 (Meiji 14). The Minister of the Right Iwakura Tomomi ordered every vice-minister (*sangi*, the equivalent of a cabinet minister) to draw up and submit a written opinion on the constitution in 1880. The opinion written by Ōkuma Shigenobu, more than any other, startled the government, and it became the spark that set off the political crisis of 1881.

Ōkuma, unlike the other vice-ministers, advocated a radical argument for opening the legislature in 1883 (Meiji 16). Moreover, in his written opinion, he proposed a British-style parliamentary cabinet system centered on a national assembly, saying "a government by constitution is a government by political parties." Hiding his report with its controversial subject matter from Iwakura and the other vice-ministers, Ōkuma tried to submit it as a secret memorial to the throne. In part owing to such clandestine actions as this, Ōkuma's position in the government was left somewhat tarnished.

Soon afterwards, a scandal erupted over corrupt property sales by the Hokkaido Development Commission. Anti-government protests began to heat up after information was leaked to the public about plans for the Hokkaido Development Commission's sale of government-owned land and assets at unusually low prices to companies tied to the government. Ōkuma was widely suspected of being the source of the leaks. It was rumored that Ōkuma, the proponent of party politics, was in a conspiracy to overthrow the government by colluding with some protestors who were out of power. So, on October 9, the government decided to stop the sale of the government-owned property at the same time that it decided to expel Ōkuma and the bureaucratic subordinates under his wing from the government. This was the political crisis of 1881 (Meiji 14).

The political crisis was a major turning point in Japanese constitutional history. After Ōkuma's ouster, an imperial rescript was issued on October 12 calling for a national assembly to be established and it was declared that it would open in 1890 (Meiji 23). Finding itself caught in a pincer movement—Ōkuma's secret memorial from within, and the Freedom and People's Rights Movement from without—the Meiji government publicly pledged, in the name of the emperor, to enact a constitution that would establish the national legislature.

Thus, the government had to get to work in a hurry to enact the constitution. Its preparation was flawless. In June, after Ōkuma's secret memorial laying out his opinion on a constitution had been discovered within the government, Iwakura compiled his own constitutional opinion piece as a countermeasure; in opposition to Ōkuma's proposed Westminster system, he offered a concept modeled on a Prussian-style constitutional monarchy. Inoue Kowashi was the author; he was the Meiji government's mastermind who later drafted the constitution. In fact, the establishment of the Meiji Constitution is unthinkable without Inoue's vigorous efforts.

Yet, it was not only the constitution that was drafted at that time. The Imperial Household Law (*kōshitsu tenpan*), which is considered a fundamental law for the state the same as the constitution (*kenpō*), was also drafted during this period (which is why the Meiji national legal system is sometimes called the *Ten-Ken* system). In addition, the Parliamentary Law, the House of Representatives Election Law, the Accounting Law, and the House of Peers Ordinance were promulgated on the same day as the constitution (February 11, 1889). While not formally constitutional law, they all were laws/ordinances indispensable for the actual functioning of the legislative and public finance system laid down by the constitution. They are called organic laws, as they are important laws that directly flesh out a constitution. Between the political crisis of 1881 and the promulgation of the constitution, there were many other important state institutions and systems continually being established. This was the period in which the Meiji state's "*kuni no katachi* (shape of the nation)" came together.

Here I would like to give my perspective on *kuni no katachi*. I wrote, above, that Inoue Kowashi drafted the Meiji Constitution. Itō Hirobumi is typically advertised at the father of the Meiji Constitution. Perhaps Itō arrogated to himself Inoue's achievement?

Inoue, certainly, had a tremendous presence in the drafting of the various articles of the constitution. When we turn to consider the creation of the panoply of national institutions that enabled the constitution to function, rather that the writing of the constitution itself, Itō's presence grows more prominent. When Itō is called the father of the Meiji Constitution, it should be understood to mean of all the institutions of state, that is, national institutions and *kuni no katachi* (constitution), rather than simply *kenpō* (constitution). (The meaning of the English word "constitution" has an original sense of the structure as well as the forming or establishing of that structure.) To understand this point, I must touch on Itō's constitutional study mission to Europe.

The year after the political crisis of 1881, Itō set out for Europe to do some constitutional research. And what he learned was the relative nature of constitutional law: that a constitution is fine insofar as it describes things in a general way. He grew aware that it is sufficient for the constitution to prescribe the structure and organization of the legislature, stipulate the rights and duties of its citizens, and enumerate the monarch's powers. That being the case, the actual enactment of the constitution does not demand that much effort. What is more important, he said at the time, is to establish the administration to enable the legislature to function when it is opened.

After returning home from his constitutional study trip, he did carry out reform of the imperial court and implement education for the emperor as a constitutional monarch. He also sought to modernize the institutions for governance by introducing a cabinet system and renovating the existing Grand Council of State (*Dajōkan*) system. In the cabinet system, any of the citizens could become a minister, regardless of their status (such as being from a noble family). He also instituted a system for the bureaucracy, and for that purpose the Imperial University was founded (1886). A recruitment system was put in place to hire men who studied at the Imperial University as civil servants to administer the state.

This series of reforms sketched out the *kuni no katachi*, a constitutional state; the promulgation of the constitution on February 11, 1889 (Meiji 22) was the finishing touch. His molding of the *kuni no katachi* is Itō Hirobumi's contribution to Japanese constitutional history.

The Meiji Constitutional System as World History Heritage

There are various possible ways of appreciating the innovativeness of the Meiji Restoration. As the classical rivalry between the "lectures" faction and the "labor-farmer" faction in the pre-war debate on Japanese capitalism over the characterization of the bourgeois revolution. As a revolution for independence or a people's revolution that beat back the foreign threat of being colonized and maintained Japan's independence as a country. Or, as a nationalist revolution that, by carrying out important reforms such as replacing feudal domains with prefectures and abolishing the four-tier social class system of the Tokugawa period, established a unified, sovereign nation.

As you can tell by the title of this chapter, I regard the Meiji Restoration as a constitutional revolution first and foremost. Consistently through various twists and turns, Meiji leaders pushed ahead with the transition to a constitutional system and the introduction of a parliamentary system, from its start in the politics of public discourse that vigorously took place at the end of the Tokugawa period. Its intended destination for some time was the very enactment of the Constitution of the Empire of Japan in 1889. We should appreciate the Meiji Restoration as a long process of revolution that spanned over 20 years.

The establishment of a constitutional system in the Meiji period, it is safe to say, has a significance in world history. We can cite two major countries in the non-Western world that came up with a constitution before Japan, Tunisia (1861) and the Ottoman Empire (1867), but neither were sustained for long and both were suspended. Japan is the rare case in the non-Western world that inherited constitutionalism successfully. Why was it possible for constitutionalism to become established in Japan? As I have run out of space here already, I shall have to put off a fundamental inquiry for another day. But I would like to leave you with a few points.

First, there is the long view. Calls for a parliamentary system of government came from within and outside of the government. But to actually achieve it, government leaders such as Kido and Ōkubo recognized the need for sufficient preparations. They firmly believed that the introduction of a constitutional system needed a slow and steady approach, never something radical or slipshod.

Second, there is the prerequisite, the nation-state. A constitutional system is one that guarantees the political participation of its citizens. This necessitates agents who are citizens able to bear the responsibility in national politics. Various measures to that end were proposed, but I would like to take the opportunity here to endorse historicism. The Iwakura Mission observed and became aware of the fact that the political systems and social organizations of each country in the Western world all differed. Moreover, historicism[3] was a fundamental trend of thought at the time. It was widely held that citizens with a shared history should be responsible for the laws and systems. After Itō's constitutional research reaffirmed this point, Japan's basic policy was set: to enact a constitution unique to the country, based on the historical traditions of the people.

Third, the relative nature of the constitution. As I just mentioned, Itō thought that a constitution, by itself, was nothing more than a sheet of paper; to breathe life into it, it was essential to have chain of institutions working in a coordinated fashion. Itō's real worth as a rare sort of leader for the constitution can be found in the fact that he both recognized that reforming the nation's institutions was inseparable from, and was one part of the process toward, enacting a constitution, and successfully implemented those institutional reforms.

Thus, the Meiji Restoration as constitutional revolution achieved results for the time being. But the promulgation of the constitution was not the end point. In fact, the start of parliamentary government saw the conflict intensify between the party-led Diet and the government dominated by several of the former domains, but finally party politics took root and there were visible signs of systemic transformations on the path to a parliamentary cabinet system.

Amid the global trend of anti-parliamentarianism, Japan, too, began adopting authoritarianism and a structure for total war in the early Shōwa period. Japanese constitutional history holds positive and negative aspects such as this. This is exactly why Japan, based on its historical experiences, is in a position to give advice and counsel to countries trying to introduce constitutional systems and to those that did so but where they are not functioning properly. The Meiji Restoration should be seen as a precious resource of knowledge for this purpose.

Bibliography: For Further Reading

Iwakura, Tomomi. 1968. *Iwakura-kō jikki* (Authentic Chronicle of Prince Iwakura). Hara Shobō.

Kido, Takayoshi. Tsumaki, Chūta and Nihon Shiseki Kyōkai (eds). 2003. *Kido takayoshi monjo dai 8kan* (The Papers of Kido Takayoshi, Volume 8). Tokyo: The University of Tokyo Press.

Mitani, Hiroshi. 2017. *Ishinshi saikō: kōgi ōsei kara shūken datsu mibunka e* (Reconsidering the Restoration: from Public Debates and Imperial Rule to Centralizing Power and Abolishing the Feudal Class Structure). Tokyo: NHK Books.

Nara, Katsuji. 2018. *Meiji ishin o toraenaosu: hi "kokumin" teki apurōchi kara saikōsuru henkaku no Sugata* (Rethinking the Meiji Restoration: The Revolution Reconsidered from an anti-"Popular" Approach). Tokyo: Yūshisha.

---

[3] The theory that social and cultural phenomena (including ideas and beliefs) are determined, and thus can be explained, by their history.

Ōkubo Toshimichi. Nihon Shiseki Kyōkai (eds). 2014. *Ōkubo toshimichi monjo: 5.* (The Papers of Ōkubo Toshimichi, Vol. 5). Tokyo: The University of Tokyo Press.

Additional Bibliography

Ōishi, Makoto. 2005. *Nihon kenpō shi daini-han* (The History of the Constitution of Japan, Second Edition). Tokyo: Yūhikaku.
A compact and condensed outline by one of the leading researchers of Japanese constitutional history who inherited the mantle from Messrs. Inada Masatsugu and Kojima Kazushi.
Takii, Kazuhiro. 2003. *Bunmeishi no naka no meiji kenpō : kono kuni no katachi to seiyō taiken* (The Meiji Constitution: the Japanese Experience of the West and the Shaping of the Modern State). Tokyo: Kōdansha sensho metier. (Published in English as: Takii, Kazuhiro. Noble, David (trans). 2007. *The Meiji Constitution: the Japanese Experience of the West and the Shaping of the Modern State.* Tokyo: International House of Japan.)
This argues that the history of the enactment of the Meiji Constitution as culturally negotiated history from the viewpoint of western legal history.
Takii, Kazuhiro. 2010. *Itō hirobumi: chi no seijika* (Itō Hirobumi: Wise Politician). Tokyo: Chūō Kōron Shinsha.
My attempt to depict Itō Hirobumi as the designer of the national system. It covers his continuous path toward achieving constitutional politics.

Chapter 2
The First Sino-Japanese War and East Asia

Takashi Okamoto

Abstract This chapter covers the First Sino-Japanese War of 1894–1895, a "watershed in world history," according to the author. It uses maps of the Korean Peninsula to shed light on other conflicts in Northeast Asia that both preceded and followed this war, which the author suggests remains unfinished and affects current geostrategic thinking. In tracing the road to war and the consequences of it, the significance of Manchuria in relation to the security of the Korean Peninsula is highlighted and the "historical deficiency of mutual understanding" lamented.

From Three Maps

The First Sino-Japanese War, which started in 1894, is one of the major events in the modern history of Japan. There are a great many books that go into the details and place it in the context of Japanese history. So it would probably be repetitive and serve little purpose for me to address the war in detail from the framework and perspective of Japanese modern history, reproducing old theories that lay somewhat outside of my particular field of expertise. Were I to discuss the topic again in my own way, I would prefer to proceed from a slightly different point of view, by asking how we should consider the First Sino-Japanese War and its significance, and then offering an answer. I should think that this approach would be more productive and constructive, if not entirely sufficient.

First, by way of an introduction to the topic, please look at the following maps. All three are maps of the Korean Peninsula; furthermore, they all depict wars that occurred there. Just getting a sense of the broad picture is fine for now. Figure 2.1 is of the First Sino-Japanese War, which, as you can tell, was fought over the Korean Peninsula. It is not the only war in history waged over the peninsula. Figure 2.2 depicts Toyotomi Hideyoshi's dispatch of troops to Korea; Fig. 2.3, the closest to us

---

The original version of this chapter has been revised. Figures 2.1–2.3 caption changed for this chapter. The correction to this chapter can be found at https://doi.org/10.1007/978-981-19-9593-4_14

T. Okamoto
Faculty of Letters, Kyoto Prefectural University, Kyoto-shi, Kyoto, Japan

© The Author(s) 2023, corrected publication 2023
M. Yamauchi, Y. Hosoya (eds.), *Modern Japan's Place in World History*,
https://doi.org/10.1007/978-981-19-9593-4_2

13

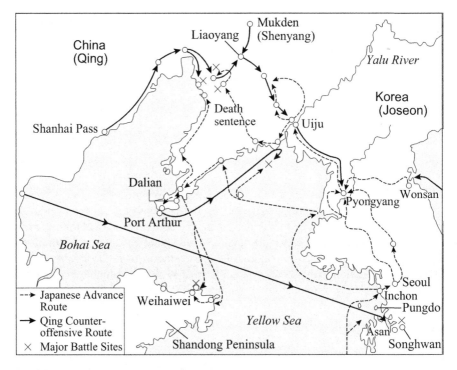

Fig. 2.1 First Sino-Japanese War (1894–1895)

in time, is of the Korean War, which broke out in 1950 and has yet to be concluded legally, with the peninsula remaining in a state of belligerence today.

You can tell just by looking at these three maps side by side that the current situation on the Korean Peninsula is a product of history. It is rather intriguing that, viewed holistically, there are commonalities running through the course of events and conditions during the 400-plus years between Hideyoshi's troop dispatch and the Korean War, notwithstanding the completely different eras and contexts in which these wars happened. The aggressor may have differed—north or south, by land or sea—but a reaction would always ensue if one side gained superiority. Against an attack from the south, military force from the continent would appear, attempting to block it from going north.

At the same time, this discussion of the three wars focuses on merely one, rather temporary, aspect of the state of affairs. However, when placed side by side for consideration, we may perhaps elaborate from a longer-term perspective that is historical and geopolitical. The status of division and conflict between the north and south on the peninsula is closely related to the balance of power of their respective hinterlands. There are examples of wars induced by changes in the power hierarchy of the continent to the north and the islands and sea to the south. In summary, this has been the situation for the past 500 years.

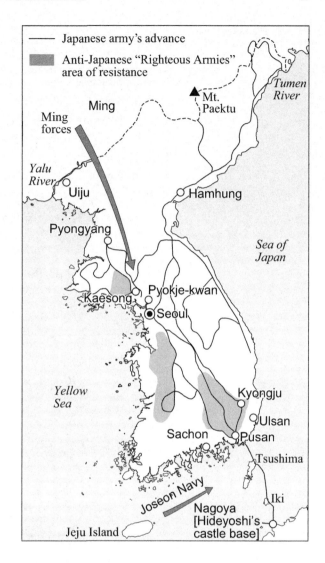

Fig. 2.2 Toyotomi Hideyoshi's dispatch of troops to Korea (Bunroku War, 1592)

The Korean Peninsula at the Center

Long before this period, the Korean Peninsula basically had never been made the battlefield for or the object of a fight between external powers historically speaking, with the exception of the Battle of Hakusukinoe in classical times. The sole example that involved the peninsula is the Mongol Invasions of Japan (1274 and 1281), when Japan fought the Mongol Empire. After gaining total control over the peninsula, continental forces then attempted to invade the Japanese archipelago; the archipelago, for its part, could not just stand and watch, it was forced to meet the invasion. This was the case up until the seventeenth century.

Fig. 2.3 The Korean War
(1950–1953 Armistice)

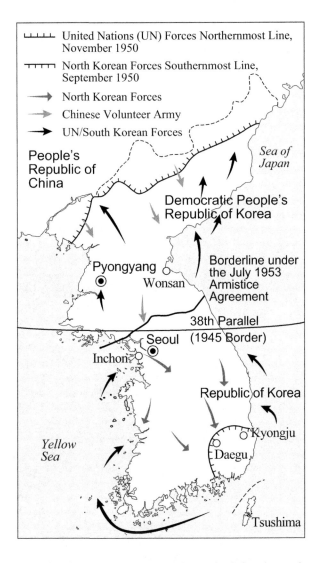

However, Hideyoshi's dispatch of troops to Korea at the end of the sixteenth century completely changed the situation, reversing the flow of movement from the archipelago across the seas toward the peninsula and continent. Leaving aside the question of whether this was good or bad, it signifies how powerful the archipelago had become. This was a situation without precedent in the histories of East Asia and the world. During its Warring States Period (fifteenth to seventeenth centuries), the Japanese archipelago had experienced a sort of high-growth period and turned into a military powerhouse. Once again East Asia had to readjust its balance of power in response to the sudden rise and emergence of the sea power, Japan.

The situation finally settled down in the mid-seventeenth century under the Qing dynasty's reign in China and the Edo government's *sakoku* national policy of

2 The First Sino-Japanese War and East Asia   17

severely limiting all foreign interaction; Tokugawa Japan, Qing China, and Joseon Korea each established various bilateral relations with the others. *Sakoku*-period Japan did not undertake political intercourse with the Qing court, maintaining trade relations only. Japan did have diplomatic exchanges with the Joseon dynasty, though relations between the central governments were little more than ceremonial. The Tsushima domain, involved with both sides, constantly kept up its ties to the peninsula.

The tributary system that had existed under the previous Ming dynasty continued between the Qing and the Joseon. It was a ceremonial, hierarchical relationship in which they referred to each other as "suzerain" (Qing) and "vassal"[1] (Joseon) and, as a rule, the suzerain did not interfere in the vassal's domestic or foreign affairs. This was how the Joseon court could almost establish diplomatic relations with Japan independently without concern for the Qing, for instance. Since the three governments were largely stable, relations between the archipelago, the peninsula, and the continent endured without any serious incidents for over two centuries.

But in the latter half of the nineteenth century, Western powers encroached on East Asia. The continent's, the archipelago's, and the peninsula's negotiations with the Western Great Powers had an impact on all their governments to a greater or lesser degree, thus necessitating another change in the existing balance of power. What arose out of that process of trial and error were the First Sino-Japanese and Russo-Japanese wars.

The twentieth century began in East Asia with the Boxer Rebellion in China and the Russo-Japanese War. A victor in both, Japan could seize the Korean Peninsula at last. Subsequently, Japan began exerting its influence on the continent and its conflict with China gradually became all encompassing. This development was not unrelated to the peninsula. Japan's fixation on Manchuria underlay its geopolitical and national security interests of how best to secure its Korean colony.

The power map of the region underwent radical change as soon as Japan, defeated in World War II, lost Manchuria and withdrew from the Korean Peninsula. Once again it was time to recalculate the balance of power among the archipelago/sea, the peninsula, and the continent. The Korean War broke out for that purpose. The outcome still defines the international situation in East Asia.

When considered like this, the trajectory of the Japanese archipelago is a critical factor in the battles fought over the Korean Peninsula. Historically since the time of its emergence in the sixteenth century until today, whenever Japan's national strength has waxed or waned, it has always meant trouble on the Korean Peninsula. It is this process that I would like to take up in addressing the First Sino-Japanese War.

---

[1] As the text indicates, the term "vassal" in the context of the Chinese tributary system is quite different than what is understood in a European feudal/modern context.

Watershed in World History

I have described the First Sino-Japanese War elsewhere in my writings as a "watershed in East Asian history" and a "watershed in world history." Understanding why only requires a brief glimpse at some simplified conditions. The war completely changed the way East Asia and the world looked between the end of the nineteenth century and at the start of the twentieth. In world history, the main players changed, with major non-Western European countries displacing the Western Europeans; in East Asia, Japan emerged as a major power. This is the moment when imperialism, or what might be called a unification or structuring of the world, finally spread to East Asia.

In general, China's modern era, in the context of East Asian or Chinese histories, begins with the Opium War in 1840. This is only the Chinese government's official historical stance, and nothing more; there is no obligation or need for Japan's study of history to adhere blindly to it. We need consider only that which conforms to historical fact. It would be best not to summarize this history from an overarching perspective as something to the effect of the Western Great Powers gained direct access to China after the Opium War and subsequent events, or their spreading influence resulted in major changes in China. That was true roughly throughout the nineteenth century.

Instead, it would be preferable to note the role of Japan, which modernized under the West's impact. It is more expedient and appropriate, at least from a big picture view of history, to assume the course of events being that the continent and peninsula both began to change at last under Japan's impact. It was after the First Sino-Japanese War that comprehensive modernization on the continent finally became an issue and even accelerated. The peninsula entered a completely new era as a Japanese colony. From this perspective, the First Sino-Japanese War can be taken as a watershed in East Asian history. We should consider the two roughly 30-year time spans before and after this watershed event. Each forms one historical cycle: the Meiji Restoration [1868] is the starting point and the Manchurian Incident [1931] the end point. We then might designate the 30 years that precede the First Sino-Japanese War "the road to war" and the 30 years that follow "after the fight."

The Road to War

The stance adopted by Meiji Restoration Japan was that the country had to modernize, to construct a national system as well as international relations in the Western style. The nearby peninsula and continent were the first hurdle at the time, especially for the Meiji statesmen. That is, their task was how to interact with the Joseon and Qing dynasties. The top fear for the Japanese islands then was a military threat reaching the archipelago via the Korean Peninsula. Such a threat on the peninsula closest to Japan engendered a great sense of crisis, whether it originated from Qing China or the Russian Empire.

If the archipelago felt that way, it would not be strange for the continent to think that way, too: that Japan, and by extension the Korean Peninsula, posed a threat to the government in Beijing. Moreover, this thought did not start with the Meiji Restoration in the latter half of the nineteenth century. The quintessential historical evidence is perhaps that the Ming court boldly sent reinforcements at the time of Toyotomi Hideyoshi's Korea expedition. What was special this time was that Japan was rapidly modernizing, with "Rich Nation, Strong Army" (*fukoku kyōhei*) its slogan. Strengthening the armed forces was the most important goal, and the resultant expansion of military power was remarkable. Surely that was the view of the Japanese islands the Chinese side had from across the sea.

Much as Meiji Japan feared a reappearance of a Mongol invasion, the continent and China feared a return of Hideyoshi's Korea expedition. It is clearly written in the Chinese historical archives: we must by no means repeat the mistakes of the Ming period. In summary, each side viewed the other as a military threat. A structure of mounting mistrust and suspicion, mutually held, lay at the root of this state of affairs. It was in this context that Japan, seeking to build modern international relations, concluded treaties with the Qing Empire and the Kingdom of Joseon. Being that this was the 1870s, these negotiations were held in a peaceful context. Yet progress was not always smooth: Japan resorted to using military force with its Taiwan expedition and it settled the matter of the status of the Ryūkyū Kingdom by incorporating the islands into its territory.

Each instance was the process of Japan exercising its control as a modern state. The Qing dynasty must have viewed these incidents as Japan rudely destroying the Chinese system of world order. So far as the Chinese side saw it, the Ryūkyūs, being separated from the continent by the sea, was not an urgent or pressing matter requiring immediate attention. What they took as an impending crisis was the Kingdom of Joseon, with the same rank in their tributary system as the Ryūkyūs. Geographically proximate to Beijing and contiguous with its territory, the peninsula had long been a militarily strategic point. The Qing government, suddenly more concerned, began strengthening its presence and pressure on the Korean Peninsula in the 1880s on the basis of their existing relationship.

These developments left the Kingdom of Joseon's statesmen and leading policymakers most perplexed. They also were the seed for remarkable factional struggles, with some advisors seeking to exploit the pressure they received from the Qing dynasty and others moving to use Japan or another Great Power. One example is the conflict between *Sadae* Party and the Independence Party. The armed clash between the two sides, in which both Japan and the Qing became embroiled, was the Gapsin Coup that took place in December 1884. Japan and the Qing dynasty concluded the Tianjin Convention as a response to this incident in which their forces engaged each other. Itō Hirobumi and Li Hongzhang agreed that, for the time being, both sides would pull their troops from the Korean Peninsula and would not make any moves there. This kept the peace in East Asia for the next 10 years.

After the Fight

Both sides pushed ahead to expand their military armaments as they continued to eye each other warily. The global balance of power had also shifted. Even if it had not, Japan was in the inferior position. It did not welcome any additional pressure on the Korean Peninsula from the Qing Empire or others. This was also tied to Japan's Foreign Minister Mutsu Munemitsu's strong motive for waging the First Sino-Japanese War. As he wrote, in order to "maintain the balance of power" in Korea with the Chinese and avoid any detrimental imbalance of that power relationship, Japan had to be prepared "to send a substantial number of troops to the peninsula." Mutsu also characterized the war as a clash between the existing old-world order of the continent and the modern international order of the archipelago:

> While we need not rehearse in detail here the origins of the long-standing Sino-Japanese struggle for power in Korea, this much should be noted: the efforts by each of the two empires to maintain its respective influence on the peninsula were virtually incompatible. Japan always regarded Korea as an independent and sovereign state, and sought to terminate Korea's ambiguous vassal-like relationship to China. China, on the other hand, loudly proclaimed that Korea was one of her tributaries by virtue of the long history of relations between the two countries. Despite the fact that Sino-Korean relations lacked several important ingredients usually recognized by international law as necessary in a suzerain-vassal relationship, the Chinese pressed for at least nominal recognition of Korea's vassalage (Mutsu 1982, p. 7–9).

In following Western-style international relations, Japan viewed Joseon as an independent state and sought to separate it from the influence of the continent. In contrast, the Qing dynasty sought to maintain the existing ceremonial, hierarchical relationship, and on those grounds tried to keep a free hand militarily on the Korean Peninsula. Ultimately, regardless of the party, the intention or goal became how to construct a balance of power with respect to the peninsula. We must not overlook this point.

Japan, as you know, won the First Sino-Japanese War. Yet, its influence on the Korean Peninsula suffered a major setback, caused by the enlargement of Russian influence stemming from the Triple Intervention. Japan felt it had to secure the Korean Peninsula at the very least, since it related to the security of the archipelago. Although it negotiated with Russia to demarcate their respective spheres of influence, they were unable to come to any agreement. And this is what led to the Russo-Japanese War.

Unchanging Essence

Japan's military victories over the Qing and Russia had an enormous influence on Qing China. Many believed that China could become stronger provided it undertook reforms like Japan's and set up a form of government like Japan's. What they were aiming to create was, in a word, a Japanese model of modernization. The *biànfǎ*

(Wuxu Reforms) and *xīnzhèng* (New Policies) reform efforts are such events in Chinese history. Nationalism was a natural outgrowth of this process. For that reason, momentum was growing in China in the twentieth century seeking the return of concessions held by the Great Powers. We can understand the deepening conflict with Japan and its evolution from the Manchurian Incident to the Second Sino-Japanese War in this context. Until the First Sino-Japanese War, the balance of power in East Asia consisted of the existing order under China and the continent and the modern Western-style international relations maintained by the archipelago (Japan). In the twentieth century, in contrast, it became a clash of nationalisms, nation versus nation, especially after the Manchurian Incident. A truly monumental shift.

We must not overlook the fact that the Manchuria question was a persistent problem throughout. To secure the Korean Peninsula, it was necessary to exert control over Manchuria (what the Qing called their "Eastern Three Provinces," which roughly corresponds to today's Liaoning, Jilin, and Heilongjiang provinces and parts of eastern Inner Mongolia). And from the continent's perspective, securing the northeast required controlling the Korean Peninsula. We can see this in the case of the First Sino-Japanese War, when Japan forced the Qing government to cede the Liaodong Peninsula, and Russia forced Japan to return the concession in the Triple Intervention (with Germany and France). This linkage between the peninsula and contiguous areas on the continent is a critical issue in the construction of the balance of power, as was apparent in the rationale for controlling both Manchuria and Korea rather than yielding Manchuria to Russia in exchange for Japanese control over the peninsula, two strategic arguments during this period.

From that perspective, we should have no trouble perceiving the Russo-Japanese War as a recurrence of the First Sino-Japanese War. The way events unfolded, Manchuria became the battlefield for the Russo-Japanese War because of Japan's stance: since it would not yield the Korean Peninsula, it deliberately started the fight from there. If that is the case, it seems as though we might also say that the First Sino-Japanese War is not over yet; the Korean War has not been officially concluded yet. After Japan renounced its colonial rule, the Korean War broke out and China came down from Manchuria to fight, a reversal of what happened in the Russo-Japanese War, from the Japanese standpoint. Yet the same interests were still at stake. The Chinese recaptured Pyongyang, long lost to them since the First Sino-Japanese War, but they were unable to keep Seoul. When considered this way, the current geopolitical balance of power is endowed with the unchanging essence of being the First Sino-Japanese War, yet unfinished.

Insufficient Understanding of History

Were I to elaborate on another of the unchanging aspects, it would be the historical deficiency of mutual understanding. This is true for the continent and the peninsula both. Frankly, I often cannot understand their words and actions. This is the case at present as well as when I read history, to the extent that it feels as though the more I study, the less I know.

In the case of the peninsula, whether the Joseon dynasty of the past or the two governments in the north and south now, there are many things beyond my grasp. It is likely that these things are specific challenges that lie in wait for us now and in the immediate future. If so, more than half the problem is in recognizing and understanding them. Trying to force understanding typically results in superficial knowledge, misunderstandings, and misinterpretations. Thus, correct understanding can only begin with the realization that we have not yet reached understanding.

It is the same as how I have addressed the problems in this chapter. For instance, earlier I touched on Chinese nationalism that emerged in the twentieth century. Though we call it nationalism, there are many points we cannot understand if we make assumptions using Western concepts of a modern state or the standards and norms for international relations. It is the same for the Korean Peninsula. How should we attempt to understand and deal with these issues, then? I believe a historical approach is effective and expedient. When thinking about the modern nation-state or about modernization, we must look back to the past, well before the turn of the twentieth century.

In the case of Japan, one must account for the fact that the political system and social structure of the Edo period became the foundation for its modernization, modern constitution, and constitutional form of government. Something similar could be said for the peninsula and the continent, though the details and situations vary. Their modernizations rest on the foundations of the political systems and social structures of the preceding Joseon and Qing periods.

Considering political systems, the rule of law tends to be a problem in both China and South Korea. Their concepts and developmental foundations for constitutional government and the rule of law are not the same things we consider them to be. The issue may be long-held and deeply embedded social structures and modes of thought. If so, a better understanding of each other will be quite a challenging undertaking, impossible to achieve overnight.

If we assume that Japan is so different from the continent and peninsula, it would not be too far a stretch to call it a "clash of civilizations." But such a conclusion has the potential to lead to another war, perhaps once again "by fate," as with the dispatch of troops to Korea and the First Sino-Japanese War. It is necessary to put mechanisms in place and figure out ways to avert such a catastrophe.

There is no reason to have expected mutual understanding between Japan and China before the First Sino-Japanese War at the end of the nineteenth century, or even well before that during the Edo and Qing periods. Nevertheless, there were long periods when peace held. Under what conditions was that possible? In that sense, there are still many things left to learn from this history. From that point, the characterization and designation of the First Sino-Japanese War is one of the events marking a change of era that continues today.

I would like to conclude this chapter by expressing the rather ordinary desire for professors who teach history to pay greater attention to history. That, I firmly believe, is one of the most important things that can be done.

Bibliography: For Further Reading

Mutsu, Munemitsu. 1983. *Kenkenroku.* Tokyo: Iwanami Bunko. [Published in English as: Mutsu, Munemitsu. Gordon Mark Berger (trans). 1982. Kenkenroku (Kenkenroku: a Diplomatic Record of the Sino-Japanese War, 1894–95). Princeton: Princeton University Press.]

Additional Bibliography

Okamoto, Takashi. 2008. *Sekai no naka no Ni-Shin-Kan kankeishi: kōrin to zokkoku, jishu to dokuritsu* (Contested Perceptions: Interactions and Relations between China, Korea, and Japan since the Seventeenth Century). Tokyo: Kōdansha sensho metier. [Published in English as: Okamoto, Takashi. The Japan institute of International Affairs (trans). 2022. *Contested Perceptions: Interactions and Relations between China, Korea, and Japan since the Seventeenth Century.* Tokyo: Japan Publishing Industry Foundation for Culture.]

Okamoto, Takashi. 2017. *Sōsho higashi-Ajia no kingendaishi1 Shinchō no kōbō to chūka no yukue: Chōsen shuppei kara Nichi-Ro senso e.* (The Modern History of East Asia Library (Vol. 1)—The Qing Dynasty and the Trajectory of China: from Hideyoshi's Korea Expedition to the Russo-Japanese War). Tokyo: Kōdansha.

Okamoto, Takashi. 2019. *Zōho Chūgoku "han-Nichi" no genryū* (The Origins of "Anti-Japaneseness" in China [Expanded edition]). Tokyo: Chikuma gakugei bunko. (First edition 2011.)

I would like to suggest the three books of mine listed above. They are all historical overviews of roughly the same time span, the sixteenth century through the start of the twentieth century. I attempted to approach the subject from different perspectives. The first book is a history of international relations focused on the Korean Peninsula. The second, while a history of East Asia with emphasis on the rise and fall of the Qing dynasty, also includes a view of the relations of Inner Asia. The third volume sketched out the societal structures of Japan and China and the political processes that shaped them. For those wishing to know more, I would encourage them to read the sources cited in these books.

Chapter 3
The Russo-Japanese War and Modern International Society

Yuichi Hosoya

Abstract The significance and reverberations of the Russo-Japanese War, the first in which a Western power had been defeated by an Asian nation, is the focus of this chapter. The war is viewed from both geopolitical and racial perspectives, with the 'Great Game' between Russia and Britain serving as a backdrop. It was a harbinger of the total wars of the twentieth century to come, the demise of the Russian Empire, and the rise of nationalism around the world.

The Russo-Japanese War in World History

The Russo-Japanese War was the first war between the Great Powers that the world witnessed as the curtain rose on the twentieth century. In addition, French diplomatic historian René Girault regarded the war as "the start of the most important transformation in modern international relations." By which he meant that it was a model for the twentieth century wars that followed, and "above all, the war [was] useful for detecting many important phenomena, to better understand the accelerating developments leading to World War I" (Girault 1998).

Understanding the Russo-Japanese War's significance in world history relates to understanding the wars of the twentieth century as well as the larger flow of history that came afterwards. To say it another way, it is vital to understand the Russo-Japanese War as the most important nodal point both for Japanese history and world history in the early twentieth century. Here I would like to discuss how the Russo-Japanese War sits within international relations history and give a general outline of how the war came about, instead of going into the details of the Japanese domestic political process surrounding the war, of which many reliable studies already exist.

Y. Hosoya
Faculty of Law, Department of Political Science, Keio University, Tokyo, Japan

© The Author(s) 2023
M. Yamauchi, Y. Hosoya (eds.), *Modern Japan's Place in World History*,
https://doi.org/10.1007/978-981-19-9593-4_3

Twentieth-Century Geopolitical Framework

The war, which broke out on February 8, 1904, was an event with considerable implications for subsequent developments in world history. To understand this point, we must have an understanding of European international politics that lay behind the Russo-Japanese War. Erupting at the far eastern edge of the Eurasian continent, the Russo-Japanese War was intimately linked with "The Great Game", the globe-spanning geopolitical rivalry between the British Empire, a leading sea power, and the Russian Empire, a continental one. It means that the interests of the British Empire were threatened by Russia's expansionism and its construction of the Trans-Siberian Railway, even as Japanese security was threatened by the spread of Russian influence on the Korean Peninsula.

The Anglo-Japanese Alliance, signed two years before the outbreak of the war, joined the fates of two maritime nations, Britain and Japan, hemming the Russian Empire in between them. If we place the Russo-Japanese War like so in the framework of global geopolitical rivalry on the Eurasian continent between a sea power and a land power, we can see how it is tied to the later framework of rivals: Britain versus Germany in two world wars as well as the United States plus Britain against the Soviet Union in the Cold War. Were we to do a geopolitical overview, within twentieth century world history, the war is characterized as a rivalry between a continental empire and maritime empire over a periphery of the Eurasian continent. We can understand Japan's actions in the Russo-Japanese War that blocked the continental power's hegemonic expansion in Eurasia as providing a model for international politics later in the twentieth century.

The outcome of the war exerted a decisive influence on international relations between major European countries thereafter. One consequence of the war, the threat posed by the Russian navy to the British Empire, vanished with the Russian Empire's defeat. That fact prepared the environment for a rapprochement between the two in 1907. To restate the point, it was the annihilation and defeat of the Russian navy, a product of the Russo-Japanese War, that became the basis for the later Anglo-Russian Entente, which in turn became the Triple Entente with France.

After that, the continental power that would square off against the British Empire in the twentieth century would shift from the Russian Empire to Germany, and even later, to the Soviet Union in the Cold War era. Thus, Japanese military activities unintentionally had an enormous impact on European international relations, spawning a new framework for rivalry. This was not something Japanese leaders were cognizant of during the war.

Japan's Victory as a Racial Menace

That Japan, a rising power in the Far East, was victorious in a war against the Russian Empire, Europe's greatest land army superpower, forced a fundamental transformation, in terms of the discussion of civilization, in international politics that had been dominated by large European countries until that point. The Russian Empire, "a white nation", was supposed to be superior to Japan intrinsically, both in terms of race and civilization. It was supposed to be impossible for the Japanese, a colored race, to beat Russia, a European power ruled by the proud Romanov family.

Japan overcame and defeated that distorted racist view, however, through a well-trained and disciplined military organization, effective government structure, and the existence of political-military relations that had gradually become integrated organically. The effect was to spread "Yellow Peril" ideology—the rise of the colored races and the ruin of the white race—among the major states of Europe, and a sense of crisis growing within the Russian and German empires. Which meant, as Girault argues, it was because "a victory of an Asian country was seen within Asia as something shockingly revolutionary." To restate it, it was because "a Yellow victory struck unease in Europeans and Americans and fanned great hopes in the peoples of Asia" (Girault 1998).

You do see such Yellow Peril commentary quite often in Western countries at the time. For instance, after the Triple Intervention following the First Sino-Japanese War, German Emperor Wilhelm II made the following argument in a letter addressed to Russian Tsar Nicholas II, his third cousin: "I thank you sincerely for the excellent way in which you initiated the combined action of Europe for the sake of its interests against Japan. . . . For that is clearly the great task of the future for Russia to cultivate the Asian Continent and to defend Europe from the inroads of the Great Yellow race" (Hirobe 2017).

Also, Frederick Cunliffe-Owen, the former British diplomat who moved to the United States, sounded the alarm in a piece in *The Washington Post* on March 31, 1904: Japanese successes over Russia have "terribly impaired the prestige. . . of the white races as a whole, throughout Asia." The rise of Japan as a modern nation as well as its victory over Russia whipped up a group of pundits to issue warnings of that kind of racial menace, an attitude often evident up through the mid-twentieth century.

Japan's victory in the Russo-Japanese War was an event that, above all, foretold the rise of Japan in international politics of the twentieth century as well as the rise of the sphere of non-Western civilization. It simultaneously reorganized European international relations and influenced enormously the very nature of international society. The international order, under European dominance until that point, inevitably underwent a significant transformation as the twentieth century dawned on the rise of America, a non-European power, as well as of Japan, a non-white power. This is where the significance of the Russo-Japanese War in world history lays.

World War Zero

The Russo-Japanese War is dubbed "World War Zero" in some recent studies, highlighting the important change of era it marks at the start of the twentieth century. One of the reasons is the recognition that the Russo-Japanese War is the origin of total war that came to symbolize the two world wars that followed. In addition, it was the first war in the twentieth century fought on a global scale between two major powers. The fact that the impact of the war was not limited to just Russia and Japan is perhaps the primary reason for this designation.

Yokote Shinji, professor emeritus of Keio University who wrote one of the finest works on the Russo-Japanese War, stated the following in one of his books:

> *The Russo-Japanese War, compared to the colonial wars that took place frequently at the time, was of a completely different kind, whether in terms of its scale, its tactical level, the level of weaponry used, or from the intimate relationship between the frontline and the home front that supported a long-term war. There had not been a war between Great Powers since the Franco-Prussian War, over 30 years earlier. Here we can see, plainly or in nascent form, the combination of trench warfare and machine guns, the capability to employ intelligence and propaganda, the coordination of land and sea forces to secure command of the sea, and almost all of the other warfare techniques that European countries will learn in the World War I* (Yokote 2005).

In fact, many military observers accompanied the two countries' military forces to monitor and analyze the war, and their reports had a great influence on later programs to strengthen military armaments. It was shocking how the battle sites at land and sea that they saw with their own eyes were so vastly different from those in nineteenth century Europe in general. Decisive fleet battles employing gigantic, armored vessels and ferocious land battles using machine guns on vast plains—the firepower and destructive power exceeded anything they could imagine. Their shock led to the subsequent augmentation of military capabilities by the Great Powers, which in turn resulted in World War I's violent battlefields.

Even so, the Russo-Japan War was not a real world war and there were just two belligerents: Russia and Japan. Moreover, the war's primary battle sites were limited to the Sea of Japan, the Korean Peninsula, and the neighboring Manchurian hinterland, so to the European powers this was nothing more than a conflict in distant lands the back side of the globe. Even calling it a total war, the modes of transportation and communication were the same as before, and so the Russian Empire severely lacked the resources for general mobilization of troops. The roles of Japan's ally Britain and Russia's ally France were completely indirect, meaning they had no direct impact on the war at all.

The important point is, the Russo-Japanese War set off a significant transformation of the structure of international relations among the major powers, which became evident in the several new diplomatic shifts that later link to World War I. With the Russian navy bearing fatal losses in its defeat in the Naval Battle of the Sea of Japan (Battle of Tsushima Strait), Russia's navy was no longer a threat to the British Empire. This fact, as I mentioned above, foreshadowed the movement toward the Anglo-Russia Entente (1907). Japan's victory is also tied to its advantageous position in Manchuria and on the Korean Peninsula, and Japan's advances on the continent gave rise to frictions with the United States and other major powers.

Above all, Russia's defeat in the war greatly damaged the authority of Tsar Nicholas II, which in combination with his imperial government's corrupt foundations, paved the way toward the Russian Revolution. The Russo-Japanese War is regarded as an influential war in world history when judged from it impacts—sparking transformations in the power balance and reorganization of treaties and alliances leading to World War I or kindling the disturbance of internal order that led to revolution. This is perhaps why some call it World War Zero. An examination of the history of the Russo-Japanese War from a global perspective offers us an understanding of the dynamism of international society that was embarking on a new era in the twentieth century.

Next, I would like to turn our attention to the Russian Empire's growing interest in its far eastern regions at the end of the nineteenth century.

The Tsesarevich's Visit to the Far East

Tsesarevich Nicholas II departed the Gatchina Grand Palace and set out on his long Eastern journey in October 1890. Joined by his cousin, Prince George of Greece and Denmark, he visited Egypt, India, Ceylon (Sri Lanka), Siam (Thailand), China, and Japan on his way to Vladivostok, a newly developing city on Russia's Sea of Japan coast, to attend the ceremony unveiling the Trans-Siberian Railway.

He was the first Russian heir-apparent to visit the Far East. Vladivostok was undeveloped land, far from the elegant imperial capital Saint Petersburg. Some in the imperial government came to believe that the Far East was important for Russia's future development, a position that Nicholas II also understood keenly. In that sense, the tsesarevich's visit to Vladivostok for the groundbreaking ceremony of the railway's operations symbolized this posture of growing interest in the Russian Far East at the time. Russo-Japanese ties during this period were quite cordial, as they had been for some time. The march toward war had yet to be heard.

Nicholas II, 22 years old, was hoping to experience all that Japan had to offer during his visit; "I want to marry a Japanese woman," he had written in his journals.

His cruiser anchored in the port of Nagasaki on April 27, 1891; Nicholas spent a relaxing evening with some of his crew at Volga, a Russian restaurant, on May 3. There the young tsesarevich met Michinaga Ei, a light-complexioned local woman in Western attire. It is said that, after enjoying a dance, the couple spent the night together. It was a fleeting romance (Morgun 2016).

The next morning, Nicholas returned to his cruiser with his memories of Japanese encounters of a non-official nature, where his ship weighed anchor for its next port, Kagoshima, on route to its final destination, Kobe. From there, he was scheduled to travel to Tokyo by land. However, on the way, he met with a failed assassination attempt in Ōtsu city in Shiga Prefecture (Ōtsu incident). Because of that, Nicholas II quickly changed his plans, returning to Kobe, canceling his Tokyo visit, and intending to go directly to Vladivostok. Even so, the incident did not ruin Nicholas' impressions of Japan. Later, he often would speak with fondness of his youthful adventure in Japan.

His Eastern journey experiences had a great influence on Nicholas, who became Tsar Nicholas II. According to historian Dominic Lieven who wrote a critical biography of the tsar, "...above all, Nicholas was intent on developing Russia's position in Siberia and the Far East. Particularly after 1900, his personal imprint on Russia's Far Eastern policy became very important" (Lieven 1994, p. 94). Many of the tsar's advisors at the time held a Eurocentric world view and downplayed the importance of developing the Far East; drawing from the experience of his journey, the tsar believed that Russia's future lay in the development of vast Siberia. His experiences are tied to the Russian Empire's expansion in Asia.

Expansion in Asia was also in vogue among the European powers then. In the late nineteenth to early twentieth centuries, they had largely completed their division and colonization of Africa and had turned their gaze on the next frontier, Asia. Especially when the Qing lost the First Sino-Japanese War (1894–95), exposing the dynasty's fragilities, Britain, Russia, France, and Germany all scrambled to aggrandize their own interests in China.

For instance, now-Tsar Nicholas II told Prince Henry of Prussia in October 1901, "I do not want to seize Korea—but under no circumstances can I allow the Japanese to become firmly established there. That would be a *casus belli*" (*ibid*, p. 98). Blocking the spread of Japanese influence in the power vacuum on the Korean Peninsula had become a key objective of the Russian government. Conversely, the apparent spread of Russian influence in the Joseon royal court exacerbated the Japanese government's fears.

Thus, the Far East after the Russo-Japanese War became the main stage on which European powers maneuvered diplomatically, a beguiling space to enlarge their influence. The Russo-Japanese rivalry over the Korean Peninsula was related to the trend in international politics. Thus, the framework for rivalry led both countries to war. But, at this stage, both countries still struggled to find the means to strengthen their friendly relations; war was by no means inevitable. Nevertheless, the important geopolitical setting existed, the context in which Russia and Japan operated, and is one reason that both countries were dragged into war.

The Era of the Great Game

We can highlight the geopolitical rivalry between the maritime British Empire and continental Russian Empire over the periphery of the Eurasian continent as being one of the most defining characteristics of international politics of this era. The framework for rivalry was called the Great Game. It was a rivalry on a global scale between the Russian Empire, with its Southern policy, and the British Empire, aiming to gain control over sea lanes of communication; they contended throughout the periphery of Eurasia, stretching from Europe through the eastern Mediterranean and the Middle East, British India, Southeast Asia, China, and on to the Korean Peninsula.

This meant that Japan became entangled in this framework for global geopolitical rivalry between the British and Russian empires with the signing of the Anglo-Japanese Alliance in January 1902. Japan was expected to use the modern military power it had employed to achieve its victory over Qing China to restrain Russia's southward expansion of its sphere of influence.

In *Diplomacy*, Henry Kissinger wrote that "Characteristically, Russia's appetite for Asian territory seemed to grow with each new acquisition." According to Kissinger, "... Russia's leaders took the position that the Far East was Russia's own business and that the rest of the world had no right to intervene" (Kissinger 1996). Russia's firm position on enlarging its territory inevitably aggravated its relations with Japan and its relations with Britain, which retained the largest interests in the Far East.

Meanwhile, Britain was actually undermining its national power as it built up its military forces in the Boer War in South Africa; ever greater military power was required to maintain the security and stability in the growing territory of the British Empire. To preserve Britain's global interests, the Fifth Marquess of Lansdowne, who was foreign secretary in the government of Lord Salisbury, felt it was necessary for Britain to abandon its policy of "splendid isolation" and actively build treaties and alliances. This led to the Anglo-Japanese Alliance (1902) and Anglo-French Entente (1904).

We can identify several factors that led to heightened tensions between Japan and Russia around the turn of the century. The first is the Triple Intervention following the First Sino-Japanese War, where Russia took the lead in cooperating with France, its treaty ally, and Germany to block Japan from keeping its Liaodong Peninsula territorial possessions. The intervention was linked to the Franco-Russian Entente while simultaneously being an expression of Russian fears about the expansion of Japanese influence in the Far East.

The fact that Japan had to return the Liaodong Peninsula to the Qing government under pressure by the three European powers orchestrated by Russia is remembered in Japan as a major disappointment and humiliation. On the other hand, it was also a significant motivation for Japan to draw closer to Britain, which had not been a party to the intervention. Secondly, Russia, which had dispatched its forces to protect its own interests in joining the multinational forces in the Boxer Rebellion (1900), continued to station the troops it had sent to Manchuria even after peace and security had been restored. The action resulted in protests by Japan and several other countries, and it was taken as an expression of Russia's territorial ambitions.

Russia at the time loathed the fact that Japanese control of the Korean Peninsula prevented its Southern policy of aggrandizing its own influence. It had started constructing the Trans-Siberian Railway to extend its power to its Far East. By securing a port that remained free of ice year-round (unlike Vladivostok), it wanted to gain command of the seas in the region. It probably saw the spread of Japanese influence on the Korean Peninsula as an obstacle to its goals.

The British Empire's efforts to enlarge its own sphere of influence in both the Mediterranean and the Far East, Russia considered an impediment. Russia sought to use military pressure to restrain Japan's behavior. Nicholas II met with Itō Hirobumi at a royal palace in the outskirts of Saint Petersburg in November 1901. Itō had resigned as prime minister earlier that May and thereafter had poured his energies into bringing Japan and Russia closer together. The tsar said the following, which Itō understood: "I firmly believe that an agreement between Russia and Japan is entirely possible, that such an entente would be valuable to us as well as to the peace in the Far East, and moreover, that putting this relationship to good use would serve to achieve even greater purposes" (Asada 2018).

So, we see that Russia did not desire a war with Japan. It found it inadvisable to remain a spectator as its own regional interests were threatened by Japan, a newly developed country that had rapidly bolstered its military power and achieved victory over Qing China. Thus, Tsar Nicholas II said, "I, myself, do not want Korea. However, I cannot allow the Japanese to set foot there. For Russia, this would be an act of war. Japanese in Korea would be like a new Bosporus in East Asia. Russia can never approve" (*ibid*).

From the phrase "like a new Bosporus in East Asia," we can understand that Russia viewed Eurasia as a whole, considering the matter of its western border, the Bosporus Strait, as being linked to the matter of its eastern border with the Korean Peninsula. In the end, Itō was unable to make the progress toward signing an agreement with Russia that he had hoped to achieve. The Japanese government preferred to ally with Britain instead of Russia. Japan's entry into alliance with Britain in 1902 was, to Russia, a considerable obstacle. The Anglo-Russian Great Game over Eurasia had evolved into a confrontation between the Russia Empire and the Anglo-Japanese alliance.

The Beginning of the Russo-Japanese War

Opinions within the Japanese government were divided between the anti-Russia hardliners (Komura Jutarō, Katsura Tarō, Yamagata Aritomo), who thought that a war with Russia was unavoidable in order to ensure Japan's national security and the independence of the Korean Peninsula, and those seeking to avoid war (Itō Hirobumi, Inoue Kaoru). Japanese public opinion, too, was split into pro-war and anti-war groupings. Yet, according to recent studies, it did not mean the two paths were always at odds, and many on both sides felt the necessity of reaching a mutual understanding with Russia through diplomatic negotiations as well as the necessity of strengthening cooperation with Britain (Chiba 2008).

For Itō, who had continued his efforts to establish a Russo-Japanese entente, it seemed hard to believe that Japan could win a war against the vast might of the Russian armed forces. Meanwhile, Russia was reinforcing the troops it had left in Manchuria after the Boxer Rebellion step by step. Furthermore, Russia's growing influence through Korean Emperor Gojong of the Great Han Empire was a source of deeper concern for Japan. Aleksey Kuropatkin, Russian imperial minister of war, visited Japan for negotiations on June 12, 1903, but since the Russian government held a low assessment of Japanese military power at the time, he did not appear to be serious in his discussion of the issue of Russian troop withdrawals from Manchuria.

As a compromise, the Japanese government put forward a proposal: Japan would recognize Russian influence in Manchuria in exchange for Russian recognition of its sphere of influence in Korea (*Man-Kan kōkan ron*). This stance acknowledged Russia's special position in Manchuria in order to avoid going to war. Russian hardliners, who held a poor opinion of Japan's national power on racial grounds, optimistically held that Russia would easily win a war if it were come down to it. It seems that the Japanese government thought that they could not reach a resolution of their problems through diplomatic negotiations as Tsar Nicholas II, too, did not feel a need to make any concessions to Japan.

The cabinet of Katsura Tarō believed that any further expansion of Russian influence on the Korean Peninsula threatened Japan's "lifeline." On February 6, 1904, Foreign Minister Komura Jutarō conveyed to Minister Roman Rosen of the Russian Embassy in Tokyo that Japan was severing diplomatic relations with Russia. Soon after, the Imperial Japanese Army advanced into the Korean Peninsula and eliminated the Russian army; the Imperial Japanese Navy wiped out the Russian Pacific Fleet anchored in Lüshun. Russian forces, insufficiently prepared for Japan's surprise attack, were unable to take appropriate action and fell into disarray for some time. The Russian government criticized Japan, saying that its surprise attack came before it formally declared war, and thus was illegal under international law. This charge was levied even though Russia had been inserting and stationing troops in Korea before the fact. Russia was ultimately unable to conclude that Japan's attack was illegal under the rules of war existing at the time.

On February 9, the Imperial Japanese Navy shelled Russia's protected cruiser *Varyag* and gunboat *Korietz* just outside the port of Inchon, and they were forced to scuttle themselves. This event worked to Japan's advantage in terms of gaining command of the seas around the Korean Peninsula. The Japanese government formally sent its declaration of war to the Russian government on February 10, after which the war commenced in earnest. Both parties entered a state of war at long last. Japan prosecuted the war to its advantage, having completed meticulous military preparations for war and shown firm unity among its political leadership. Divided between Lüshun and Vladivostok, the Russian fleet was handed a catastrophic defeat, unable to display its anticipated military capabilities when confronted with the ingenious tactics of the Imperial Japanese Navy.

The Portsmouth Peace Treaty

The Russian people were upset over the series of lost battles and the added miseries in their lives imposed by the war their tsar had started. Their discontent boiled over on Bloody Sunday, January 9, 1905. The losses among the people caused by the drawn-out war are connected to the increasing instability of Russian society in which the Russian Revolution later happened. With its Baltic Fleet essentially destroyed in the Naval Battle of the Sea of Japan on May 27–28, Russia completely lost control over the sea. When the fleet arrived in the Sea of Japan after a long seven-month passage from the Baltic Sea in Europe, a journey spanning half the globe, it had already lost the will to fight.

Wielding deft command of its modern naval vessels, Japan's combined fleet lost only three torpedo boats, resulting in an overwhelming victory that sent shockwaves throughout the world. Within Russia, anger at the pitiful results of the war (such as the disgrace that the Russian Imperial Navy's commander-in-chief had become a prisoner of war) precipitated widespread riots nationwide as they directed their anger against the tsar. Russia had lost both the popular support needed to continue fighting and the number of naval vessels sufficient to regain command of the sea.

Japan saw its military expenditures hit 1.8 billion yen owing to the necessity of assembling a sizable force to continue fighting with the enormous Russian military. The Japanese government found it impossible to continue bearing such costs. The mood for seeking peace was brewing on both sides.

Peace treaty negotiations began on August 9, 1905 just outside of Portsmouth, New Hampshire through the good offices of US President Theodore Roosevelt. The plenipotentiaries representing each side at the peace talks were Komura Jutarō, Japan's foreign minister, and Sergei Witte, Russia's former finance minister. Japan was unable to obtain the financial reparations or all the territorial concessions it had initially hoped for. Back in Tokyo, Itō Hirobumi thought that Japan could not continue fighting the war as it was eroding the nation's strength. So, through his strong appeals, the peace Treaty of Portsmouth was signed on September 5, 1905, putting an end to the Russo-Japanese War that had stretched on for 18 months.

What Was the Russo-Japanese War?

In his book, Yokote Shinji succinctly argues the significance of the Russo-Japanese War: "The Russo-Japanese War was a major event in which an Asian country that had set up the new Meiji system fewer than 40 years before beat Russia, a European power. It was a clear demonstration of the fact that a non-European power could challenge a European great power in a war and win, provided it could deftly implement reforms learned from the Europeans. This, you might say, was the ideology that the Russo-Japanese War begat" (Yokote 2005).

In twentieth century history, this "ideology that the Russo-Japanese War begat" spread throughout the world in the blink of an eye. Motivated by this ideology, though heedless of the intentions of Japanese leaders or the later path Japan had travelled, many non-European countries began the fight to escape from colonial rule. Indeed, this ideology and their passion, by altering world history, created the history of the twentieth century. The irony is that, even as Japan encouraged the non-- Europeans' efforts to decolonize, it later took a path that resulted in the expansion of its sphere of influence, seeking natural resources and national security, and justifying its conduct with the same principles used by the European colonial powers.

The total number of military and civilian personnel that took part in fighting the Russo-Japanese War on the Japanese side topped 1.08 million; the number of Russian troops transported by Trans-Siberian rail was on the order of 1.29 million. The number of war dead is put at 84,000 for Japan and over 45,000 for Russia (*ibid*).

Indeed, such statistics clearly show that it was a large-scale war calling for all the nation's energies, appropriately called a "total war." The rise of nationalism to mobilize the citizens in this way was indispensable.

The Japanese people, having paid an enormous sacrifice, had anticipated that the country would get territory and reparations, more than it had from the First Sino-Japanese War. But Russia held to a hardline posture at the peace talks, appearing ready to resume hostilities. Japan was in no position to fight Russia again given its lack of reserve troops, equipment, and logistics. Inferior in terms of national power, Japan felt it had to accept a peace treaty with only limited gains: the Southern Karafuto (southern part of Sakhalin Island), the Liaodong Peninsula leaseholds, and reimbursement for expenses used to care for Russian prisoners of war. Discontent with such a peace treaty, citizens gathered in Hibiya Park on September 5 and proceeded to protest violently, setting the home minister's residence ablaze. Nationalism is both the vitality that is critical to wage war as well as the pressure complicating diplomatic compromise.

The Russo-Japanese War originated in the rivalry between Japan and Russia over the spreading of influence on the Korean Peninsula. So, Japan's victory resulted in Japan occupying the superior position on the peninsula. The First Japan-Korea Agreement signed August 22, 1904 was an important step toward Japanese colonization of Korea. After the war, with Korea now placed within its sphere of influence, Japan began to feel the need to spread its influence in Manchuria, Korea's hinterland, in order to protect its interests on the peninsula.

The rampant nationalism and enormous toll in citizen's lives in the Russo-Japanese War, the first war between two major countries in the twentieth century and the first total war in history, foretold the tragedies humanity would encounter later that century. For Japan, which successfully underwent rapid modernization in the latter half of the nineteenth century, it was also an opportunity to affirm that the path that Meiji leaders had chosen was not a mistake. The Russo-Japanese War, associated as it is with the origin of total war and to Japan's construction of a modern nation, also occupies a special place in world history in the sense that it is a union of the histories of Asia and Europe. Modern international society reached a new stage of development with the Russo-Japanese War.

Bibliography: For Further Reading

Asada, Masafumi. 2018. *Nichiro kindaishi: sensō to heiwa no hyakunen* (The Modern History of Japan and Russia: A Hundred Years of War and Peace). Tokyo: Kōdansha gendai shinsho.

An outline of the history of the Russo-Japanese War focused on diplomacy that grants a deep understanding of the background of the process leading to war. A valuable book depicting the historical overview of Japan-Russian relations.

Chiba, Isao. 2008. *Kyūgaikō no keisei: nihon gaikō 1900–1919* (The Formation of Old Diplomacy: Japanese Diplomacy 1900–1919). Tokyo: Keisō Shobō.

Girault, René. Watanabe, Hirotaka et al (trans/eds). 1998. *Kokusai kankeishi 1871–1914nen: yoroppa gaiko minzoku to teikoku shugi* (Diplomatie européenne, nations et impérialisme: histoire des relations internationales contemporaines. T. 1, 1871–1914). Tokyo: Miraisha.

The French authority on diplomatic history lays out European international relations of the time from the comprehensive perspective of "international relations history," synthesizing developments in military diplomatic history and socio-economic history. We can understand the moves of the European Great Powers that took place in the run up to the Russo-Japanese War.

Hirobe, Izumi. 2017. *Jinshu sensō to iu gūwa: kōkaron to Ajia shugi* (Race War Myth—Yellow Peril and Asianism). Nagoya: The University of Nagoya Press. [English version from Kaltenbronn Schwarzwald 16/IV 95 found at http://www.gwpda.org/wwi-www/willnick/wilnicka.htm]

Kissinger, Henry. Okazaki, Hisahiko (trans). 1996. (Diplomacy). Tokyo: Nihon Keizai Shinbunsha. [English publication from Simon & Schuster.]

Lieven, Dominic C. B. 1994. Nicholas II: Twilight of the Empire. New York: St. Martin's Griffin.

Morgun, Zoya. Fujimoto, Wakio (trans). 2016. *Urajiosutoku: nihonjin kyoryūmin no rekishi 1860–1937nen* (The Japanese Mosaic of Vladivostok, 1860–1937). Tokyo: Tōkyōdō shuppan.

Yokote, Shinji. 2005. *Nichiro sensōshi: 20seiki saisho no taikokukan sensō* (The Russo-Japanese War: the 20th Century's First Major War). Tokyo: Chūō Kōron Shinsha.

The highest standard of historical research that you can read in the Japanese language on the Russo-Japanese War, replete with international research findings. As the author is a giant in the field of Russian political history, it is especially detailed on developments on the Russian side.

Additional Bibliography

Minamizuka, Shingo. 2018. *Rendōsuru sekaishi: jūkyūseiki sekai no naka no nihon* (Linked to World History: Japan in the World of the Nineteenth Century). Tokyo: Iwanami Shoten, 2018.

A study by an eminent historian laying out the linkages between European international relations and East Asian trends from an innovative viewpoint. One can understand that developments in Japan are deeply embedded in world history.

Steinberg, John W.; Menning, Bruce W.; Shimmelpennick van der Oye, David; Wolff, David; and Yokote, Shinji (eds). 2005. *The Russo-Japanese War in Global Perspective. World War Zero.* Leiden: Brill.

Chapter 4
World War I and the Origin of Sino-Japanese Conflict

Sōchi Naraoka

Abstract This chapter focuses on World War I and the origins on Sino-Japanese conflict, attributing the Twenty-One Demands as the primary source of the latter. Japan's efforts to resolve the Manchuria question underlies its issuance of the Demands, which alienated the West and is viewed by many Chinese as the start of "Japan's invasion of China." Yet, the author suggests that conflict between Japan and China was not necessarily inevitable.

The Difficulty of Evaluating the War Historically[1]

In contrast to the consensus reached in Europe on the causes, timeframe, and historical significance of World War II, historical assessment of that war remains unfinished in East Asia. There are many reasons for this, but one can be found in the remarkable complexity of the sequence of events leading to the outbreak of that war in East Asia, compared to Europe.

The war has many names in Asia. The Pacific War (also known as the Greater East Asian War or Asia-Pacific War) that broke out in December 1941 was fought as part of the world war that had already started in Europe in 1939. Japan had been fighting the Second Sino-Japanese War (which it previously referred to as the China (*Shina*) Incident, then the Japan-China (*Nikka*) Incident, in the absence of a formal declaration of war), which was incorporated into World War II. It meant that after December 1941, Japan was involved in an all-out war with the United States, Britain, and the Netherlands, as well as with China. The causes of, as well as sequence of events leading to, the start of this war, however, are very complicated and leave room

---

[1]*This chapter revises and expands upon "'Nitchū tairitsu no genten' to shite no taika nijūikkajō yōkyū" ("The Twenty-One Demands as the Source of Sino-Japanese Conflict") published in the September 2015 issue of Chūō Kōron magazine.*

S. Naraoka
The Graduate School of Law, Kyoto University, Kyoto, Japan

© The Author(s) 2023   39
M. Yamauchi, Y. Hosoya (eds.), *Modern Japan's Place in World History*,
https://doi.org/10.1007/978-981-19-9593-4_4

for many possible views. It may be clear from this brief synopsis, then, that exactly what to call this war remains a topic of debate.

There are multiple views on the starting point and length of the war. This was a war of aggression, part of the war that began in 1928 with the assassination of Zhang Zuolin, according to the judgment reached by the Tokyo Trial (the International Military Tribunal for the Far East) after the war's end. Recently, however, the Manchurian (Mukden) Incident (1931) has received more emphasis in general, and so there is a strong basis in Japan for viewing the period from that incident to the end of the war in 1945 as "the Fifteen Years' War." Meanwhile, the general emphasis in China had been placed on 1937, the outbreak of the Second Sino-Japanese War, and so they often used the expression "the Eight Year War of Resistance against Japan." But in 2017, Beijing released a statement noting that the period for the "Anti-Japanese War" would be revised from "Eight Years (1937–1945)" to "Fourteen Years (1931–1945)." Consequently, there exists a diverse set of views even regarding the chronology of the conflict between Japan and China. No matter where one stands, however, the fact remains: antagonism between Japan and China worsened in the 1930s until it morphed into an all-out war.

The Twenty-One Demands as the Source of Sino-Japanese Conflict

How and when did relations between Japan and China become antagonistic? There are a wide range of opinions on this, too. Starting with the oldest, we could look for the causes in the First Sino-Japanese War (1894–1895). Japan, the victor, compelled the Qing to promise to pay a huge sum of reparations and hand over Taiwan and the Liaodong Peninsula (Japan returned the latter because of the Triple Intervention). The Allied Nations in World War II had thought to return postwar East Asia to its status quo before the First Sino-Japanese War. In the Cairo Declaration they issued in 1943, the United States, Britain, and China demanded the return of Taiwan and "all the territories Japan has stolen from the Chinese." The San Francisco Peace Treaty, which entered into force in 1952, reaffirmed this line of thought; Japan lost all the colonies it had acquired after the First Sino-Japanese War.

This does not mean, however, that the First Sino-Japanese War caused a decisive rift to open in Japan-China relations. The great wave of Chinese students going to study in Japan is emblematic of the trending thought following the Qing's defeat that, to strengthen the nation, China needed to learn from Japan. In fact, many Chinese visited Japan after the war, including Liang Qichao, Sun Yat-sen, Wang Jingwei (born Changming), and Chiang Kai-shek. It is thought that, since Qing China was not a nation-state, the general populace had a very weak sense of having lost the war. Antagonism between Japan and China gradually increased when Japan sought to enlarge its Manchurian interests after winning its war against Russia (1894–1895), from which Japan acquired the Liaodong Peninsula and South

Manchuria Railway. But a friendly atmosphere and active people-to-people exchanges existed around the time of the Xinhai Revolution (1911). You might characterize this period of Japan-China relations as still full of possibilities and far from unwavering conflict.

I believe that what destroyed these ties and triggered the rapid intensification of conflict between Japan and China were the "Twenty-one Demands" that Japan handed to China in 1915. The document that Ōkuma Shigenobu's second cabinet presented to the Yuan Shikai administration in January comprised five groups of demands seeking the enlargement of Japan's interests:

Group 1: Japanese assumption of German interests in Shandong Province;
Group 2: expansion of Japanese interests in South Manchuria and Eastern Inner Mongolia;
Group 3: joint Japan-China administration of the Hanyeping Iron & Coal Co., Ltd.;
Group 4: no further Chinese concessions to foreigners along its coastal regions;
Group 5: placement of Japanese political, financial, and military advisors in the Chinese government; a partial merger of their police forces; Japanese commitment for military supplies to China; etc. (Japan later characterized Group 1–4 items as "demands" or "requests"[2] and Group 5 items as "wishes".)

Although it had protested vigorously, the Chinese side was forced to accept all but a part of these demands in the end. May 9, the date these demands were accepted, is remembered in China as the "Day of National Humiliation." It might be taken as the origin of anti-Japanese sentiment.

The Manchuria Question: The Source of the Twenty-One Demands

The Twenty-One Demands, which cover a rather wide range of items, was a Japanese attempt to aggrandize its interests in China at a stroke. Why did the Japanese government put forward such strong demands so suddenly?

The question of Manchuria was in the background. With its win in the Russo-Japanese War, Japan acquired a colony in mainland China for the first time, becoming a continental state. After signing the peace Treaty of Portsmouth with Russia and the Beijing Treaty of 1905 with the Qing, Japan took over the special interests that Russia held in Manchuria, such as the Liaodong Peninsula leaseholds and administration of the South Manchuria Railway. Many Japanese were dissatisfied with their government's failure to get reparations despite having paid a tremendous cost in lives lost in the war (symbolized by the Hibiya Riots following the signing of the peace treaty), and so their hopes for the Manchurian interests were that much stronger. Until the war, Manchuria was thought of as a dangerous land out of

---

[2]The term *yōkyū* encompasses these English meanings.

Japan's reach, in mighty Russia's shadow. That image changed with Japan's victory, and Manchuria became associated more as a place having "special ties"—contiguous to the Korean Peninsula, increasingly incorporated into Japan's sphere of influence—as well as a land for advancing Japanese commerce and industry and for emigration and development.

Japan's advance into Manchuria did proceed rapidly after the war. Japan increased its interests in South Manchuria's rails, mines, and coalfields under the legal basis of the Beijing Treaty of 1905, its related agreement, and secret minutes. Accordingly, the number of Japanese residing in Manchuria grew from fewer than 4000 before the war to over 76,000 in 1910. Manchuria came to be regarded as an object of sentimentality and nostalgia, land won in exchange for 100,000 brave souls and 2 billion yen from the state coffers. The push for further advances in Manchuria grew stronger within Japan after it annexed Korea in 1910. Not without reason did Europe, America, and China show greater concern that, after the Korean annexation, Japan might be trying to make Manchuria a second Korea.

The interests that Japan acquired in mainland China were not secure. The dates were set for returning these Manchurian interests—1923 for the Liaodong Peninsula, 1939 for the South Manchuria Railway—and extending the period of the leaseholds was not guaranteed. After its war with Russia, Japan was constantly aware of its diplomatic task: how to extend the leaseholds for its interests in Manchuria. With the 1911 Xinhai Revolution and the founding of the Republic of China the following year, Chinese nationalism grew stronger, and the focus turned to rights recovery, regaining concessions that China had made to the Great Powers. As its interests in Manchuria were no exception, Japan experienced a growing sense of crisis at home. After the start of the revolution, the Imperial Japanese Army and anti-foreign hardliners insisted on a policy of intervention, with one objective being the retention of interests in Manchuria. Such intervention did not happen, since the second cabinet of Saionji Kinmochi was following policies of non-interference in China's domestic affairs and maintaining the status quo in Manchuria. But it should be apparent that an elevated sense of crisis over maintaining the Manchurian interests already existed during this period.

One of the most capable Japanese diplomats at the time keenly aware of the need to resolve the Manchuria question was Katō Takaaki. While serving as the Ambassador to the United Kingdom in January 1913, Katō met with Foreign Secretary Edward Grey and gained his understanding regarding the extension of the Manchurian leasehold period that was looming in 10 years. Taking up the foreign minister position in the second Ōkuma Shigenobu cabinet the following year, Katō aimed to resolve the Manchuria question. It was undoubtedly what he emphasized most when putting forward the Twenty-One Demands; the Group 2 demands addressed the Manchuria question. In short, resolving the Manchuria question, one of the biggest pending matters that Japanese diplomacy faced after the Russo-Japanese War, was the trigger for the Twenty-One Demands.

Outbreak of World War I and the Twenty-One Demands

The extension of the Manchurian leasehold periods was unilaterally advantageous for Japan and held absolutely no merits for China, so getting China to accede to it was rather challenging. Chinese acceptance would require something valuable in return, something that World War I suddenly offered to Japan.

World War I was a major conflict fought by nearly all the world's leading countries, divided into the Allied Powers (Britain, France, Russia) and the Central Powers (Germany, Austro-Hungary). It was sparked by the Austro-Hungarian declaration of war against Serbia on July 28, 1914, and by August 4, Germany, Russia, France, Belgium, then Britain had joined the fight. Under Foreign Minister Katō's powerful leadership, Japan entered the war on August 23 on the side of the Allied Powers, citing the Anglo-Japanese Alliance as the rationale. Japan forced Germany to surrender its South Sea islands in October and occupied its leasehold territory on China's Shandong Peninsula around Jiaozhou Bay. Along with purging German influence in the Asia-Pacific region, Japan acquired the right to ask to take over German interests after the war, thus achieving its expected aim in joining the war.

These, however, were not Katō's primary purposes for entering the war. His foremost objective was to use the return of the newly acquired German interests on the Shandong Peninsula as a bargaining chip to gain larger interests from China—resolution of the Manchuria question. Had Japan not seized it, Germany could have leased the territory for 99 years (i.e., through 1997) under the terms of the convention respecting the lease of Jiaozhou signed in 1898. By engendering goodwill through the conditional return of this area, Katō thought to pressure the Chinese side to extend the period for returning the leases in Japan's Manchurian interests. In other words, what prompted the offer to resolve the Manchuria question in exchange for resolving the Shandong question was the Twenty-One Demands.

Reaching a compromise on the Twenty-One Demands may not have been that difficult if Katō had negotiated with China after paring down the discussion to just the Manchuria question (Group 2) and the Shandong question (Group 1). The Western Great Powers had not shown any objection to the substance of Groups 1–4 when Japan informally briefed them after the Twenty-One Demands had been presented to China. China's negative reaction and refusal were perhaps inevitable. But in the end, China acceded to Japan's ultimatum, a reduced set of demands that included the key parts of Groups 1–4 but omitted the Group 5 items. And barring any unforeseen circumstances, it was believed that resolving the Manchuria question through diplomatic negotiation was not outside the realm of the possible.

The actual diplomatic negotiations over the Twenty-One Demands were very disorderly. There are three reasons why they were so disorderly: the agitated state of Japanese public sentiment, Katō's clumsy diplomatic leadership, and the Chinese side's skillful resistance.

Around the outbreak of World War I, Japanese public opinion became excited, believing a good opportunity had arrived for Japan to expand its interests in China, the perfect time since the European powers had no spare capacity to be involved with

China matters. So, the Ōkuma cabinet was under pressure to act. Unable to restrain this "expansion fever" coming from every corner of the country, Katō and his Ministry of Foreign Affairs did not limit the demands to just the Manchuria and Shandong questions, and instead piled on every issue pending at the time, and ultimately wound up with the bloated Twenty-One Demands. One gets a sense that the Twenty-One Demands was, in effect, just an exhaustive list of issues in the Japan-China relationship after the Russo-Japan War. That Japan foisted such a large list of demands upon China is the fundamental cause of the disorder in the diplomatic talks.

Around the time of Japan's entry into World War I, there was a groundswell of opinion in China that, naturally, Tokyo would return the Shandong concessions to China. This was the context in which the government of Yuan Shikai approached the diplomatic talks with Japan, and it maintained a firm posture throughout. By skillfully leaking information regarding the talks to the public at home and abroad, the Yuan administration succeeded in fomenting domestic public opinion against Japan and increasing the Western Powers' wariness toward Tokyo. The term Twenty-One Demands was something the Chinese side began using to stoke this anti-Japanese trend, and the appellation eventually stuck throughout the world.

Meanwhile, because its negotiating plans lacked clarity and consistency, Japan often found itself playing catch-up in the talks and in managing public opinion. Katō was put in a situation where he was unable to make any concessions, because a general election was scheduled for March and the public mood remained agitated. Tokyo's attempt initially to keep the Group 5 demands secret from the Western Powers played a major role in hardening the attitude of Britain and the United States against it. Japan sent China an ultimatum in early May that omitted the Group 5 "wishes" and successfully got China to accept most of the items from Groups 1–4 of the Twenty-One Demands. While Japan did achieve its expected objectives after great effort, it came at the significant cost of contributing to a vigorous anti-Japanese movement in China and increasing the West's mistrust of Japan.

The Twenty-One Demands badly tarnished the image that China had of Japan. Britain, France, and Russia all held more special interests in China, but presenting the Twenty-One Demands made Japan the sole enemy that was impeding China's efforts to build a new nation. There were large-scale boycotts of Japanese goods throughout China, and many Chinese students studying in Japan returned home. It was the first time that such large-scale and organized anti-Japanese protests had happened. The Twenty-One Demands had indeed become the source for later conflict and antagonism between Japan and China. (For details, please refer to Naraoka 2015.)

How to Consider the Twenty-One Demands

Some people do not think the Twenty-One Demands was problematic whatsoever, being the sort of diplomacy often undertaken under imperialism. For instance, Tamogami Toshio, former chief of staff of Japan's Air Self-Defense Force, has written, "Some people say that this [Japan compelling China to accept the Twenty-One Demands] was the start of Japan's invasion of China, but if you compare these demands to the general international norms of colonial administration by the great powers at the time, there was nothing terribly unusual about it" (Tamogami 2008).

Certainly, the Western Great Powers continued to pursue their traditional imperialistic diplomacy during World War I. It is widely acknowledged that the division of the former Ottoman Empire's territories by Britain and France is the source of the problems in the Middle East we have today. To restore *Italia irredenta*, Italy left its Triple Alliance with the Central Powers and entered the war after getting a guarantee from the Allied Powers about acquiring these perceived Italian interests under foreign rule. The United States, too, conducted military interventions in Mexico, Haiti, and the Dominican Republic, and made Nicaragua a protectorate. Perhaps Japan's Twenty-One Demands does not even rise to the level of this conduct by the western Great Powers.

When Japan had briefed the Western Great Powers about Groups 1–4 soon after presenting China with the demands, none of them showed any particular concern. They protested vigorously, however, when they later learned of the existence of the Group 5 items. The demands in Group 5, they believed, not only infringed on their own vested interests, they went against the principles regarding China that the Great Powers, including Japan, had affirmed until that point—territorial integrity, equality of opportunity, and the "Open Door"—and included substance that would interfere in China's domestic affairs.

The purpose of the Anglo-Japanese Alliance, as revised in 1911, was "[t]he preservation of the common interests of all Powers in China by insuring the independence and the integrity of the Chinese Empire and the principle of equal opportunities for the commerce and industry of all nations in China." So, Britain, which saw Group 5 demands at cross-purposes to this, strongly pressed Japan to reconsider its demands. France also voiced deep concerns about Group 5 items. The attitude of the United States was rather hardline. It viewed the Twenty-One Demands as running counter to the Takahira-Root Agreement (1908) that laid down such concepts as "the principle of equal opportunity for commerce and industry" and "preserv[ing] the common interest of all powers" in China. So, after Japan and China concluded negotiations and reached agreement, the United States released a diplomatic note in the name of Secretary of State William Jennings Bryan that took the position of repudiating the outcome of the talks in its entirety. Even though the US attitude—attempting to advocate for China from the moral high ground by emphasizing universal values (often termed "missionary diplomacy")—is quite exceptional, Britain and the other European Powers considered the Twenty-One Demands as having gone too far. From the point that it instilled in the West a strong distrust toward Japan, the Twenty-One Demands undoubtedly became a source of future problems.

How should the Demands be viewed in the context of relations with China? Generally, in China the Twenty-One Demands is taken as the "starting point for Japan's invasion of China." Therefore, Yuan Shikai is deemed a "collaborator and traitor to his country" and his foreign policies are criticized heavily.

Such criticism is unavoidable perhaps, in light of the fact that he ultimately did accept the majority of the demands. Yet, a detailed examination of the negotiating process reveals how skillfully the Yuan government managed these diplomatic talks. It attempted to prolong them, fanned anti-Japanese opinion by leaking information about them to the press in China and overseas, and got the Powers to rein in Japan. The Yuan administration's negotiating policy extracted a key Japanese concession, the dropping of Group 5 items. (For an appraisal of Yuan's diplomacy, please refer to Kawashima 2014.)

Militarily weak, the Yuan government had no choice but to concede, but it had resisted Japan using all the powers it had. The popular dissatisfaction with the extent of concessions made poured over into an upsurge of Chinese nationalism, an energy that exploded in the May Fourth Movement (1919) after the end of World War I. Considering the history up to that point of Japan unilaterally enlarging its interests in Manchuria, it is quite possible to see the Twenty-One Demands as the starting point for China's counteroffensive. By resolving the Manchuria question and acquiring new special interests besides, Japan gained the advantage in the short term but at the considerable cost of losing the faith and trust of the Chinese people. The Twenty-One Demands did narrow the potential for friendship and cooperation between Japan and China.

Could Japan-China Conflict Have Been Avoided?

This does not mean, however, that Sino-Japanese conflict was inevitable after the Twenty-One Demands. Throughout the 1910s, Japan built a degree of amicable relations with Duan Qirui, Zhang Zuolin, and other regional military leaders and continued to support the path of mutual understanding with Sun Yat-sen, Chiang Kai-shek, and other revolutionaries. (Incidentally, Sun Yat-sen did not regard the Twenty-One Demands in a completely negative light because it did lead to the overthrow of the Yuan government.) After World War I, the Hara Takashi cabinet rebuilt a policy of cooperative diplomacy with the West and attempted to construct a new relationship with China on the basis of non-interference in its domestic affairs and emphasis on commercial ties. Even Katō Takaaki, the man responsible for the Twenty-One Demands, keenly regretted his own failed policies, and so during his time as prime minister (1924–1926) pursued a steady policy of international cooperation (Shidehara Diplomacy). Relations between Japan and China in the 1920s still retained an ability to right itself, and the two countries struggled to find ways to resume friendly ties.

I would like to highlight two factors that led to the failure of these efforts and deepened Japan's conflict with China: a mistaken view, widely held among the Japanese, that China would do everything Japan's way and strong public support for expanding Japanese interests on the Chinese mainland.

As I mentioned above, the Twenty-One Demands grew out of a fever for aggrandizing Japan's special interests, a sentiment found throughout the country. Popular opinion remained extremely hawkish after the demands were presented, with the majority in political circles, the military, the business world, and the media calling on the government to achieve the demands. Just a minority calmly observed the diplomatic negotiations over the Demands; popular sentiment was on the boil. As an illustration of this, one widely used expression of that time was a "Monroe Doctrine for Asia" (the concept that Japan should determine matters in Asia, along the lines of the US Monroe Doctrine in the Americas).

This hardline attitude toward China fell silent for a while after World War I but reemerged energetically in the latter half of the 1920s with the Shandong Expeditions, the assassination of Zhang Zuolin, and the Manchurian Incident. Thereafter, Japan fell into a repetitive pattern: some politicians and members of the army would clamor for expanding interests on the Chinese mainland, with the media and public opinion following in their footsteps, and the government being dragging along behind them. The policy-making process during the Twenty-One Demands reincarnated, you might say. The Twenty-One Demands is an example of the Japanese government, dragged along by popular opinion, advancing headlong into mainland China, an experience from which we should learn very important lessons.

Bibliography: For Further Reading

Tamogami, Toshio. 2008. *Nihon ha shinryaku kokka de atta no ka* (Was Japan an Aggressor Nation? [True Interpretations of Modern History Prize-Winning Essay]). [English from the APA site https://ajrf.jp/ronbun/pdf/vol01_eng.pdf]

Additional Bibliography

Kawashima, Shin (eds). 2014. *Rekishi no naka no nihon seiji, 3 Kindai chūgoku o meguru kokusai seiji* (Japanese Politics in History (Vol. 3): International Politics surrounding Modern China). Tokyo: Chūō Kōron Shinsha.
A publication of Mr. Kawashima's dissertation, "The Twenty-One Demands and Japan-China Relations: a Reconsideration—with a focus on the Chinese Response," that clearly lays out the Chinese side's reaction to the Twenty-One Demands.
Naraoka, Sōchi. 2015. *Taika nijūikkajō yōkyū towa nandattanoka: daiichiji sekai taisen to nitchū tairitsu no genten* (What is the Historical Meaning of the

21 Demands? World War I and the Origin of Sino-Japanese Conflict). Nagoya: The University of Nagoya Press.

A study analyzing the Twenty-One Demands from the perspectives of the intent and the background for Japan's putting them forward, developments in popular opinion and the Great Powers, and the influence of domestic politics.

Yamamuro, Shin'ichi; Okada, Akeo; Koseki, Takashi; and Fujihara, Tatsushi (eds). 2014. *Gendai no kiten daiichiji sekai taisen* (The Starting Point of the Contemporary: The First World War (Vol. 1)—A Global War). Tokyo: Iwanami Shoten.

A publication bringing together dissertations that consider the connections between World War I and East Asia from a global vantage point.

Chapter 5
Transformational Period in Japan-China Modern Relations (1910s to 1930s)

Shin Kawashima

Abstract The chapter details various transformations in relations between Japan and China from 1900s to 1930s. The Qing dynasty's collapse coincided with the period of the Boxer Rebellion, the formation of Chinese nationalism, Japanese acquisition of Russian interests in Manchuria, and the Xinhai Revolution. The Twenty-One Demands were a turning point in Japan-China relations, even as both countries entered World War I to bolster their own national interests. The Washington Treaty System did not prevent the gradual collapse of Great Power cooperation over China and the outbreak of the second Sino-Japanese War.

Reversal of the Power Balance in Japan-China Relations

From Equal to Unequal

Generally speaking, the modern period of Japan-China relations opens with the Sino-Japanese Amity Treaty of 1871. It is called an equal treaty, mutually recognizing limited consular jurisdiction (in contrast to extraterritoriality). Whether from the arguments made in the negotiation process or from Article 6 stipulating that communication between the two countries would be written in Chinese (a Chinese translation was required for any documents sent in Japanese), you could conclude that the Qing held the advantage (Okamoto and Kawashima 2009).

"Japan won the First Sino-Japanese War, an East Asian confrontation between the Qing dynasty, an aging, waning power, and Japan, a newly developed power under the Meiji Restoration." While not mistaken, this perspective found in Mutsu Munemitsu's *Kenkenroku*, inter alia, is incapable of capturing the complexity of Japan-China relations in the late nineteenth century. The Qing were in a superior position on the Korean Peninsula in the 1880s, even militarily, following the Imo

S. Kawashima
Department of International Relations, The Graduate School of Arts and Sciences, The University of Tokyo, Tokyo, Japan

© The Author(s) 2023
M. Yamauchi, Y. Hosoya (eds.), *Modern Japan's Place in World History*,
https://doi.org/10.1007/978-981-19-9593-4_5

Incident and Gapsin Coup, having dispatched Yuan Shikai there as a resident military and political advisor. Even as it maintained tributary relations with the Joseon, the Qing strengthened its control over the kingdom. In the latter half of that decade, the Qing augmented its Beiyang Navy, purchasing large-scale warships from Europe, and ordered it to patrol the eastern side of the Korean Peninsula in the Sea of Japan from its naval bases on the Shandong and Liaodong peninsulas starting in 1886. Qing China was not simply an old power wasting away in its decrepitude.

Japan did beat the Qing in the First Sino-Japanese War; equipment and training are credited as the primary factors for its victory. Under the Treaty of Shimonoseki (1895), Japan not only obtained Taiwan to colonize and an indemnity of 200 million taels of silver, the Qing also agreed to accord Japan the same status as the Western Great Powers. More specifically, Japan acquired unilateral extraterritoriality and most favored nation status, and the Qing lost tariff autonomy with respect to Japan, too. This did not result in an immediate shift in the power balance between the two nor did it mean the worsening of bilateral ties. Chinese intellectuals, such as those involved with the Hundred Days of Reform (Wuxu Reforms), showed a willingness to learn from Japan.

The Boxer Rebellion and Great Power Cooperation

During the Boxer Rebellion of 1900, the Qing had formally declared war on the Western Great Powers as a domestic measure and so, after losing to the Eight-Nation Alliance, it signed the Beijing Protocol (Xinchou Treaty). Under the treaty, the Western Great Powers gained 450 million taels of silver in reparations (the Boxer Indemnities) and the right to place guards in the Legation Quarter and station troops in the area from the coast to Beijing. The treaty also stipulated that the Qing would set up a Ministry of Foreign Affairs as the organization to conduct its diplomacy. Behind this treaty, the most comprehensive between the Qing and the Western Great Powers since the Treaty of Tianjin (1858), lay the Western Great Powers' principles of the Open Door and maintaining China's integrity, their support for the Qing's construction of a modern nation, and their cooperation with respect to extending loans to China. Japan became truly incorporated into the Great Power relationship toward China through its participation in the Beijing Protocol.

Under the name of [Emperor] Guangxu's New Policies, the Qing undertook reforms to build a modern state with the support of the Western Great Powers. Modern systems and institutions for law, education, and the military (primarily army) were introduced. Imperial civil service examinations were abolished in 1905 and an academic record under the new school system became a condition for civil service employment. For that reason, many young Chinese men attended universities in Japan, the least costly and most convenient place to obtain a degree. From Japan, they learned about Western (more than Japanese) law and state institutions. Even so, the time spent in Japan became their personal experience with a modern state.

The Formation of Chinese Nationalism

After the First Sino-Japanese War, the Western Great Powers gained leased territories along the Chinese coast and constructed naval bases there as a center for their
spheres of influence. This carving up of China by the Western Great Powers, conduct
that went hand-in-hand with Social Darwinist thinking, greatly alarmed Chinese
intellectuals and spurred a rapid growth in patriotic spirit. The first decade of the
twentieth century is the period when we begin to see the shape of China emerge, as
the Qing rule gradually became unified and centralized over areas that had been
separate until that point: Manchuria, Mongolia, Tibet, Xinjiang (Xinjiang Province
was established in the 1880s), and the provinces where the majority of residents were
of Han ethnicity. As it rapidly built a modern state in this space, the Qing tried to
extend its control over these societies more than it had previously. Burdened by
heavy indemnities, the Qing faced many problems on the financial front, so it had no
option but to proceed with modern state building by either depending on foreign
loans or shifting the financial burden onto these societies. Such financial limitations
arising out of the construction of a modern state became one of the causes of the
Xinhai Revolution.

The opening of the twentieth century is also known as the period for nurturing the
consciousness of "China" and "Chinese people." It is said that Chinese nationalism
manifested through several incidents, including exclusionary US immigration acts,
the Humankind Pavilion incident in Japan (the problematic incident at the Fifth
National Industrial Exhibition in Osaka (1903) where Ainu, Korean, and Ryūkyū
people were exhibited in a human zoo designated the "Anthropological Pavilion"),
and the Anti-Russian Movement (1903) against Russia's continued occupation of
Manchuria. Certainly, the Yuanmingyuan (Old Summer Palace) had been destroyed
and the capital pillaged during the Second Opium War (Arrow War) with Britain and
France, yet there had not been a large reaction then. Beginning in the early 1900s, in
contrast, Chinese who had studied abroad and urban residents would protest vigorously against even diplomatic proceedings (Yoshizawa 2003). At the same time, a
relative perspective was spreading that saw the world as a group of nations, side by
side, and designated the Qing Empire as one country in that world
(Kawashima 2004).

The Russo-Japanese War and South Manchuria Interests

Russia did not withdraw its troops from Manchuria after the war against the Boxers,
nor did it withdraw all of them after having talks about their withdrawal. This
(in)action not only upset the Chinese public, it stoked growing criticism from the
Western Great Powers on the principle of their cooperation with respect to the Qing
Empire. In the Japanese historical context, after the (Russian-led) Triple Intervention, the slogan "enduring unspeakable hardships for the sake of revenge" was part

of the fabric leading up to the Russo-Japanese War. In contrast, one of the causes of that war in the view of Chinese history was the fact that Russia had smashed the Western Great Powers' cooperation regarding the Qing and continued to do so even after the Anglo-Japanese Alliance was signed. Russia was the first to disrupt this Great Power cooperation.

The Qing Empire was neutral for the Russo-Japanese War, but the Chinese initially leaned somewhat toward Japan's side. It was possible to regard Japan, in opposing the Russian occupation of Manchuria, as an ally from the Qing's perspective. After the war's conclusion, the Japanese government bestowed honors and awards on many Qing bureaucrats, in fact. Once the realization sank in that Japan had just acquired the interests in Manchuria in place of Russia after all, it fueled a backlash against Japan.

The Russo-Japanese War resulted in Japan paying a cost of many lives lost for a gain of the South Manchurian interests, without any indemnity. Moreover, the lease period for the Guandong (Kantō) Leased Territory including Lüshun and Dalian was 25 years starting in 1898, and many other interests were time limited, including the railroad. Subsequently, Japan sought to extend the leases of its interests in South Manchuria to make them more secure, an objective that became a source of confrontation for Japan with China as well as with the Western Great Powers.

The Western Great Powers had strengthened their cooperative relations around the time of the Russo-Japanese War, recognizing each other's special interests in China. From China's standpoint, however, this stronger Great Power cooperation over China meant greater difficulty in revising the unequal treaties and recovering its national rights.

Situation at the Time of the Xinhai Revolution

The Xinhai Revolution began October 10, 1911 in Wuchang in Hubei Province. Subsequent developments from the destruction of the Qing Empire to the foundation of the Republic of China (ROC) continued until 1913, when countries recognized the ROC government. The Qing dynasty, which had relied on foreign loans to implement its policy of nationalizing the railroads and had entrusted their management to foreigners, faced a strong pushback over the low purchase price from the powerbrokers who had originally provided the funds to construct the railroads in the regional societies. A movement protesting railroad nationalization happened in Sichuan Province and the army in Hubei Province left to go suppress it. While it was away, a revolution arose in Hubei Province, which declared its autonomy from the Qing dynasty. Thereafter, all provinces south of the Yangtze River Basin declared their autonomy and their representatives organized a government: the Republic of China, founded in Nanjing on January 1, 1912, with Sun Yat-sen as its provisional president. As the Qing court still existed in Beijing at that time, there was a standoff between two governments, one in the north and one in the south. Britain served as a mediator between the two.

Irrespective of the Anglo-Japanese Alliance, Japan tried its own approach to the situation in China, heedless of British intentions, as it now felt it had become a "first-class power" through its war victories against the Qing and Russian empires. Britain carried out its good offices between the Nanjing and Beijing governments without sufficient coordination with Japan, too.

Although the north-south conference resulted in the collapse of the Qing dynasty, the emperor continued to reside in the Forbidden City after his abdication, and Yuan Shikai established a government based on the Qing's civil service and military. This government succeeded to the various treaties the Qing Empire had entered into. The Republic of China was revolutionary: the republican state, established after the Qing dynasty had been rejected, was a repudiation of imperial institutions. On the other hand, as a state that inherited the Qing dynasty's foundations, it had an aspect of the historical virtuous successor to a Chinese emperor who abdicated rather than leave the throne to an heir. Japan opened diplomatic relations with the new state in the autumn of 1913. Continuing to cooperate, the Great Powers supported Yuan Shikai, whom they called "the strongman."

Turning Point: The Twenty-One Demands

China and World War I

World War I was the first international issue Yuan encountered, even as he maneuvered to increase his own authority by defanging the institutions of China's assembly-led republican state. China declared neutrality, lacking the military might to fight the Great Powers and fearing that its own lands might become battlefields because of the presence of German, British, and Japanese forces. After consultations with neutral China, Japan, having entered the war, jointly attacked Germany's base in Jiaozhou Bay with the British and occupied the Shandong Peninsula. Japan justified its action by saying it would return these German interests to China, but it continued to rule Shandong until 1922. World War I presented new turning points for Japan-China relations and for relations among the Great Powers with respect to China. The Twenty-One Demands presented January 18, 1915 was one of the most serious.

What Was the Twenty-One Demands?

The Twenty-One Demands was 21 demands/requests that Japan gave to President Yuan Shikai of the ROC government in Beijing. At the time, Ōkuma Shigenobu was Japan's prime minister, Katō Takaaki was foreign minister, and Hioki Eki was minister to China. The Twenty-One Demands is deeply etched in modern Chinese history as a display of Japanese aggression against China that exploited the opportunity of European nations' inattention to Asia because of their all-consuming focus on World War I, as well as a display of the traitorous nature of the Yuan government, which caved to the Japanese government and accepted its demands in hopes of getting its agreement to support Yuan to become emperor (Tang 2010). In Japan, the Demands, especially the handling of the Group 5 items mentioned below, is spoken of as one example of a mistake in Japanese diplomacy (Naraoka 2015).

The demands/requests were categorized into five groups. Group 1 concerned Japan's taking over German interests on the Shandong Peninsula that Japan now occupied; Group 2 concerned the interests in South Manchuria that Japan had gained from the Russo-Japanese War, the extension of lease periods as well as the enlargement into eastern Mongolia; Group 3 dealt with the Hanyeping Iron & Coal Co. Ltd.; and Group 4 dealt with the territorial integrity of China. Foreign Minister Katō had given the Great Powers advance notice of Groups 1–4, but not Group 5, which comprised the Chinese government's employment of Japanese political, financial, and military advisors, the creation of a joint Sino-Japanese police force, and other items.

Japan dropped the Group 5 items from the January 18 version of its 21 demands, reworked it into 24 articles, and presented that on April 26, 1915; it issued an ultimatum on May 5, which the Yuan government accepted on May 9. These 24 articles were the basis for the two treaties signed and 13 diplomatic notes exchanged on May 25. (These are known as the "Min 4 treaties" in Chinese history; Min 4 is the fourth year of the Republic, or 1915.)

Why Was the Twenty-One Demands a Turning Point?

We might call the Twenty-One Demands something that shows Japan's view or attitude toward China, a post-Russo-Japanese War sense of superiority, a first-class power mentality, the development of a China policy unbound by the Anglo-Japanese Alliance. In other words, while the Europeans were too busy with World War I to pay attention to Asia, Japan pressed China (a neutral in that war) on the Shandong Peninsula. Japan, having used the Anglo-Japanese Alliance as the rationale to join the war against Germany, occupied that peninsula under the pretext of returning these interests to China but had not. Instead, it sought to retain them, conditioning their return on the extension of the leases on its South Manchurian interests gained in the Russo-Japanese War (i.e., the Guandong Leased Territory including Lüshun and Dalian had a 25-year period, and had to be returned to China in 1923).

In addition, there is the matter of the Group 5 items that Japan did not disclose in its briefings to the Great Powers. Japan's actions were recognized as disrupting Great Power cooperation. That is perhaps why Great Power cooperation vis-à-vis China was reaffirmed at the Washington Conference held from 1921 to 1922. Researchers of Japanese diplomatic history, therefore, emphasize that the Twenty-One Demands would not have been such a major issue if Japan had not included the Group 5 items. Yet, the Twenty-One Demands left deep scars in the Japan-China bilateral relationship, and subsequently being friendly toward Japan become taboo in China; even in relations among the Great Powers over China, Japan came to be viewed as a problem.

Furthermore, there are various explanations for why Japan presented the Group 5 items, such as they were bargaining terms, or they were actually "requests" (not "demands"), or both. Those in charge of China's diplomacy at the time, notably Cao Rulin and others who had studied in Japan, explained that these Group 5 items were bargaining terms frequently employed in Japanese diplomacy and so their approach in the talks was to completely ignore them, which is what they did in fact. Thus, the Group 5 content was not included among the 24 articles that Yuan accepted on May 9, 1915.

The Problem of Yuan Shikai's Diplomacy

Aside from not discussing the Group 5 items, the Chinese government's negotiating plans for the Twenty-One Demands assumed that China would have to accept the items regarding the interests on the Shandong Peninsula (Group 1) and those in South Manchuria, which were Japan's core Group 2 demands. Lacking the military power to resist the Japanese military, China decided to try to use its standing as a neutral country to regain these interests in the peace treaty after the end of the Great War in Europe. Moreover, it presumed that, by appealing to the Great Powers after the war, the treatment of the South Manchuria interests would revert to that in the original treaty. The ROC negotiating plan as well as the actual talks were careful and thorough, and consistent with the international environment and national abilities at the time.

In point of fact, research on the Twenty-One Demands negotiating process remains insufficient. One argument in Japanese academia, strongly influenced by the memoirs of Paul Samuel Reinsch, US minister to China at the time, holds that Yuan Shikai's government had conducted talks with Japan under America's influence. But there is hardly any evidence indicative of that to be found in China's diplomatic archives. Yet, contemporaneous diplomatic assessments and books written in the early 1930s (for instance, Wang, 1932–1934) paint a relatively more positive picture of the Yuan administration's diplomacy related to the Twenty-One Demands. When the Guomindang and the Chinese Communist Party later criticized Yuan, his Twenty-One Demands diplomacy also came under criticism.

China Enters World War I

Negative sentiment toward Japan grew in China in conjunction with the Twenty-One Demands. Meanwhile, there was a textbook controversy around the time of Japan's occupation of Shandong, and the Japanese government protested to the Chinese government that Chinese textbooks were anti-Japanese. A boycott of Japanese products, mainly in urban areas, also happened during this period.

Japan made attempts to improve its deteriorating ties with China, of course. President Li Yuanhong and Premier of the State Council Duan Qirui led the ROC government after the 1916 death of Yuan Shikai, who had fumbled around with efforts to revive the imperial system in his later years. Duan, who had inherited control from Yuan over everything military related, was the one Japan approached. Japan sought to improve relations with Duan in stages by providing a huge amount of loans. Since all government loans to the Chinese government were undertaken by cooperation among the Great Powers, Japan constantly referred to it as lending by private citizens. These were the Nishihara loans, extended in the name of Nishihara Kamezō. Duan certainly succeeded in strengthening his own base of support with these loans, and his subordinates, such as Xu Shuzheng, reoccupied Outer Mongolia and some of his troops even joined the Siberia Intervention.

For the ROC, 1917 was a decisive year. It entered World War I as a member of the Entente, declaring war on Germany and Austria on August 14. The ROC had already lodged a protest and severed diplomatic relations, but there had been a debate domestically whether to enter the war. Joining the war did not mean sending troops to European battlefields, because there were still fears that China would again become the battleground or be invaded if it were to get embroiled in the war.

President Li, cautious about entering the war, and Duan, a member of the pro-entry faction, argued repeatedly in the first half of 1917, and ultimately Duan won the advantage and Feng Guozhang became president. The international community, particularly the United States, hoped that China would enter the war, and even Japan gradually came to support China's entry. Entry into the war meant for Duan that he could further bolster his support base with additional loans from Japan and other foreign countries, but it also held several merits for Beijing.

First, it meant the possibility of revising China's unequal treaties with Germany and Austria. Second, it meant that, by participating in the postwar peace talks as one of the victors, Beijing could make the issue of the Twenty-One Demands and Chinese recovery of the Japanese-occupied Shandong Peninsula a focus of that venue. Third, it would be able to join the postwar League of Nations as a founding member state, very important in terms of elevating its international status. Fourth, by declaring war, China could at least stop paying the Boxer Indemnity to Germany, which was paid the largest amount, which was the most urgent matter for Beijing. Japan, Britain, and all the Great Powers had said that, were China to declare war, they would defer its payment of the Boxer Indemnities for 5 years beginning December 1917. By entering the war, China had hoped that it might obtain new loans in addition to the temporary relief from its financial burden, paying the Boxer Indemnities.

The Merits of Entering the War

China became a victor by entering the war. It was its first win against a great power since the Opium War. It meant the possibility of joining the League of Nations as a founding member state. However, the prospects seemed rather dim regarding the elimination of the various treaties and notes exchanged that implemented the Twenty-One Demands, including the extension of the South Manchurian lease periods, and the recovery of Germany's Shandong interests.

China had sent plenipotentiary representatives to the 1919 Paris Peace Conference; as the peace conference approached, anti-Japanese movements were growing at home. Also, in part owing to the influence of US President Woodrow Wilson's principle of national self-determination, China had expectations for "truth" and "justice" at the Paris Peace Conference and in the League of Nations, that is, rectifying the unequal treaties and the Great Powers' heavy-handed conduct and realizing a more ideal world order.

However, even the support that Wilson had initially pledged to China was impossible because Britain, France, and Japan had reconciled their mutual interests. The ROC delegation was suddenly faced with the possibility it would walk away empty-handed. Against that backdrop, the May Fourth Movement occurred in Beijing on May 4, 1919. It is very easy to understand the basic question the demonstrators had: why was a victorious China unable to recover the loser Germany's special interests in China? During this period, a suspicion already lurked among the students who had started the protest that the governments of Yuan Shikai, and both Li Yuanhong and Feng Guozhang with Duan Qirui had been engaged in a traitorous diplomacy with Japan, so they began to denounce those responsible for the Chinese government's negotiations with Japan on an individual basis. Certainly, the "Japan School," the cadre of Japan hands who had studied in Japan, gradually lost their positions in the Ministry of Foreign Affairs throughout the 1910s.

Many of the men who formed the core of China's delegation at the Paris Peace Conference had studied in the United States. That is true of V.K. Wellington Koo (Gu Weijun), Alfred Sao-ke Sze (Shi Zhaoji), and Chengting Thomas (C.T.) Wang (Wang Zhengting). Delegation head Lou Tseng-Tsiang (Lu Zhengxiang) had been a civil servant since the Qing dynasty.

Once they understood that the Shandong interests were to be transferred from Germany to Japan in the Treaty of Versailles, the peace treaty with Germany, they investigated ways to sign the treaty while making a reservation regarding just that article. They were worried about Article 1 of the treaty, that signatories to the treaty became founding members of the League of Nations. The problem for the diplomats in Paris was whether not signing the Treaty of Versailles meant that China would be ineligible to join the League of Nations. Faced with the May Fourth Movement, Beijing instructed them to sign in the end, even if the treaty were to include the Shandong clause and that the Shandong interests would go to Japan. Discovering that the first article of the Treaty of Saint-Germain-en-Laye with Austria contained the same language regarding League of Nations founding membership, however, the

Paris delegation confirmed that China could join the League by signing this peace treaty and so decided not to sign the Treaty of Versailles.

China and Germany concluded a bilateral peace treaty in 1921. China recovered German concessions and its public property within China, and the payment of the Boxer Indemnity to Germany was terminated, of course. Germany and China established a relationship based on equality.

China's decision not to sign the Treaty of Versailles meant that Japan directly took over the German interests in Shandong Province. The transfer contributed to a rise in anti-Japanese criticism in China. Japan at this time was pursuing a policy of cooperative diplomacy, handed down from Hara Takashi to Shidehara Kijūrō, that aimed to be conciliatory toward nationalist emotions by developing cultural programs toward China and eschewing the use of military force against China, but these trial efforts did not produce enough positive results in China. From the perspective of Japanese history, Japan embraced the contemporary global trends of anti-colonialism and forswearing war, and it tried to restore cooperation in its foreign policies concerning China. From China's perspective, these efforts are usually regarded as a continuation of Japanese aggression against China primarily in economic and cultural terms.

To understand Japan-China relations, it is necessary to separate their bilateral relationship from that of the Great Power relations concerning China. The situation was now that bilateral ties showed hardly any signs of improvement even when Great Power cooperation was good. Indeed, after the Nine-Power Treaty (discussed below) the anti-Japanese protests in the first half of 1923 had just about wound down and an active movement to aid Japan started up in China after the Great Kantō Earthquake later that year. However, subsequent revelations of the murder of Wang Xitian and the massacre of Chinese laborers in the Tokyo area meant that Japan-China relations did not return to the status before the Twenty-One Demands.

The Washington System and Its Problems: The Chinese Perspective

China and the Nine-Power Treaty

The Washington Conference was held in 1921–1922 to discuss various matters including Great Power cooperation that World War I had thrown into disarray, the extension of the Anglo-Japanese Alliance, and naval arms reduction. The conclusion of the Nine-Power Treaty restored Great Power cooperation over China, and institutionalized cooperation between Japan, the United States, and Britain on the issue of naval arms reduction. This cooperative framework is called the Washington System. As Akira Iriye has brought up, there is an aspect of this framework that set the stage for the argument explaining how Japan resorted to war when this framework collapsed (Iriye 1965). The Nine-Power Treaty, which once again stipulated Great Power cooperation with respect to China and China's territorial integrity, was the third comprehensive treaty concerning China after the Treaty of Tianjin (1858) and the Beijing Protocol (1901).

The important difference is that China did not take part in this treaty as a defeated belligerent. At the Washington Conference, China presented Ten Principles outlining a path for revising the unequal treaties, some of which were reflected in the Nine-Power Treaty. In contrast to the emphasis placed on renewed cooperation among the Great Powers on China, this treaty neither provided a security framework for the ROC government in Beijing nor did it establish a path for treaty revision.

The Chinese government was confronting new financial problems. It was obvious that ROC government finances would fall into a precarious state if China's repayment of the Boxer Indemnities, temporarily deferred when China entered World War I, were to restart in December 1922. Neither Beijing nor the Great Powers heralding China's integrity did anything to save the country from fiscal bankruptcy.

Meanwhile, the talks in Washington did bring about one concrete blessing for China. Though not a part of the Washington Conference, Japan and China signed a Treaty for the Settlement of Outstanding Questions Relative to Shandong, returning the leasehold territory and other interests to China and, for the moment, settling the Shandong question that had been pending since the Twenty-One Demands in 1915.

China and the Washington System

If one were to give a lecture in a Chinese academic setting on the relationship between the Washington System and Chinese diplomacy, the difficulty would be determining what to talk about aside from explaining the fact that the Washington System meant cooperation between Japan, Britain, and the United States. The 1920s is the period when the "Nationalist revolution" culminated in the establishment of the Nationalist government in Nanjing: with the decline of the Beijing government, signatory to the Nine-Power Treaty, the Guomindang was in the ascendancy, holding its first party congress in Guangdong in 1924, founding a Nationalist government in 1925, then undertaking the Northern Expedition to unify the country.

Sun Yat-sen and his colleagues had started a military government in Guangdong in 1917, proclaiming it the central government of the ROC. This Guangdong government, however, played no direct part in the Washington System. Also outside of the framework of this system, moreover, was the Soviet Union, which supported the Guomindang, had strong ties to the Zhang Zuolin regime in Manchuria, and had even concluded an agreement with the Beijing government in 1924 (Sakai 1992). Similarly, Germany, which had restarted diplomatic relations on an equal basis with China in 1921, was outside this Washington System.

When the government in Beijing collapsed in 1928, Zhang Zuolin (then the head of that government) fled to Mukden (Fengtian) by rail, where he was assassinated by a bomb placed by Japan's Kwantung (Kantō) Army. Succeeding to his father's power base upon his death, Zhang Xueliang chose to subordinate himself to the

Nationalist government in Nanjing at the end of 1928 with the Northeast Flag Replacement (the December 29 announcement replacing all national flags in Manchuria with the "Blue Sky, White Sun" flag of the Nationalist government), marking the end of the Northern Expedition and the reunification of China. The Soviet Union had been the main foreign influence supporting the forces of the Northern Expedition.

Meanwhile, the Nine-Power Treaty signatories, who had recognized the Beijing government, had not established close ties to the government in Guangdong and yet had done little to help the government in Beijing to survive. For instance, after the Beijing government resumed paying out the Boxer Indemnities at the end of 1922, France demanded that it pay in gold francs, refusing to accept payment in francs, which had depreciated since France left the gold standard. Until Beijing accepted that condition, France did not attend talks aimed at restoring China's tariff autonomy. Ratification of the Nine-Power Treaty, signed in February 1922, finally occurred in August 1925. A conference to discuss restoring tariff autonomy began 2 months later, which meant that when China actually recovered this right at the end of the decade, it was the Nationalist government in Nanjing that obtained it, rather than the Beijing government, by then defunct.

The Northern Expedition and Revolutionary Diplomacy

Sun Yat-sen opened the first National Congress of the Guomindang in Guangdong in 1924; as he tolerated the Communist Party, Chinese Communist Party members who became Guomindang party members also attended the Congress. After Sun's death in 1925, the May 30th incident occurred in Shanghai. Originating as a labor strike at a Japanese cotton mill in Shanghai, things came to a head when a British policeman in the international settlement, confronting the mass of protestors on May 30, fired shots which killed several protestors. This incident precipitated an anti-imperialist movement. It also provided impetus for the Northern Expedition, carried out by the National Revolutionary Army (NRA) led by Chiang Kai-Shek, starting in 1926. In the course of the Northern Expedition, however, Chiang staged a coup on April 12, 1927 in Shanghai and purged the Communist Party members from the Guomindang and NRA ranks.

The diplomatic slogan the NRA trumpeted throughout the execution of its Northern Expedition was "revolutionary diplomacy." Properly speaking, revolutionary diplomacy meant instantly making null and void all the unequal treaties and agreements signed by previous governments in order to construct new, equal relations. But, in the case of China during that period, it meant the movement, linked to the NRA's Northern Expedition, for recovering rights China lost through those agreements. Founded in 1927 and achieving national unification the following year, the Nationalist government in Nanjing had succeeded to the treaties signed by the Qing Empire and the Beijing government. Not only was it unable to implement revolutionary diplomacy, even when opportunities for treaty revision arose, the government followed a *daoqi xiuyue* concept of amending a treaty's terms a little at a time when it comes up for renewal, an approach that produced some results after the Nationalist government assumed the Beijing government's seat in negotiations on such issues as tariff autonomy.

Japan apparently felt the slogan was a threat to its special interests in Manchuria and mainland China. Revolutionary diplomacy's primary target was not Japan, but Britain, which possessed the most interests in China. When the NRA demanded the return of concessions, Britain returned those in Jiujiang and Hankou (part of Wuhan now) along the Yangtze River, and later, even the leased territory of Weihaiwei on the northeast coast. Bearing the brunt of nationalist fervor in the May 30 incident, Britain showed a relatively conciliatory posture toward the Northern Expedition.

In contrast, Japan stuck fast to its harsh stance, decisively going through with three Shandong Expeditions. It signified a policy reversal, away from Shidehara diplomacy of cooperation with Britain and the United States and avoiding the use of military force in China, inviting Chinese nationalism to train its sights on Japan. We can surmise the psychological impact this had on China, particularly after the Jinan Incident in 1928 (in which Imperial Japanese Army (IJA) troops clashed with the NRA in Jinan, Shandong Province over Japan's expeditionary forces dispatched to Shandong), from the anecdote that Chiang Kai-Shek started writing *xuechi* (cleanse the humiliation through revenge) in his journal every day. Such events as the NRA attack on the Japanese consulate general in Nanjing (the Nanjing incident of 1927) caused national sentiment to worsen on the Japanese side, too. Public opinion in each country, to a greater extent that ever seen before, became an important driver in the policymaking of both governments.

Nationalist Government in Nanjing

At the time of the ROC's founding in 1912, the aim was a republican system based on parliamentary democracy. Successive great presidents starting with Yuan Shikai, however, shirked the push to make it a true republic with a strong legislative authority. In the 1920s, Sun Yat-sen expounded upon his three-stage political system—military government; political tutelage; then constitutional government— saying that the time was not ripe for realizing a republican system. The "Nationalist government" designation indicates that this was the period of political tutelage under the political guidance of the Guomindang, and the head of government was no longer called the "president" but the chairman of the Nationalist government.

The government was strongly influenced by the Soviet Union: the party guided the state and excelled at using propaganda, mobilization campaigns, and other related methods. If the Beijing government was a nineteenth century-style administration inherited from the Qing dynasty, the Nationalist government was a twentieth century-style administration. The bureaucracy was composed of both civil servants carried over from the Beijing government and Guomindang bureaucrats; the military was made up of forces under the government's direct control, based on the NRA, and regional military forces. The business world, represented by Jiangsu-Zhejiang financial interests, was also a major class of support.

The Great Powers sought to maintain their cooperation with respect to this Nationalist government in Nanjing, but they remained cautious, particularly about moving their legations to the capital, Nanjing. Yet, Germany, which had inked an equal treaty with China, and the Soviet Union had already set off on different paths from the other Great Powers, and as China itself was gaining in national power. Perhaps the Nine-Power Treaty had already ceased to function as the framework for Great Power cooperation as it had been. The ROC government successfully strengthened coordination with the League of Nations and several of the League's cooperative projects were started in China.

The Nationalist government in Nanjing finally succeed in recovering tariff autonomy in 1928–1929. Taking over these negotiations started by the previous Beijing government resulted in a stronger financial base and brought with it the Great Powers' recognition of the government. The 3-year period starting 1928 was rare one, as the ROC government was able to exert its control over almost all the areas it claimed as its own territory. Yet, the regional military powers and the Communist Party were still going strong within the country, and there was a leadership struggle within the Guomindang. The financial market crashes in 1929 and the Great Depression that ensued also affected East Asia, but the region recovered quickly compared to the United States and Europe. As the 1930s opened, Japan and China were headed for all-out conflict and Great Power cooperation over China was crumbling, too.

The Manchurian Incident and the Collapse of Great Power Cooperation

The Manchurian Incident happened on September 18, 1931. In a very short period, the Kwantung Army went on to capture nearly the whole of Manchuria. Confronted with this development, Zhang Xueliang, then absent from Mukden quelling unrest in the countryside, avoided war with the Kwantung Army, in part owing to Chiang Kai-shek's instructions. Chiang in Nanjing decided to follow a plan of "first internal pacification, then external resistance"—stabilize the home front by wiping out the forces of regional military powers and the Communist Party, and then on that basis confront the foreign threat, i.e., Japan.

The Nationalist government sought to resolve problems at the diplomatic table while avoiding military conflict. One venue was in connection with the Nine-Power Treaty, where China's territorial integrity was a fundamental stipulation, but the Great Powers were non-responsive. Another was the League of Nations, where Japan was a permanent member and China was a non-permanent member of the Council; China charged Japan with violating the League's Covenant. The logic of collective security was in China's favor. After deliberations, a fact-finding body led by Lord Lytton was sent to East Asia. At the League, Japan and China argued over the report that this Lytton Commission had compiled on the entire recent history of East Asia and submitted to the international body. Even though the report had acknowledged Japan's special interests in Manchuria, it stated sovereignty over the region belonged to China, and proposed putting Manchuria under an international administration, a plan that Japan vociferously rejected. Japan gave notice in March 1933 that it would withdraw from the League of Nations. At the time, there were quite a few countries that had left the League, so Japan's withdrawal was not an indication that it would be immediately isolated from international society. It was one event that did signify a clear breakdown of Great Power cooperation with respect to China.

During this period of fact-finding, the Japanese and Chinese militaries had clashed in Shanghai in January 1932 (in what is called the (First) Shanghai incident), and Japan founded a new country, Manchukuo, that March. The Manchurian Incident was concluded by the Tanggu Truce that Japan and China signed on May 31, 1933. Yet, Japan continued to make incursions into provinces in North China and Inner Mongolia afterwards.

Second Sino-Japanese War and "The Fourteen-Year War"

Nowadays, China's national history curriculum teaches the "Fourteen-Year War" concept: that the timeframe of the Second Sino-Japanese War is 1931–1945, which means that it began with the Manchurian Incident. China had long viewed the starting point of the war with Japan as the July 7, 1937 Marco Polo Bridge Incident, which contemporaneously was seen as the "Eight-Year War of Resistance," a view that emphasized the cooperation between the Chinese Communist Party and the Guomindang following the December 1936 Xi'an Incident (Zhang Xueliang detained Chiang Kai-shek, who had been fixated on wiping out Communist forces, to advocate the end of the civil war between the Guomindang and the Communist Party to resist Japan through national unity). In contrast, the Xi Jinping administration's aims for recently setting the Manchurian incident as the war's starting point could be, first of all, to stop emphasizing the Second United Front that entailed cooperation with the Guomindang in Taiwan at present, and second, to refocus its history on nationalism over modernization by prolonging the period of the war of resistance against Japanese aggression.

As a matter of fact, there are considerable challenges and many difficulties to designating this entire period as a war, especially from 1933, when the Tanggu Truce put a stop to the Manchurian Incident, to the Marco Polo Bridge incident in 1937. Of course, since Japanese incursions into Northern China did continue, if they were an indicator of aggression, it would be possible to consider the Manchurian Incident the starting point. Even allowing that Japan and China were both preparing for war in 1933–1936, you cannot say that they were in a state of war.

The Nationalist government imposed many obligations on the areas ruled by regional military leaders and the Communist Party, reasoning that it ought to rule these regions directly; it implemented currency reform as part of that effort, which resulted in the government amassing currency. The Xi'an Incident came about through the cooperation between Zhang Xueliang (who had moved from Manchuria to Shaanxi Province) and the Communist Party (which had marched to Yan'an in northern Shaanxi) to oppose this Nationalist government pressure on the regional military leaders and Communist Party. It was not as though China started a war with Japan right after the conclusion of the Xi'an Incident. The Marco Polo Bridge Incident happened on July 7 over half a year later. Moreover, it was not right after the incident but toward the end of July that both sides began to have a sense that the war had started. We begin to see full-scale combat start on August 13, 1937 in the Battle of Shanghai (Second Shanghai Incident).

The Second Sino-Japanese War signified a rupture in bilateral relations, yet the two sides held many peace talks. Most ended in failure over the issue of recognition of Manchukuo or the lack of trust in the relationship. Great Power cooperation over China had already collapsed because of the Manchurian Incident, and the existence of Manchukuo became a flashpoint between Japan and the United States, for which no common ground could be found, as evidenced by the 1941 Hull Note (the US proposal for Japan submitted by Secretary of State Cordell Hull at the final stage of Japan-US negotiations).

Bibliography: For Further Reading

Iriye, Akira. 1965. After Imperialism: The Search for a New Order in the Far East, 1921–1931. Harvard University Press.

Kawashima, Shin. 2004. *Chūgoku kindai gaikō no keisei* (The Formation of Modern Chinese Diplomacy). Nagoya: The University of Nagoya Press.

Naraoka. Sōchi. 2015. *Taika nijūikkajō yōkyū towa nandattanoka: daiichiji sekai taisen to nitchū tairitsu no genten* (What is the Historical Meaning of the 21 Demands? World War I and the Origin of Sino-Japanese Conflict). Nagoya: The University of Nagoya Press.

Okamoto, Takashi and Kawashima, Shin (eds). 2009. *Chūgoku kindai gaikō no taidō* [Fomentation of China's Modern Diplomacy] Tokyo: The University of Tokyo Press, 2009.

Sakai, Tetsuya. 1992. *Taishō demokurashī taisei no hōkai: naisei to gaikō* (The Collapse of the Taishō Democracy System: Domestic Politics and Diplomacy). Tokyo: The University of Tokyo Press.

Tang, Qihua. 2010. *Bei "feichu bupingdeng tiaoyue" zhebide beiyang xiuyue shi* (1912–1928) (Treaty Revision Campaign of the Beijing Government, 1912–1928: Out of the Shadow of the "Abrogation of Unequal Treaties"). Beijing: Social Sciences Academic Press.

Yoshizawa, Seiichirō. 2003. *Aikoku shugi no sōsei: nashonarizumu kara kindai chūgoku o miru* (Fomenting Patriotism: Viewing Modern China through Nationalism). Tokyo: Iwanami Shoten.

Wang, Yunsheng. 1932–1934. *Liushi nian lai zhongguo yu riben* (Sixty Years of China and Japan). Da gong bao she.

Additional Bibliography

Hatano, Sumio; Tobe, Ryōichi; Matsumoto, Takashi; Shōji, Jun'ichirō; and Kawashima, Shin. 2018. *Ketteiban nitchū sensō* (Definitive Edition: The Second Sino-Japanese War). Tokyo: Shinchōsha.
A book on the Second Sino-Japanese War that takes both the Japanese and Chinese perspectives into account. In particular, it depicts Japan's history from the view of the political, military, and financial histories.
Kawashima, Shin. 2010. *Shirīzu chūgoku kingendaishi2 Kindai kokka eno mosaku: 1894–1925* (Series on China's Modern History (Vol. 2): Groping for a Modern State: 1894–1925). Tokyo: Iwanami Shinsho.
A work concerning Chinese history from the end of the nineteenth century to the mid-1920s. I would recommend referencing it together with the third volume of that series by Ishikawa Yoshihiro, *Revolution and Nationalism*.
Sakurai, Ryōju. 2015. *Kahoku chūton nihongun: giwadan kara rokōkyō eno michi* (Japan's North China Army: The Path from the Boxer Rebellion to the Marco Polo Bridge). Tokyo: Iwanami gendai zensho.
A comprehensive book on the Japan's North China Army in the period between the Boxer Rebellion and the Marco Polo Bridge Incident. Helps to understand changes in the Imperial Japanese Army in North China.

Chapter 6
The Manchurian Incident and Party Cabinets

Michihiko Kobayashi

Abstract This chapter covers the turbulent years (1926–1932) when Japanese diplomacy towards China was in a state of flux and party cabinets were in decline. The increasingly uncontrollable Kantō Army, in an attempt to protect Japanese interests in northeast China, assassinated Zhang Zuolin, caused the Manchurian Incident, and expanded military operations into Manchuria, thus causing harm to Japan's relations with China and the United States. The question of the imperial prerogative of supreme command, the politicization of the Japanese Imperial Army, and the efforts of successive Japanese cabinets to achieves political stability form a complex story that ultimately led to the founding of the puppet state of Manchukuo.

Historical Background

As a result of the Russo-Japanese War Japan acquired the Guandong Leased Territory (to be returned to China in 1923) and the South Manchuria Railway from Lüshun to Changchun (scheduled return in 1939). Japan gained additional concessions with the Beijing Treaty (Treaty and Additional Agreements Between Japan and China Related to Manchuria December 1905) such as the right to construct the Andong-Mukden Railway (between what is now called Dandong and Shenyang). Also, construction of a competing line parallel to the South Manchuria Railway was clearly forbidden in the secret articles of the treaty and the right to construct and operate the Jilin-Changchun Railway was one of the enumerated items for ongoing negotiation. The exceedingly vague delineation of these South Manchurian rights provided the scope for conflict between Japan and China.

Later, with the second Ōkuma Shigenobu cabinet's Twenty-One Demands (1915), Japan forced the government of China to swallow a term extension for, and enlargement of, its South Manchurian rights, which stoked intense Chinese

M. Kobayashi
Center for Fundamental Education, The University of Kitakyushu, Fukuoka, Japan

M. Yamauchi, Y. Hosoya (eds.), *Modern Japan's Place in World History*,
https://doi.org/10.1007/978-981-19-9593-4_6

nationalism and gave rise to "revolutionary diplomacy," a coercive Chinese diplomatic approach for rights recovery (Naraoka 2015).

Starting with Hara Takashi's (1918–1921), successive Japanese administrations sought to secure the country's interests in Manchuria by using the local military leader, Zhang Zuolin, as a buffer, since he had adopted a position of coexistence with Japan. But Zhang Zuolin was not a man to be satisfied by staying quiet in Manchuria. He made frequent forays into the Central Plains of Northern China, seeking to gain hegemony there, and returned to Manchuria and Japan's protection when he failed, a performance he repeated several times. This resulted in a gradual buildup of friction with Japan, which sought stability for its South Manchurian interests (the remainder of this chapter draws heavily from Kobayashi 2010).

The Shandong Expedition and the Assassination of Zhang Zuolin

In 1926, Zhang Zuolin skirmished with the National Revolutionary Army (NRA), led by Chiang Kai-shek, that had come north. The Seiyukai cabinet of Tanaka Giichi dispatched troops to Shandong three separate times (1927–1928). Although the troops did protect the Japanese residents there, their objective was to stop China's national revolution from spreading to Manchuria. They also allowed Zhang Zuolin to withdraw peacefully back to Manchuria. However, the Kwantung Army (the Imperial Japanese Army (IJA) garrisoned in Manchuria) had already given up on Zhang; Kōmoto Daisaku and other senior staff officers had decided to back his son, Zhang Xueliang, as the new leader of Manchuria.

Kōmoto and his Kwantung Army comrades blew up Zhang along with his whole train carriage in the outskirts of Mukden (Fengtian) on June 4, 1928 (known in Japanese as "A Certain Important Incident in Manchuria"). Instead of becoming a puppet of the Kwantung Army, however, Zhang Xueliang joined forces with the Nationalist government of Chiang Kai-shek.

Kōmoto's objective was to replace the head of the Northeast China military clique and nothing more; any idea of using military force to combine Manchuria and Inner Mongolia and create an independent state was not even a consideration at first. The fact that he and his comrades were not punished by a court martial for the method they used, political terrorism, is related to the trend of that era growing within the IJA, especially the Kwantung Army—a lack of military discipline and actions taken arbitrarily without prior authorization.

Prime Minister Tanaka and the IJA senior ranks had intended to hold a military trial as a matter of course. However, they encountered strong criticism from anti-foreign hardliners among the civilian bureaucracy and the Seiyukai. Like at the time of the Shandong Expeditions, there were more hardliners in the influential political parties than in the military; Tanaka, who had a difficult time trying to control his own party, gave in to their demands and dealt with Kōmoto and comrades with administrative punishments. Since that decision angered the emperor, the Tanaka cabinet was left with no choice but to resign en masse in July 1929.

The Hamaguchi Cabinet's New China Policy

The two Minseito cabinets that followed—led by Hamaguchi Osachi (his army minister was Ugaki Kazushige) and Wakatsuki Reijirō (his second; Army Minister Minami Jirō)—made a major shift in Japan's policy toward China. They supported the Nationalist government's push to modernize and construct a nation of laws by providing Chinese policemen training for public officials in Japan, lifting the ban on arms exports to the Nationalist government and the Northeastern Army, and similar measures (Kobayashi 2004). Foreign Minister Shidehara Kijūrō and Finance Minister Inoue Junnosuke believed that, as Japan's South Manchuria interests were economic interests, bilateral political frictions would resolve themselves so long as Japan and China strengthened their economic coordination.

The lynchpin in this policy framework outlined above was Japan's lifting of the gold embargo (Japan's return to the international gold standard took place in January 1930). That move presumed a stable regional order in the Far East; an essential pre-condition to lifting the embargo on gold was keeping the IJA under control at home and abroad. Hamaguchi had more confidence in his own ability to govern after the army, under Ugaki's lead, made its position clear of supporting the cabinet in the wake of allegations that the government's signing of the London Naval Treaty on disarmament violated the emperor's prerogative of supreme command (1930).

However, the political scenarios that Hamaguchi and his supporters had envisioned were starting to go awry. Zhang Xueliang made another incursion into Northern China, prompted by the Central Plains War. His Northeastern Army had made progress strengthening its aerial warfare capabilities and modernizing its armaments, such as poison gas equipment. Its anti-Japanese stance was also striking. A plan to lay a rail line originating in Huludao that would run parallel to the South Manchuria Railway is an example of its increasingly aggressive political propaganda. Anti-Japanese leaflets distributed around Mukden that looked like and were called "lost maps" designated Taiwan and Korea as well as Okinawa, Amami Ōshima, and even Tsushima as territories that should be restored to China.

"Economic Diplomacy" Hits a Dead End

Tensions increased rapidly in Manchuria between the Northeast Army and the Kwantung Army. A group within the Kwantung Army centered around staff officers Itagaki Seishirō and Ishiwara Kanji started looking for realistic possibilities to use armed force to split Manchuria and Inner Mongolia off from the rest of China. They held absolutely no illusions about economic diplomacy. They believed it self-evident that the interests and rights in South Manchuria were imbued with a political significance, and just calling them economic interests did nothing to alter the situation. Even supposing Japan and China could construct a win/win economic relationship, unless that were linked to an easing of political and military tensions, you could not hope for stability with respect to the Manchuria question.

Ishiwara concluded that the leaders of the Northeast Army clique, whoever they may be, would always hold ambitions of advancing into the Central Plains. In other words, the Northeast Army clique's very existence was a cause of instability in the Manchurian situation, and so to overcome this vicious circle the only course left for Japan was to take bold action, separate Manchuria from mainland China, and either establish an independent state or a new Japanese territory.

Political Leadership in Flux

In the meantime, the Great Depression had started with Western stock market crashes in October 1929 emanating shockwaves that hit Japan, leading to growing discontent in the Japanese home islands as well as in Manchuria regarding the policy package of fiscal retrenchment and cooperative diplomacy of the Shidehara/Inoue team. In October 1930, Prime Minister Hamaguchi was felled by a right-wing assassin's bullet in Tokyo Station (he died the following August). The second Wakatsuki cabinet that followed tried to find a way out of this predicament by cutting the IJA budget. Within the IJA, a political trend that opposed arms reductions was gaining momentum; seeing which way the wind was blowing, Ugaki resigned as army minister and became the governor-general of Korea.

To summarize the political power situation post-Hamaguchi/Wakatsuki: party cabinet dysfunction brought with it a reduction across the board of integrated institutional capabilities. Emperor Shōwa tended to abstain from active involvement in politics, an aftereffect of his personal rebuke of Prime Minister Tanaka; his advisors, the *genro* (elder statesman) Saionji Kinmochi and Lord Keeper of the Privy Seal Makino Nobuaki, held different opinions on whether the emperor's role in politics should be indirect or direct. There was factional discord within the IJA and the Imperial Japanese Navy (IJN) and the embers of conflict were smoldering within the Kwantung Army. Unlike their predecessors Hara Takashi or Katō Takaaki, prime ministers Wakatsuki Reijirō and Inukai Tsuyoshi sorely lacked the ability to control their own parties, which set the stage for popular opinion to exert a growing and remarkably powerful influence on national politics in the run-up to a general election.

From an overall perspective, the IJA was becoming more active politically even as it was riven internally by widening discord and conflict among various schools and ranks, between the headquarters and the field armies, within the Kwantung Army, between the Ministry and General Staff Office, and among the senior and middle grade officers.

Political power was in a state of flux. Enough potential remained for political parties to come out on top of the military through a process of realignment, with political actors making and breaking temporary alliances. The situation regarding the military's ascendancy remained highly unpredictable until the summer of 1931.

Politicization of the Imperial Japanese Army

Stepping back for a moment, let us examine why the IJA became so politicized.

Created amid the turbulent Meiji Restoration, the IJA was designed and set up as "the emperor's army," a concept based on the public fiction (*tatemae*) that the supreme being of the emperor was detached from sundry political disagreements. That means that the emperor's army was created as a civil service-style, nonpolitical military force.

We begin to see minute cracks in this apparatus to maintain systemic stability, which the emperor's army was intended serve as, after the appearance of series of "dangerous ideologies" that flatly rejected the monarchy (the 1910–1911 High Treason incident: a socialist-anarchist plot to assassinate the Emperor Meiji), a trend that energized activities consistent with the international Communist movement (Japan Communist Party founded in 1922).

A crisis of the National Polity (*kokutai*) roused a band of young commissioned officers, who organized a range of study groups in 1927–1928: the Double-Leaf Society (*Futaba-kai*); the Thursday Society (*Mokuyō-kai*); and a merger of the two, the One Evening Society (*Isseki-kai*). These groups vigorously debated the Manchuria-Inner Mongolia question, the system and institutions necessary to support total war, and other ideological issues. This did not mean, however, that they were already on the path to fascism and war. Core members, like Nagata Tetsuzan, held fundamental doubts concerning the plan to use armed force to carve off Manchuria and Inner Mongolia, questioning the merits of taking these regions if it meant going to war; even the talk of a system for total war was, at the start, merely a search for how to create a support structure under party cabinet control.

Economic disruptions caused by the Shōwa Financial Crisis and similar events aggravated Japan's existing internal and external crises. Some younger officers, inspired by increasingly radicalized, highly idealistic interpretations of the National Polity, formed anti-bureaucratic groups, and in the style of men of high purpose at the end of the Tokugawa era (shishi), began to get involved in various plots for a coup d'état. One of these groups was the Cherry Blossom Society (Sakurakai) in which Hashimoto was a central figure. This group of political soldiers who would not submit to bureaucrat control was the very type that the Meiji army had purged from its ranks.

The Formation of Linked Crises: Korea, Manchuria, North China, Shanghai

An "arc of instability" (Korea—Manchuria—North China—Shanghai) was taking shape on the continent during this period. If a conflict happened at one of these points, it had the potential to send sparks flying immediately to neighboring regions. Apart from Shanghai where the IJN had its Yangtze River Fleet, the IJA had area armies garrisoned in these regions (Japanese Korean Army, the Kwantung Army, and Tianjin Garrison Army); whenever one of these mechanisms to protect the empire was engaged in operations, it carried the risk of inducing an enlargement of the incident.

Frictions were growing between Japan and Chinese authorities over managing problems in the Korea-Manchuria border zone, which had become the military stronghold of the Korean independence movement. The Wanpaoshan Incident occurred in July 1931: Japanese and Chinese authorities intervened in a violent altercation over water rights between Chinese residents and Korean migrants at Wanpaoshan in the outskirts of Changchun. As news of the incident was reported in Korea, in exaggerated form, there was a rash of sudden occurrences of persecution of and violence toward ethnic Chinese throughout the country, most seriously in Pyongyang (the Korean Incident).

Contributing factors underlying these incidents were the widening income gap that accompanied economic growth in Korea and the surge in the number of Koreans from lower income levels immigrating to Manchuria. The Japanese government, abhorring an influx of these Koreans to the home islands, planned their discharge into Manchuria, which caused a massive increase in tensions between ethnic Chinese and Koreans where they ended up, setting the stage for such incidents to occur.

It seems likely that the longer it took to deal with the incident, the anti-Chinese uprisings might evolve into a movement for Korean independence. Even though the Korean Incident quieted down before long, it did not imply that the original issues were resolved. And so, the issues of Koreans in Manchuria later proved to be a growing constraint on the Wakatsuki cabinet's policy of non-expansion (Kobayashi and Nakanishi 2010).

How the Manchurian Incident Came About and Played Out

On September 18, 1931, the Kwantung Army blew up the South Manchuria rail line at Liutiao Lake in the suburbs of Mukden (Fengtian) and, calling it the handiwork of the Chinese, assumed total control over Mukden. The Liutiao Lake Incident was the start of the Manchurian Incident. As is widely known, the Kwantung Army pushed past the Japanese government's non-expansion policy to seize the whole of Manchuria and ultimately wound up inventing a "Manchukuo," which declared independence in March 1932. But the Manchurian Incident is not about the Kwantung

Army's electrifying military actions. It is about the political battle, full of twists and turns, between the Kwantung Army and the government. That political process can be divided into the following three periods:

First period: the period of chaos from the outbreak of the Liutiao Lake Incident through the October Incident (mid-September through mid-October of 1931). The second Wakatsuki cabinet laid down its "non-expansion policy" and kept the Kwantung Army's area of operations restricted to the land belonging to the Manchurian Railway and the area along the leased railroad.

Second period: the period of the second Wakatsuki cabinet's counteroffensive (mid-October through mid-December of 1931). The Kwantung Army sought to break the non-expansion line by going north to Qiqihar or south to Chinchow but was prevented from doing so by temporarily delegated orders from the chief of the IJA General Staff Office. The emperor temporarily delegated his supreme command authority to the chief of the Army General Staff, who then exercised this authority to issue orders to troops in the field without needing the emperor's approval, on an ad hoc basis, for instance, in the middle of the night.

Third period: the period of confrontation between the Inukai cabinet and the Imperial Way Faction (anti-Chōshū faction) in the army (mid-December 1931 through May 1932). Inukai had persistently refused to recognize Manchukuo, but he was assassinated in the May 15 Incident.

This signaled the end of a practice of the two major political parties taking turns governing, an era called *kensei no jōdō* (the established procedures under the constitution), and it raised the curtain on the era of "Shōwa Restoration" driven by young army officers. Let us examine the features of each of these periods, below.

The True Status of the Kwantung Army

Proclaimed as the elite, the Kwantung Army was actually nothing more than divisions rotated in from the Japanese main islands (the second Division from Sendai at the time) and its effective strength was just 8800 soldiers; moreover, its rear logistics units (the Transportation Corps) that supported the army's operations in the interior remained behind in Sendai. Being an armed force meant to protect Japanese special interests in Manchuria, the Kwantung Army was basically only able to fight along the route of the railroad.

The opposing Northeast Army possessed a huge fighting force of about 220,000 men but was saddled with a mishmash of troops and many mounted bandits. The Japanese predicted that, if they could strike Mukden and paralyze its chain of command, the Northeast Army would probably fall into disarray.

Even if that were so, occupying the whole of Manchuria would require additional troops dispatched from Korea and the main islands. The budget for reinforcements that the Wakatsuki cabinet (with Shidehara and Inoue) approved was quite small.

No sooner had the Liutiao Lake Incident occurred than the Wakatsuki cabinet very clearly laid out its policy of non-expansion, flatly rejecting the Kwantung Army's requests for additional troops and support. Without having an order from the emperor to act, Japanese Korean Army commander Hayashi Senjūrō decided on his own initiative to provide "critical emergency assistance" to the Kwantung Army, ordering his subordinate 39th Mixed Brigade to advance on Mukden. This action was obviously illegal. Yet, fearing chaos in Manchuria, Wakatsuki gave his approval on the condition that the Kwantung Army pull back to the territory belonging to the Manchurian Railway (September 21, 1931).

Policy of Non-expansion and "Peace Keeping" Deployments

Coinciding with the rout of the Northeast Army, peace and stability in the Manchurian interior suddenly worsened. There were frequent reports that remnants of the defeated army were looting and committing violent acts against ethnic Koreans residing in Manchuria. Strict application of the non-expansion policy was able to lower the risk of the Kwantung Army running rampant, but it did not put a brake on the decline in security in Manchuria, especially in the interior. As Shidehara put it, if the situation were left alone, "it would give rise to a situation where control of Korea would not be easy."

The Wakatsuki cabinet had to work to restore peace in Manchuria while skillfully controlling the Kwantung Army, a situation that caused the occasional slight ripple in his government's policy of non-expansion. The public safety issue, itself, was a suitable tool prepared by Ishiwara and his comrades to get the government to swallow the bitter pill, their requisitions for military reinforcements. During this period, the Kwantung Army gradually enlarged the area in which it dispatched troops, nominally for the purpose of keeping the peace, going as far as Jilin and places along the railroad leased by the South Manchuria Railway.

The Wakatsuki cabinet, having established its non-expansion policy, resisted this move by geographically restricting the Kwantung Army's area of operations. Army Chief of Staff Kanaya Hanzō cooperated with Shidehara to try and squelch the Kwantung Army's maneuvers and mischief making.

The Movement Toward Forming a Political Majority: October Incident and the Movement to Cooperate with the Cabinet

Meanwhile domestically, radical elements of the Cherry Blossom Society tried to overthrow the Wakatsuki cabinet in a military coup d'état. But they were all rounded up in advance (the October Incident of October 17, 1931), which resulted in a reshuffling of the radicals in the IJA General Staff Office, making it easier for Kanaya to take control of the office.

The October Incident shocked the political world. Joining forces, the two major political parties formed a Seiyukai/Minseito coalition cabinet that included army moderates (Kanaya, Ugaki, Shirakawa Yoshinori). It was accompanied by a gathering momentum to take greater control over the whole army. This movement to cooperate with the cabinet soon went out of fashion because Finance Minister Inoue, who was increasingly confident of his ability to control the Kwantung Army, made an economic policy U-turn (reimposing a ban on gold exports), which generated a strong backlash. Thus, the opportunity for uniting political forces was lost.

Incidentally, that the Wakatsuki cabinet did not make the October Incident public, and just let Hashimoto and the other perpetrators off with very light punishments, was a political expedient to avoid Kanaya's resignation (the Imperial Way Faction had been scheming Kanaya's transfer). Even though the circumstances were what they were, this was yet another instance where the importance of military regulations and discipline was ignored, as was the case of the incident involving Zhang Zuolin's assassination.

Meanwhile, Zhang Xueliang had established a military government in Chinchow (Jinzhou) in the southern part of Manchuria, in an effort to maintain his nominal authority to rule over Manchuria. Ishiwara Kanji, and his comrades plotted a Chinchow offensive and the Japanese Tianjin Garrison Army also decided to attack Chinchow. Were that garrison army to be mobilized, the theatre of conflict would have expanded into Northern China. Without consulting others, Ishiwara had Chinchow bombed on October 8, a development that stunned the international community. Some League of Nations members loudly called on Japan to withdraw its troops by a certain deadline. On October 11, army headquarters strongly admonished the Japanese Tianjin Garrison Army, narrowly preventing the Manchurian Incident from escalating to the "North China Incident."

The Kwantung Army, Boxed In: The Exercise of Supreme Command Authority and the Depletion of Military Force

Over the next month, a fierce tug-of-war played out between the Kwantung Army, which sought to break through the non-expansion policy line with excuses of needing to improve public safety and safeguard Japan's special interests, and the cabinet and IJA General Staff Office, which was trying desperately to block it.

The following list of chains of events illustrates this tug-of-war:

1. the dispatch of the Nenjiang detachment (800 men) to the outskirts of Qiqihar, which resulted in a skirmish with Ma Zhanshan's army, which led the Kwantung Army to deploy the main force of the second Division without consultation (November 4, 1931), ended with a temporarily delegated order to stop the advance (November 5).

2. the second Division's advance into Qiqihar (November 17) ended with a temporarily delegated order to pull back.
3. the fourth Mixed Brigade's advance on Chinchow under the pretext of an uprising in Tianjin further south (November 27) ended with a temporarily delegated order to withdraw the troops (November 27–28).

The only case where the government's consent was received before the fact was the first: the dispatch of the Nenjiang detachment was for the purpose of repairing the railway. The rest were instances of Ishiwara and his comrades acting without proper authorization. Shidehara and his colleagues were overly optimistic about their ability to control the Kwantung Army, thinking that they had stymied its plots. In fact, its engagements with Ma Zhanshan's army and the brutal cold weather of northern Manchuria were depleting the Kwantung Army's (second Division's) fighting force. To ensure the Kwantung Army's ability to maintain the peace, the government allowed the fourth Mixed Brigade's deployment to Manchuria in exchange for the 39th Mixed Brigade's return to Korea (November 7). The measure was careless, to say the least, for Ishiwara took these fresh, well-honed young troops and immediately sent them to attack Chinchow. But this action, too, was prevented by a temporarily delegated order.

Through close coordination, the party cabinet and IJA General Staff Office successfully thwarted the Kwantung Army from breaking out of the non-expansion line to the north or south in the last part of November. International opinion was gradually shifting and there was increasing talk in the League of Nations of the concept of a mandate for Manchuria to be administered by Japan.

"I'm at my wits' end." Having concluded that it was not feasible to create an independent Manchuria or a Manchuria/Inner Mongolia territory, Ishiwara suddenly began to insist that they needed to make Manchuria a League of Nations mandate (December 2, Ishiwara, "Whither the Manchuria-Mongolia Question?") The Kwantung Army had been driven into a box.

Reversal: Foreign Minister Shidehara's Infringement on Supreme Command Authority

The situation with the United States suddenly changed, however, with Secretary of State Henry L. Stimson's remarks to the press (the morning of November 28, 1931 in Japan). Stimson had spoken about his understanding, based on Foreign Minister Shidehara's assurances passed through US Ambassador to Japan William Cameron Forbes, that the Kwantung Army would take no hostile operations toward Chinchow. When the Japanese evening newspapers reported Stimson's remarks and the assurances that Shidehara, of his own accord, had made to Stimson about Kwantung Army operations, it was met with deafening criticism that he had violated the emperor's prerogative of supreme command over the military (Banno 1985).

Charging a violation of the prerogative of supreme command was like bringing out a secret weapon or playing a trump card; many powerful politicians heard the allegations, turned their backs on Wakatsuki's Minseito cabinet, and began to attack it simultaneously. This proved to be a fatal blow to Shidehara, Army Minister Minami, and Army Chief of Staff Kanaya Hanzō who were the cabinet's unifying political force. They lost the authority to use temporarily delegated orders. The supposedly finished Kwantung Army gained new life; the return of the 39th Mixed Brigade to Korea was postponed on December 10. Itagaki Seishirō, a high-ranking staff officer in the Kwantung Army, seized the initiative for the planning and organizing of Manchukuo. Within the IJA, Araki Sadao and others of the Imperial Way Faction denounced Minami and Kanaya (who was transferred on December 23). After Wakatsuki's second cabinet was forced to resign en masse, Inukai Tsuyoshi established a Seiyukai cabinet on December 13, in keeping with the established procedures under the constitution (*kensei no jōdō*).

The Inukai Cabinet's Secret Negotiations with China

Concurrent with the formation of the Inukai cabinet, Army Minister Araki and Deputy Chief of Staff Masaki Jinzaburō, both Imperial Way Faction members, assumed their posts and seized power. As they had always shown favor toward the Kwantung Army, it now truly became impossible for the IJA General Staff Office (headed by Prince Kan'in Kotohito) to keep the Kwantung Army under control.

Inukai cunningly intended to pull back on the reins and gain greater control after briefly increasing the number of troops in Manchuria. Reinforcements were dispatched on December 17, the first Independent Mixed Brigade to the Kwantung Army and the first Independent Mixed Regiment to the Japanese Tianjin Garrison Army. However, the Tianjin Garrison used these new forces in its attempt to put its "North China Strategy" into operation.

It was time to fight poison with poison. The Inukai cabinet announced December 27 that it would exercise its right, recognized by the League of Nations, to pacify its territory ("suppress bandits"), and the Kwantung Army seized Chinchow on January 3, 1932. This was a desperate measure to prevent the Japanese Tianjin Garrison Army from taking unauthorized actions, which would have meant enlarging the theatre of conflict to include Northern China.

During this time, Inukai had been coordinating with the Guomindang government of Sun Fo (or Sun Ke, son of Sun Yat-sen) regarding support for a new government in Manchuria. He was seeking a policy to control the situation in Manchuria through an international police force to keep the peace, with the IJA providing the bulk of the force. There was a push on the Chinese side, in fact, to use the Kwantung Army to get rid of Zhang Xueliang, and its occupation of Chinchow was the first step (Katō 2007).

Harbin Deployment: Shifting Political Mood Over Supreme Command Authority

Emperor Shōwa impatiently urged the government to start negotiations with Zhang Xueliang and to withdraw the independent mixed brigade from Manchuria. Though it upset Inukai's plans, he could not go against the emperor's wishes. The IJA General Staff Office moved ahead with arrangements to reduce some of the forces in Manchuria, and officers in the IJA senior ranks, like Uehara Yūsaku and Ugaki Kazushige, expressed their agreement (January 6–11, 1932). The shock from the Stimson incident was rapidly being repaired.

On January 8, there was a failed assassination attempt on the Emperor Shōwa by a Korean man (the Sakuradamon Incident). The Imperial Way Faction worked out a plan to force the whole cabinet to step down, but the emperor's confidence in Inukai did not waiver. The state of affairs rested on a foundation of the emperor, Inukai, and the Control Faction in the IJA.

The only thing that could restore these declining fortunes was to use strong medicine of deploying troops to Harbin. Honjō Shigeru, the commanding officer of the Kwantung Army, sounded out Araki and Army Chief of Staff Kan'in about the Harbin dispatch on January 27, and Kan'in immediately approved. Unlike with the Qiqihar operation the year before, he had not sought approval in advance from the cabinet.

Following the Stimson incident, civilian officials were sensitive to the issue of infringing on the supreme command authority, so no one complained about the army's high-handedness. The political mood as regards supreme command authority was clearly shifting. In the end, even the IJA General Staff Office's plans for a partial troop withdrawal were retracted (February 1), and Imamura Hitoshi and other Control Faction members were reshuffled all at once (February).

Outbreak of (First) Shanghai Incident

Yet another major incident occurred on January 28: the (First) Shanghai Incident.

Many parts of this incident remain unclear. Evidence of plots can be found on both the Japanese and Chinese sides (Roku 2001). But, if we recall that there were military officers seeking political ties within the Kwantung Army, the Imperial Way Faction, the Fleet Faction/Naval aviators group, and the perpetrators of the May 15 incident (see below), I believe it highly unlikely that the outbreak of the (First) Shanghai Incident and events in Manchuria were completely unrelated.

The incident stemmed from a clash between Japanese residents and local Chinese; the Imperial Japanese Navy (IJN) made the initial response. The incident escalated from January 29 to February 2, becoming a skirmish; encountering stiff Chinese resistance, Japan quickly mobilized one army division (the ninth) and sent in the IJN's first Air Fleet (aircraft carrier *Kaga*). In early February, the IJN carried out a personnel purge against members of the Treaty Faction, which did not favor deploying troops. The Chinese army, firmly believing it was waging the war of resistance, forced the IJA into such a hard fight that, in the end, Japan had to reorganize and dispatch the Shanghai Expeditionary Army (the 11th and 14th Divisions) commanded by Shirakawa Yoshinori. "The Imperial Japanese Army must never suffer a defeat to the likes of the Chinese army." Now, even Inukai longed for a "ceasefire through victory." At the time, the emperor had verbally conveyed his wish for a ceasefire to Shirakawa, and so keeping that in mind, Shirakawa managed to secure a ceasefire after the general offensive (March 3).

The Founding of Manchukuo

The state of Manchukuo in Manchuria, which took the Xuantong Emperor, Puyi, for its leader, declared its independence on March 1. As this is the date memorializing the 1919 *Manse* Demonstration (the Korean *Sam-il* independence movement), it naturally stoked the anger of Korean nationalists. Japanese general Shirakawa became one of the victims of a terrorist bombing on April 29 (the Shanghai Emperor's Birthday Celebration incident).

Yet, the incident did not lead the Japanese side to renege on the Shanghai ceasefire agreement. Inukai requested the support of Ugaki and Uehara so that talks with the Nationalist government would continue. After the chain of tragic events in Shanghai, however, it was not realistic to think it was possible to successfully complete negotiations. While simultaneously dragging out the recognition of Manchukuo, Inukai intimated that he was settling the situation in Shanghai according to the emperor's wishes, which incurred the wrath of civilian right-wingers and naval young officers. Inukai, too, became a victim of political terrorism in the May 15 incident.

In Conclusion

The Saitō Makoto cabinet recognized Manchukuo on September 15, 1932, and the Japanese and Chinese militaries exchanged treaty instruments for the Tanggu Truce in May 1933, aiming to bring the Manchurian Incident to a close. Yet conditions later escalated into what would become the Second Sino-Japanese War in 1937, as the Kwantung Army and its sympathizers forged ahead with schemes to partition Northern China.

That the First Sino-Japanese and Russo-Japanese wars had been concluded in a relatively short time was because none of the belligerents had lost their ability to govern. Also, Japan's withdrawal of its troops from Siberia in 1922 was possible precisely because the Bolsheviks had established control over the Far East.

One major reason why the Manchurian Incident was not resolved completely, speaking from the Japanese side, was that power in Japan was dispersed—and the Kwantung Army's series of uncontrolled actions is only one aspect of this situation. It would be quite an irony of history if one of the factors contributing to the ascendancy of the IJA in the 1930s was the dissolution of Yamagata Aritomo's bureaucratic clique during the period of Taishō Democracy (established after the First Sino-Japanese War, it was the preeminent, pro-army clique composed of elements from the former feudal domains; it later split into the Imperial Way and Control factions).

Bibliography: For Further Reading

Banno, Junji. 1985. *Kindai nihon no gaikō to seiji* (Modern Japanese Diplomacy and Politics). Tokyo: Kenbun Shuppan.

Kobayashi, Michihiko. 2004. "Nihon rikugun to chūgen taisen—1929–31nen" (The Imperial Japanese Army and the Central Plains War: 1929–31) in *Kitakyūshū shiritsu daigaku hōseironshū v32 n1* (2004-6): 1–34.

Kobayashi, Michihiko. 2010. *Seitō naikaku no hōkai to manshū jihen: 1918–1932* (The Collapse of the Party Government and the Manchurian Incident: 1918–1932). Kyoto: Minerva Shobō.

Kobayashi, Michihiko and Nakanishi, Hiroshi. 2010. *Rekishi no shikkoku o koete: 20-seiki nitchū kankei e no shinshiten* (Beyond Historical Awareness: A New Perspective on 20th Century Japan-China Relations) Tokyo: Chikura Shobō.

Katō, Yōko. 2007. *Shirīzu nihon kingendaishi, 5 Manshū jihen kara nitchū sensō e* (Japanese Modern History Series (Vol. 5): From the Manchurian Incident to the Second Sino-Japanese War). Tokyo: Iwanami Shinsho.

Naraoka, Sōchi. 2015. *Taika nijūikkajō yōkyū towa nandattanoka: daiichiji sekai taisen to nitchū tairitsu no genten* (What is the Historical Meaning of the 21 Demands? World War I and the Origin of Sino-Japanese Conflict). Nagoya: The University of Nagoya Press.

Roku, Shakushun [Lu, Xijun]. 2001. *Chūgoku kokumin seifu no tainichi seisaku: 1931–1933* (Chinese Nationalist Government's Japan Policies: 1931–33). Tokyo: The University of Tokyo Press.

Additional Bibliography

Kitaoka Shin'ichi. 2012. *Kanryōsei to shite no Nihon Rikugun* (The Japanese Army as Bureaucracy). Tokyo: Chikuma Shobō.

A persuasive study of the bureaucratization of the Imperial Japanese Army in the Shōwa period, which led to the outbreak of war and, ultimately, to Japan's defeat by preventing the civilian cabinets' effective control over the armed forces.

Shimada, Toshihiko. 2005. *Kantōgun: zai man rikugun no dokusō* (The Kwantung Army: Independent Action by the Imperial Japanese Army in Manchuria). Tokyo: Kōdansha gakujutsu bunko.

A historical overview of the Kwantung Army from its creation to its destruction. A classic work written in the 1960s.

Tobe Ryōichi. 2016. *Nihon rikugun to chūgoku: shinatsū ni miru yume to satetsu* (Imperial Japanese Army and China: Dream and Fiasco of the China Hands). Tokyo: Chikuma gakugei bunko.

A study the Army's "China hands," who represented the deep connection between the Imperial Japanese Army and China.

Usui Katsumi. 1974. *Manshū jihen: sensō to gaikō to* (The Manchurian Incident: War and Diplomacy). Tokyo: Chūkō shinsho.

A classic volume that made full use of diplomatic historical methods. The analysis of the (First) Shanghai Incident in particular is outstanding.

Chapter 7
Disarmament Conferences and a Crisis of Diplomacy in the Interwar Period: The Road to World War II

Ken Kotani

Abstract This chapter focuses on the international system following World War 1 and efforts to create peace and stability through the League of Nations' collective security, outlawing war, and various disarmament conferences. It covers the crises of diplomacy related to the expansionist Hitler regime that culminated in the rise of fascism in Italy, the Munich Conference, and the eventual outbreak of World War II.

Introduction

World War I, brought to a close by the Armistice of 11 November 1918, had resulted in over 20 million deaths, an astonishing, heretofore unseen number. The "Great War" indeed, it easily surpassed the largest wars fought in Europe until then: the Thirty Years' War of the seventeenth century and the Napoleonic Wars of the nineteenth century. The countries that experienced the war contemplated carefully the steps they could take so as to never again endure a war of this magnitude. These included introducing a system of collective security with the Treaty of Versailles (the League of Nations' Covenant) and the Locarno Treaties; enacting the Pact of Paris outlawing war (Kellogg-Briand Pact); and holding international conferences for the purpose of disarmament. A mere 21 years later, however, World War II started on September 1, 1939.

One of the major causes of World War II was the establishment of the regime of Adolf Hitler in Germany with its pursuit of a policy of foreign expansionism. British historian A.J.P. Taylor, arguing the counterpoint in *The Origins of the Second World War*, pointed out the role that British and French passivity played in inciting German arrogance. The debate over the war's causes has been lively ever since. Arguably, the personalities of the British, French, German, Italian, and Soviet leaders had brought on the war. In addition to these factors, it may be necessary to look at such

K. Kotani
College of Risk Management, Nihon University, Tokyo, Japan

© The Author(s) 2023
M. Yamauchi, Y. Hosoya (eds.), *Modern Japan's Place in World History*,
https://doi.org/10.1007/978-981-19-9593-4_7

issues as the domestic political situations in each country, the international system of the time, and international conditions outside of Europe, as well. In this chapter, I shall present a general overview of the origins of World War II in Europe, seasoned with some insights on these other issues.

Post-WWI International System

The balance of power policies of every country in Europe were thought to be a cause of World War I. US President Woodrow Wilson called for the formation of a general association of nations (League of Nations), a concept of building collective security arrangements, in his "Fourteen Points" address outlining principles for world peace. The Treaty of Versailles, which put collective security in writing, and the Pact of Paris (1928), which outlawed wars of aggression, provided the basic rules for this system.

The postwar peace in Europe was built upon the scapegoating of Germany, one of the defeated Central Powers in the war. Germany was obliged to pay 132 billion gold marks in reparations (in the 1921 London schedule of payments), an enormous sum that the country was still paying off in the twenty-first century. In addition, it lost 40,000 square kilometers of territory and seven million of its population. In the 1925 Locarno Treaties, its western border zone with France and Belgium was demilitarized and the signatories pledged to treat it as inviolable. Such measures sought to restrain Germany by force, but the collective security arrangements and legal aspects to support those measures were left extremely ambiguous.

First of all, the collective security system, logically being between major powers and their potential adversaries, had difficulty functioning; absent any strong compulsion, states found it hard to intervene in a conflict in a region lacking any connection to their own national interests. Although Article 16 of the League of Nations' Covenant clearly states that any member disregarding the League's covenants will be "deemed to have committed an act of war" and will immediately be subject to sanctions, it had a fatal flaw, in that each member had the right of refusal, so there was no obligation to sanction or use military force against an aggressor. The fact that a key country, the United States, did not join the League meant that this system was in a precarious state right from its foundation.

In addition, the Kellogg-Briand Pact, by failing to provide a clear definition of a war of aggression, was interpreted to permit only wars of self-defense. But it held almost no validity as a treaty and, as international legal scholar Shinobu Junpei pointed out, "the Pact, far from outlawing war, was an endorsement legitimating the conduct of war in general" (Shinobu 1941). There was a nagging feeling, even in those days, that idealism had gotten too far ahead of the institutions that shaped postwar international relations, as suggested by a remark Winston Churchill made in a speech: "The League shall never replace the Grand Fleet." That is, the international institutions of the interwar period were not set up to deal with countries that did not abide by the system or take the solidarity and cooperation of its member countries seriously, nor were they designed to suppress with force countries that attempted to destroy the system using force.

There was an idea, however, to limit each country's military strength through a variety of disarmament conferences. Article 8 of the League of Nations' Covenant obligates members of the League to reduce national armaments, with the League itself to play an important role in providing a venue for multilateral discussions on the matter.

Disarmament Conferences: Successes and Setbacks

Relatively many international conferences on disarmament were held in the interwar years. The characteristic of disarmament conferences of this period is that the humanitarian argument for the complete abolishment of poison gas and bomber aircraft as inhumane weapons existed alongside the strategic argument that reducing naval vessels and ground warfare armaments possessed by all countries would decrease the possibility of war. Of the two, strategic arms limitations made relatively more progress.

The Washington Naval Conference (1921–1922) and the First and Second London Naval Conferences (1930, 1935–1936), for instance, all concluded with treaties signed, whereas the Geneva Naval Conference (1927) and the Geneva Conference for the Reduction and Limitation of Armaments (1932–1933) did not. Perhaps the most successful was the Washington Naval Conference, which brought together the five sea powers of the era (Britain, the United States, Japan, France, and Italy) to avoid a naval arms race in vessel construction by setting quantitative limits on both aircraft carriers and battleships. The Washington Conference established a broader framework for international cooperative security called the Washington System, one aspect of which was naval disarmament.

As the Great Depression that started in October 1929 in the United States reverberated worldwide, governments turned to measures serving their own national interests, rather than to international cooperation, to overcome the crisis. Countries with many colonies, such as Britain and France, aimed to protect their national industries and currency by solidifying their own economic bloc, leaving Japan and Germany to suffer considerable economic damage. Amid such conditions, the Manchurian Incident occurred September 18, 1931, an event the Japanese public supported enthusiastically. The Imperial Japanese Army (IJA) carried out the Manchurian Incident from a national security perspective, to resolve the Manchuria question, but the incident ultimately harmed Japan's international standing. Britain appeared willing to come to terms with Japan in the League of Nations but, facing opposition from League members on the issue of recognizing Manchukuo, Japan announced March 27, 1933 that it would be withdrawing from the League.

Nevertheless, the British government held out a sliver of hope for the Second London Naval Treaty Conference scheduled for 1935. But the preliminary and exploratory talks in 1934 broke off, with the United States locked in competition with Japan, each rebutting the other's assertions, and the US pursuit of idealistic calls for arms reduction in total opposition to Britain's push for realistic limits.

Japanese Ambassador to the United States Saitō Hiroshi formally notified Secretary of State Cordell Hull of Japan's intent to terminate the Washington Naval Treaty in the afternoon of December 29, 1934 (Washington time). As the treaty would cease to be in force 2 years following such notification, Japan had arranged for the date to coincide with the timing of the London Naval Treaty's expiration at the end of 1936. On March 25, 1936, Britain, the United States, and France signed the Second London Naval Treaty, its key features being the mutual notification of naval vessel construction plans and the setting of qualitative limits on vessels. Despite being asked, Japan refused to join.

The absence of treaties in the naval arena meant that a future naval construction arms race was inevitable after 1936. Starting in fiscal year 1937, the Imperial Japanese Navy (IJN) implemented a massive naval buildup around plans to construct the battleships *Yamato* and *Musashi* under the Third Naval Armaments Supplement Program (*maru-san*). As if to counter this, the US government enacted the Naval Act of 1938 in May of that year (the Second Vinson Act) that mandated a 20% increase in strength of the US Navy. The British government, too, commenced plans for a large-scale buildup over 1936–1939, setting the Royal Navy's strength at the level of the combined naval strengths of Japan and Germany, and constructing seven battleships, four aircraft carriers, and 20 cruisers. Thus, one wing of the interwar international order, the Washington System, was crumbling, and the naval arms race that everyone had feared had come to pass.

The Geneva Conference on the topic of European disarmament opened in February 1932. It convened 62 countries from around the world to discuss limits on all offensive weapons, land, naval, and air. Two points of interest were the debate over whether to regard tanks, submarines, and bombers as offensive weapons, and thus restrict their use, and whether France, Europe's largest land and air power, would actively take arms reductions measures. Using the League of Nations' Covenant to its advantage, Germany, then subject to the severest limitations on military armaments, argued that every country, and not only Germany, must face an equal set of restrictions, a position that France completely disagreed with.

Germany's potential national power, though reduced by the Treaty of Versailles' arms limitations, far surpassed that of France. In contrast to France whose lands became World War I battlefields, Germany saw its industrial belt survive the war largely unscathed; the German population was also 20 million larger than France's. In addition, France arguably needed to maintain the Versailles system and keep suppressing Germany for the sake of its own national security, as France owed a sizable debt to the United States and Britain. The issue was whether Germany would continue to consent to that state of affairs.

Supposing France were to permit Germany to rearm, Paris would require a security guarantee from London. The French government planned to take no measures on arms reductions without a firm commitment for assistance from Britain. Yet, the Ramsay MacDonald government remained uninterested in the issue of disarmament and French national security. The British government's attitude during this period did not encompass a spirit of international cooperation.

The unenthusiastic attitude of Britain and France toward arms reduction and limitation gave Germany the excuse it needed to insist on a principle of equality in armament. In protest, Germany pulled out of the Geneva Conference in October 1933 and withdrew from the League of Nations, as well. Early that year, Adolf Hitler had become the German chancellor on January 30, and his government was secretly moving ahead with a military expansion program. The Führer's aims were vast: to isolate France in Western Europe and thereby destroy the Versailles system, and to expand the German military in order to acquire *Lebensraum* in the east. So, naturally, the British and French postures against disarmament in Geneva provided Germany with an excuse to rearm. Germany declared its intent to rearm on March 16, 1935, tripling the strength of the army and building a new Luftwaffe at a stroke. Anticipating the true threat from German rearmament, the British government had already approved Expansion Scheme A in July 1934 to build up the Royal Air Force (RAF).

The years 1933–1934 might be characterized as the turning point of the interwar period. Idealism seeking international cooperation and peace was in retreat; realism, and the turn toward military expansion to establish one's own national security, was on the rise. Not every country reacted this way to conditions during this period. British Prime Minister MacDonald and French Prime Minister Aristide Briand had to pursue their realistic policies amid a general domestic trend of idealism, which complicated the issues. It was said that British members of parliament, reacting to the report on the RAF extension scheme, could be heard asking as to the purpose of the military buildup.

A Crisis of Diplomacy

Britain, France, and Italy issued the final declaration of the Stresa Conference in April 1935, affirming a tripartite coalition in opposition to Germany's declaration to rearm. To defend against German expansion in eastern Europe, Paris also concluded the Franco-Soviet Treaty of Mutual Assistance with Moscow on May 2, 1935. These moves were of the old tradition, measures to maintain the balance of power by relying on separate alliances, rather than through a system of collective security as stipulated in the Locarno Treaties. However, a coalition among Britain, France, Italy, and the Soviet Union should have had enough power to restrain Germany. A just 2 months after its declaration, however, the Stresa Front abruptly collapsed because the British government separately concluded the Anglo-German Naval Agreement. It was the start of Britain's appeasement policy to Germany.

Meanwhile, Italian *Duce* Benito Mussolini announced the invasion of Ethiopia on October 2. The League of Nations responded by imposing economic sanctions against Italy; they were faltering half-measures from the start. Mussolini warned Britain and France that their participation in applying economic sanctions would bring about war with Italy. The two countries, foreseeing a confrontation in Europe with Germany, did not welcome making Italy an adversary over some distant country in Africa; they even devised the Hoare-Laval plan, attempting to provide justification for Italy's aggressive actions. When newspapers reported on the plan in December, the British public erupted in anger, forcing Foreign Secretary Samuel Hoare to resign. Despite urgent entreaties from the Ethiopians, the League of Nations took no action. This is the moment when the League's collective security system fell apart.

Exploiting the disorder stirred up by the Ethiopia question, Germany boldly moved to occupy the Rhineland on March 7, 1936, abrogating the Locarno Treaties that had designated that area as a demilitarized zone. France had two options to respond: take a firm stance militarily or pursue a peaceful policy diplomatically. Confronted with an unequivocal act of aggression, France could have exercised its right of self-defense militarily under the terms of the Locarno Treaties, without waiting for League of Nations' arbitration. The day following Germany's occupation, French Foreign Minister Pierre-Étienne Flandin requested the French military to deploy some army units, but Army Chief of Staff Maurice Gamelin, fixated on defensive operations along the Maginot Line, did not accede to his request. If Britain and France had cooperated at this stage, even if it meant war, they just might have been able to crush the German army. Decision makers and the public opinions of both countries continued to shy away from resolute action that might lead to war. British Prime Minister Stanley Baldwin remained indifferent to the French position, saying that the German move was not act of aggression. Since it was dangerous for France to act alone without a firm British commitment of assistance, Paris ultimately chose the option to avoid confronting Germany directly.

A.J.P. Taylor summarized this French response to the Rhineland Occupation: ". . . they closed their eyes to it and pretended that it did not exist." (Taylor 1961, p. 114) Furthermore, the Popular Front cabinet of French Prime Minister Léon Blum prioritized domestic economic sanctions over diplomacy. France was unable to take decisive policies against Germany because its national power was in decline during this period (weakening economy, decreasing birthrate) and the political situation was unstable.

France's actions made its neighbors uneasy. Belgium decided to withdraw from its military accord with France and declare itself neutral. The governments of the eastern European parties to the French-leaning Little Entente (Czechoslovakia, Romania, Yugoslavia) indicated their disillusionment with Paris' attitude. Even Moscow abandoned Franco-Soviet cooperation, turning instead to a Berlin-leaning diplomacy and concluding the German–Soviet Trade and Credit Agreement (1939). France, for the most part, became isolated in Europe. Britain, the ally France should have been able to depend on, had only just started to increase the strength of its army, so going to war with Germany was not yet feasible. "No one then breathed about [German] sanctions," wrote British Under-Secretary of State for Foreign Affairs Robert Vansittart about contemporary conditions. "The Labour Party indeed expressly repudiated them. Our obligation, had said Sir Herbert Samuel for the Liberals, was 'not to arm but disarm.' The Conservative majority sat tight"

(Vansittart 1943, p. 53). A League of Nations Council meeting was held in London on March 14, 1936; although the Council did recognize that the German occupation of the Rhineland was a violation of the Treaty of Versailles, it ultimately was unable to take any action whatsoever.

All too quickly, Hitler achieved his objective of dismantling the system established by the Versailles and Locarno treaties. His adversaries, Britain and France, sought to win over Italy as a stopgap measure to give themselves time to rearm. On July 4, 1936, both governments lifted the economic sanctions that they had imposed related to Ethiopia, hoping to improve ties with Italy. But Germany acted first. With the outbreak of the Spanish Civil War in July, Germany and Italy backed the regime of Generalissimo Francisco Franco, and the two announced the creation of a Rome-Berlin axis on October 25. Britain and France had been outmaneuvered once again. British Prime Minister Neville Chamberlain, naturally alarmed, wanted to make friendly approaches to Italy regardless of how it looked; disagreeing, his Foreign Secretary Anthony Eden resigned.

Britain was confronted with a thornier challenge when the Second Sino-Japanese War erupted on July 7, 1937. Even though the Japanese government had hammered out a strategy to simultaneously advance north on the continent and south into the South Seas under its Fundamentals of National Policy of August 7, 1936, it would be more fitting to say the Second Sino-Japanese War was the result of chance overlapping with opportunism, instead of design. The Japanese-German Anti-Comintern Pact concluded November 25, 1936 began to link the situations in Europe and East Asia.

Much like the situation France faced in Europe, the British in East Asia did not have the means to oppose Japan alone, without US support. Since the League of Nations still seemed dysfunctional, Britain did what it could, persistently engaging Japan in negotiations and giving itself more time by providing China with assistance. The Guomindang government did not want the situation in Europe to deteriorate further, having concluded that Britain and the Soviet Union would seek to appease Japan if it did. Preparing for the worst, the premier of the Republic of China, Chiang Kai-shek began to consider forging closer ties to the United States. Each of these countries had no choice but to proceed while carefully observing the situations in both Europe and East Asia.

The Outbreak of World War II

Germany's annexation of Austria on March 13, 1938 (Anschluss) gave greater clarity to the shape of Italo-German ties. Italy originally opposed the annexation of Austria, but Mussolini gave his consent. Hitler's next target was the Sudetenland in Czechoslovakia. Formerly a part of the Austro-Hungarian Empire, it had been annexed by Czechoslovakia after World War I despite having three million German-speaking inhabitants, some of whom started a campaign seeking self-determination. Czechoslovakia, for its part, signed a mutual assistance treaty with

France in 1924 that obligated Paris to provide military assistance for Czechoslovakia's defense in the case of a German military invasion. The problem in practice, however, was that Germany already had so surpassed France in terms of air power that France was could not to defend itself in a time of national crisis.

Here too, Britain's attitude and approach was the key. Chamberlain was not enthusiastic about defending Czechoslovakia; on the point of self-determination of ethnic groups, he appeared to show understanding for Germany. The French government briefly considered a policy of countering Germany by including the Soviet Union, which had signed its own mutual assistance pact with Czechoslovakia. But, given the British government's deep-rooted mistrust of the Soviet Union, Franco-Soviet discussions did not even commence.

In this context, the Munich Conference opened on September 29, 1939. Participants included Hitler, Chamberlain, and French Prime Minister Édouard Daladier; Italian *Duce* Mussolini moderated. Representatives of Czechoslovakia and the Soviet Union were not even invited to the conference. Chamberlain pressed ahead with an appeasement policy toward Hitler, acknowledging German claims for the cession of the Sudetenland. For Chamberlain, defending Czechoslovakia was unrealistic and British public opinion would not allow the option of waging total war against Germany for that purpose. The British people felt a deep aversion to war notwithstanding their domestic preparations such as air raid shelters readied against German bombs and distribution of poison gas masks. Even Daladier, initially sympathetic to the Czechoslovaks, simply followed Chamberlain's lead in Munich.

Criticizing Chamberlain and Daladier for their policy of appeasement has a touch of judging in hindsight quality to it. Contemporary public opinion welcomed the British and French politicians for both seeking to avoid war, a position that had public backing, and then achieving that goal. The German people, too, fêted them as heroes. Even US President Franklin D. Roosevelt praised the outcome for a time.

The outcome of the Munich Conference, however, caused a major shift in the situation in Europe. Distrustful of Britain and France, the Soviet Union drew closer to Germany in order to establish its own security arrangements. Hitler became convinced that Britain and France would try to avoid war, no matter the sacrifice. He soon aimed to seize the whole country of Czechoslovakia not just the Sudetenland, but before that he set his sights on Poland.

The basic concept with Poland closely resembled the issue with the Sudetenland. Germany undertook negotiations with Poland over returning the Free City of Danzig, where most inhabitants were of German descent, but talks broke down on March 26, 1939. Unlike with Czechoslovakia, the plans of Britain and France did not include compromise. Were Germany to take possession of Danzig, it would stabilize its eastern border and enable it to obtain strategic natural resources from the region. Therefore, Britain and France both regarded the issue of Poland as one that might cause troubles for them later. The Franco-Polish mutual assistance treaty of 1921 obligated France to come to Poland's aid. Britain preferred to join with Poland rather than the Soviet Union. The British government had engaged the Soviet Union in talks of a military alliance throughout April and May of 1939, but after failing to get any meaningful results, concluded a mutual assistance treaty with Poland on August

24, 1939, preparing together with France for a German invasion of Poland. It remained unclear how the two countries would defend Poland, however.

The Soviet Union, meanwhile, rapidly drew closer to Germany. The two had been engaged in secret talks that came to fruition on August 23 with the Soviet-German treaty of non-aggression (Molotov–Ribbentrop Pact). Having thus secured its rear, Germany carried out a sudden invasion of Poland on September 1. Two days later, Britain and France declared war on Germany in accord with their mutual assistance pacts with Poland. The Soviet Union, on the basis of the secret protocol to its non-aggression pact with Germany, attacked Poland from the east on September 17. Thus, World War II began.

In Conclusion

E.H. Carr, a British historian and former diplomat, tried to glean lessons from international relations in Europe in the interwar years. In *The Twenty Years' Crisis*, Carr argued with a sense of urgency that moralistic utopianism was being superseded by authoritarian realism. Following the Occupation of the Rhineland, however, British and French compliance with German demands, Carr argued, was based on their understanding that Germany's demands followed a certain logic, rather than to hold off the crisis. In other words, that the Treaty of Versailles, which formed the foundation of European international security system in the interwar period, was itself unreasonable for Germany. Nevertheless, the Hitler regime cannot shirk its responsibility for the war by blaming structural problems in international relations.

We also tend to overlook the issue of time. So quickly did the chain of events unfold in the latter half of the 1930s, it is hard to say that countries had enough time for analysis and consideration. France, antagonistic to Germany throughout the interwar period, tried to overcome this confrontation through a policy of allying with several countries, but there had not been time enough to build relationships of trust and so they all were hastily assembled. According to American international relations scholar Stephen Walt, an alliance requires a certain amount of time before it can function properly, time to build a relationship of trust and to institutionalize the alliance. So, looking at developments from 1935 to 1939, you might say there was not nearly enough time for that.

During that interval, the sole constant is that Hitler's Germany always moved before other countries could act, leaving Britain and France continually outmaneuvered. Democracies clearly need time for politicians to reach concensus amongst themselves and to make policies that take public opinion into consideration. Japan, too, concluded an alliance with Germany and Italy, feeling as if it was about to "miss the bus." However, like Hitler, who for a time seemed to be doing quite well, both saw their grand strategies end in failure by making adversaries ultimately of the United States and the Soviet Union, both.

Bibliography: For Further Reading

Shinobu, Junpei. 1941. *Senji kokusaihō kōgi, dai-1kan* (Lectures on International Law in Wartime, Volume 1). Tokyo: Maruzen.

Taylor, A.J.P. Yoshida, Teruo (trans). 2011. *Dai-niji sekai taisen no kigen* (The Origins of the Second World War). Tokyo: Kōdansha Gakujutsu Bunko. [Originally published as: Taylor, A.J.P. 1961. *The Origins of the Second World War.* New York: Simon & Schuster Paperbacks.]

A book on the topic of the origins of World War II that caused a stir. While there are some objections to the book, the content is suitable as a general statement.

Vansittart, Baron Robert Gilbert. 1943. *Lessons of my Life, by the Rt. Hon. Lord Vansittart.* London: Hutchinson.

Additional Bibliography

Carr, Edward Hallett. Hara, Yoshihisa (trans). 2011. *Kiki no nijūnen: risō to genjitsu* (The Twenty Years' Crisis: The Ideal and the Reality). Tokyo: Iwanami Bunkō. [Originally published as: Carr, E.H. 1946. *The Twenty Years' Crisis, 1919–1939: an Introduction to the Study of International Relations: by E.H. Carr.* London: Macmillan.]

A consideration of European international relations in the interwar period, it is also renowned as an international political science textbook. There are two translations, an old and new; the newer one is easy to read.

Murray, Williamson; Knox, MacGregor; and Bernstein, Alvin (eds). Ishizu, Tomoyuki; Nagasue, Satoshi (trans). 2007. *Senryaku no keisei: shihaisha kokka sensō. gekan* (The Making of Strategy: Rulers, States, and War [Last Volume]). Tokyo: Chūō Kōron Shinsha. [Originally published as: Murray, Williamson; Knox, MacGregor; Bernstein, Alvin (eds). 2009. *The Making of Strategy: Rulers, States, and War.* Cambridge: Cambridge University Press.]

The British, US, French, German, and Soviet military strategies in the interwar period are written about in detail from various standpoints.

Nye, Joseph S., Jr.; Welch, David A.; Tanaka, Akihiko; and Murata, Kōji (trans). 2013. *Kokusai funsō: risō to rekishi* (International Conflict: Theory and History). Tokyo: Yūhikaku. [Originally published as: Nye, Joseph S., Jr.; Welch, David A. 2013. *Understanding Global Conflict and Cooperation: an Introduction to Theory and History (Ninth Edition).* Boston: Pearson.]

A textbook for international security studies, its fourth chapter is a detailed commentary on the international politics of the interwar years.

Ōi, Takashi. 2008. *Ōshū no kokusai kankei 1919–1946: furansu gaikō no shikaku kara* [European International Relations, 1919–1946—from the angle of French Diplomacy] Tokyo: Tachibana Shuppan.

Very knowledgeable on French diplomatic policies of the interwar period.

Chapter 8
The Southward Advance and Going to War with the United States: The Road to World War II

Atsushi Moriyama

Abstract This chapter examines how and why Japan ended up going to war with the United States in 1941. It discusses the concept of the "Southward Advance," highlights the linkage between developments in Europe and Japan's national policies, and examines key moments in joint military-government deliberations to avoid or pursue military conflict. It concludes with a brief summary of the results and lessons of Japan's defeat.

Japan and Rapid Changes in the European Front

As hopes dimmed for "Operation Kiri," peace feelers seeking direct talks with Chiang Kai-shek to resolve the Second Sino-Japanese War that had become a quagmire, in Europe, Nazi Germany commenced its western offensive. The German army got the ball rolling by invading Norway in early April 1940, surmounted the defensive battle pitched by the three Benelux countries from May 10, and forced France to surrender on June 22. It had taken possession of nearly the whole of western Europe.

Many Japanese went wild with enthusiasm, as if they had forgotten Germany's breach of trust a mere 10 months before (Germany signed a non-aggression pact with the Soviet Union, effectively blowing up moves to strengthen the Anti-Comintern Pact). They thought that Germany's victories would lead to the collapse of the old Anglo-centric world order. They also hoped that the defeat of the home countries of the colonies in Southeast Asia—the Dutch East Indies (modern day Indonesia) and French Indochina (present day Vietnam, Laos, and Cambodia)—would mean that Japan could obtain their natural resources to develop its economy.

Those forces seeking to "renovate" domestic and foreign policy, such as freeing Japan from the Anglo-American international order, toppled the pro-status quo

A. Moriyama
School of International Relations, University of Shizuoka, Shizuoka, Japan

© The Author(s) 2023 95
M. Yamauchi, Y. Hosoya (eds.), *Modern Japan's Place in World History*,
https://doi.org/10.1007/978-981-19-9593-4_8

Fig. 8.1 Prime Minister
Konoe Fumimaro (National
Diet Library)

Fig. 8.2 Foreign Minister
Matsuoka Yōsuke.
(Photobook: 50-Year
History of Constitutional
Government)

cabinet of Yonai Mitsumasa to form another cabinet headed by Konoe Fumimaro. The key policies of this second Konoe cabinet were strengthening the national defense, reforming diplomacy, and advancing into Southeast Asia (the "southward advance"). The Imperial General Headquarters-Government Liaison Conference on July 27 adopted the "Outline of Japan's Policy in Coping with Changing World Conditions" ("the July 27 outline") which also considered the use of force in the southward advance. The foreign minister in the cabinet was Matsuoka Yōsuke, who could boast of a popularity among the Japanese public on par with Konoe (Moriyama 2017). Matsuoka released a statement on August 1 that set his foreign policy line on the construction of a Greater East Asian Co-Prosperity Sphere, one that also encompassed the southern areas under the Dutch and French empires (Figs. 8.1 and 8.2).

Japan did not just make a mad dash southward in accordance with the national policy agreed at the time, however. A vague, ambiguous national policy, hurriedly adopted amid the feverish mood of Germany's western offensive, the July 27 outline gave rise to divergent interpretations immediately following its adoption (regarding the situation of such dual competing theories of the national policy, see Moriyama 2012, 2016). The Army General Staff Office, most inclined to use force, was ready to go to war against Britain if it would hasten that country's defeat. Yet, some held more cautious views on using military force that would, with high probability, invite military conflict with the United States as well as Britain. The Imperial Japanese Navy (IJN), notably, believed that war with the United States was unimaginable, though it did welcome the Imperial Japanese Army's (IJA) change of focus away from its traditional northward advance policy to the southward advance (the IJN thought the latter was the basis for bolstering its own preparedness). Since all the key players held their own concept of what the southward advance meant, the stationing of Japanese troops in northern French Indochina is when the policy began to unravel.

Stationing Troops in Northern French Indochina and the Tripartite Pact

As the intentions for the southward advance became more convoluted, Japan demanded that IJA units be allowed to station troops in French Indochina, nominally to resolve the Second Sino-Japanese War. France accepted the Matsuoka—Arsène-Henry agreement on August 30, 1940, which held that, in exchange for Japan respecting its territorial sovereignty, French Indochina would engage in economic cooperation with and provide military facilities to Japan (though limited to the objective of operations against Chiang Kai-shek). However, some IJA officers who aimed to use this opportunity for seizing the region through force of arms ran amok, engaging French forces in combat. Though those responsible were reassigned, most returned straight away to IJA central. Undeniably, an atmosphere of approval did exist within the IJA regarding the desire to capture the region through military force.

At the same time, negotiations were progressing on the Tripartite Pact, an alliance between Japan, Germany, and Italy (concluded on September 27), which Matsuoka wrapped up single-handedly, unlike the talks to strengthen the Anti-Comintern Pact that the IJA was pushing for. Matsuoka was said to have been enamored of the concept of incorporating the Soviet Union into the Tripartite Pact to form an anti-Anglo-American four-country bloc.

The IJN had been firmly opposed to strengthening the Anti-Comintern Pact, but this time switched to a position of acceptance provided the issue of automatic entry into the war cleared the hurdle (in the case where Japan, Germany, or Italy was attacked by a third country—notionally the United States—that had not yet entered World War II, whether the other two countries would enter the war was thoroughly decided independently). In exchange, the IJN called on the government to complete preparations for war while using diplomacy to avoid going to war. The international environment surrounding Japan became harsher. The Tripartite Alliance severely damaged US public opinion toward Japan, and the Dutch East Indies, too, began taking a stricter attitude toward economic cooperation (which acquiesced just after the defeat of Dutch) with Japan.

Adjusting the Faltering Concept of the Southward Advance

The southward advance as conceived by the IJA rested on the premise that avoiding war with the United States was possible so long as Japan limited its war adversaries to just Britain and the Netherlands (the Anglo-American divisibility school). However, the IJN insisted that, because any move involving Britain would necessarily force US entry into the war (the Anglo-American indivisibility school), Japan should use military force only in the case of self-reliance and self-preservation. Both sides could not bridge the gap. Given the lack of agreement between the army and navy, the path of least resistance was to strengthen Japanese influence in French Indochina and Thailand by any means short of war. At that moment, the border dispute between Thailand and French Indochina flared up at the end of 1940, and Japan stepped in to arbitrate. Using this opportunity, the IJA and the IJN incorporated plans to acquire bases in southern French Indochina and to conclude a military alliance with Thailand into the national policy.

However, Matsuoka halted those plans. A vocal proponent of capturing Singapore, Matsuoka was thought to have speculated that the army and navy were not ready for war. So long as they were not prepared to seize Singapore, Matsuoka rejected the measures for Thailand and French Indochina as meaningless, and so the IJA and IJN could only back down. In addition, Britain, which misinterpreted Japan's conduct as a military advance in the south, spread the story of a crisis in the Far East beginning in the first half of February 1941, which caused the IJN to fold (Kotani 2004; Moriyama 2016). Right after establishing arbitration to prevail on French Indochina to begrudgingly cede some territory to Thailand, Matsuoka set out on a trip to Europe, confusing the IJA and IJN.

Concluding the Japanese-Soviet Neutrality Pact and the Start of Japan-US Talks

Matsuoka received a warm and enthusiastic welcome in Germany and Italy, and on his return trip he concluded the Japanese-Soviet Neutrality Pact in Moscow on April 13, arriving home in Japan in high spirits. It appeared as though Japan, Germany, Italy, and the Soviet Union had established a quadripartite bloc. Matsuoka believed he could use this potential to Japan's advantage in negotiations with the United States, having already laid the groundwork for such talks by reaching out to US Ambassador to the Soviet Union Laurence Steinhardt in Moscow.

Matsuoka found a draft understanding between Japan and the United States for a gradual settlement in the Orient waiting for him upon his arrival in Japan on April 22. The emperor, Konoe, and the IJA and the IJN all had expressed eager support for this quasi-private sector-initiated diplomatic proposal, which skillfully papered over the conflict between Tokyo and Washington and contained favorable conditions, such as having the United States serve as a go-between in resolving the Second Sino-Japanese War. Whether he sensed some kind of ruse or was simply vexed remains unclear, but Matsuoka sabotaged the Japan-US talks.

The Argument for Stationing Troops in Southern French Indochina and Foreign Minister Matsuoka

An attaché of the army that returned from Thailand submitted a report on April 16, "Japanese forces have little presence, still have a long way to Go" (Daihon'ei 1998). French Indochina was beginning to balk at exporting rice to Japan, citing poor pick-up as an excuse (a series of poor harvests made it necessary for Japan to import foreign rice). In addition, the Dutch East Indies had strongly rejected the broad requests that Japan had made in bilateral trade talks, which subsequently foundered. Britain began turning up economic pressure, fearing that Japan would send the resources it was obtaining from the southern areas to Germany via the trans-Siberian Railway. In order to achieve a breakthrough in this feeling of deadlock, the IJA and the IJN sought to have Matsuoka reopen policy measures toward Thailand and French Indochina that had been left unresolved for far too long.

Matsuoka rejected their request using similar rhetoric as before. And so, they escalated the content of their policy measures to station troops and establish bases in southern French Indochina. They also sought to persuade Matsuoka by expressing their readiness to go to war with the United States. Matsuoka's bluff, which had worked until then, was no longer effective against an adversary who showed a firm determination not to give in. As a result, he was forced to act decisively. Regardless of its dramatic declaration to go to war with the United States, the IJA and the IJN, aside from just a portion, did not think that stationing troops in southern French Indochina would provoke war with the United States. Mid-level staff officers busily occupied themselves drafting documents to convince Matsuoka about the need to station troops. But these documents were so unconvincing, their drafters quipped, "those who disagreed [with the stationing] would not see the necessity after reading [the documents], whereas those who already agreed would" (ibid.).

Matsuoka briefly approved the stationing of troops in southern French Indochina, but immediately reversed himself. This transpired in the context of measures to respond to the impending start of hostilities between Germany and the Soviet Union. Matsuoka called for a reconsideration of the stationing numerous times from mid-June into July. He changed the grounds for his opposition, switching to the northward advance over the capture of Singapore, and confounded everyone around him by expounding a hardline argument that surpassed even the IJA's hardline views.

The Start of War Between Germany and the Soviet Union and Japan's Response

Germany commenced its attack on the Soviet Union on June 22, 1941; intelligence concerning that attack had conveyed to Japan by June 5. Confronted with the need to draft response measures, Japan determined a new national policy, "Outline of the Imperial National Policy in view of the Changing Situation," ("July 2 Outline") at the Imperial Conference on July 2.

The July 2 Outline made settlement of the China Incident (the Second Sino-Japanese War) a priority, yet it also mentioned advances northward and southward: "taking steps to advance south, and depending on changes in the situation, ... involve a settlement of the Northern Question as well." Moreover, since the July 2 Outline included language that "we must prepare to go to war against Great Britain and the United States," there is a tendency to misinterpret it to mean that Japan had made a decision for war against the United States at this stage already. But, as mentioned above, the IJA and the IJN understood this as a countermeasure against Matsuoka. It is evident reading other sections of the July 2 Outline that such assertiveness was, on the contrary, nothing more than an appeal for the position of preparing for the northward and southward advances (resorting to force would be decided "independently" with regards to the German-Soviet war or possible US entry into the war) (Ike 1967). What was specifically settled was only to proceed with already established measures for Thailand and French Indochina. Yet, it became possible to move ahead with preparations for using force in both the north and south on the basis of this national policy.

The Start of the Kwantung Army's Special Exercises

News of Germany's steady advance reinvigorated the argument for the northward advance, especially among the Army General Staff Office. If Soviet forces in the Far East were weakened by redeployments to the Western front, it generated a once in a lifetime opportunity. The issue was the degree of Soviet weakness that would allow Japan to use force more effectively. Proponents led by Tanaka Shin'ichi, chief of the first bureau (operations), Army General Staff Office, pushed to mobilize the Kwantung Army immediately and, in concert with German actions, shake the persimmon tree, causing the *shibugaki* (unripe persimmons) to fall (thus, the *shibugaki* school of thought). In contrast, the cautious Military Affairs Bureau was of the opinion that Japan should wait until Soviet troop strength in the Far East dropped to a level where engagement became almost unnecessary (the *jukushi* (ripe persimmons) or "laying low and awaiting one's chance" school of thought).

There was consensus within the IJA, however, to prepare to attack the Soviet Union. First Bureau Chief Tanaka's direct appeal to Army Minister Hideki Tōjō bore fruit, and it was determined July 5 after the Imperial Conference that the IJA would mobilize half a million men. It was the start of special exercises by the Kwantung Army. August 9 was selected as the deadline for commencing hostilities, so as to end operations before the hard winter frost arrived. The cautious factions within the Army Ministry took it upon themselves to remain watchful until that very day, so that the Army General Staff Office would not take any unauthorized actions (Nishiura 2013).

Foreign Minister Matsuoka's Reluctance and His Dismissal from the Cabinet

Around this period, Matsuoka was opposed to all those around him regarding the matter of proceeding with negotiations with the United States. Concerning the draft Japan-US understanding that made the disputes between the two countries artfully disappear, Matsuoka sought to negotiate by using a harder-line proposal. For instance, under the proposed draft, the United States would counsel Chiang Kai-shek toward peace linked to Japan's guarantee of a troop withdrawal from China; the May 12 Japanese draft made no mention of this troop withdrawal and now read that the United States would counsel peace having understood and accepted the existing treaties agreements between Japan and the Wang Jingwei government. At the Imperial General Headquarters-Government Liaison Conference, Matsuoka became quite emotional by arguing that US entry into the war in Europe had to be prevented at all costs, otherwise it would be the destruction of world civilization. Thus, he asserted that the scheduled convoys (groups of transport ships with supplies to aid Britain that were protected by the US fleet) must be blocked. For those ministers and high command officers around him, putting an end to the China Incident (Second Sino-Japan War (soon to hit the 4-year mark)) was the first priority. They assumed Matsuoka is about to lose a perfect opportunity to achieve that goal.

The United States responded to the proposal of the Japanese side with an unofficial proposal on May 31 and an official counterproposal which it handed to the Japanese side on June 21. To the latter was appended an oral statement from US Secretary of State Cordell Hull saying that talks would be very difficult so long as "some Japanese leaders in influential official positions" repeatedly made pro-German remarks that influenced Japanese public opinion, and he hoped for a clearer indication that the Japanese government wished to pursue courses of peace (Department of State 1943).

Though it avoided naming him, the statement's content challenging Matsuoka enraged him. At the July 12 liaison conference, Matsuoka demanded a retraction of the oral statement and insisted on cutting off talks, perplexing everyone around him. In the end, the liaison conference decided to continue talks and to send the Japanese counterproposal by telegraphic cable, but Matsuoka decided to send just a cable demanding the retraction of Hull's oral statement, paying no mind to the counter-proposal. Prime Minister Konoe, long exhausted by the inability to reach consensus with Matsuoka, finally decided to have his entire cabinet resign, so as to oust Matsuoka from his position as foreign minister.

The Third Konoe Cabinet and Stationing Troops in Southern French Indochina

Under the system of the Meiji Constitution, the prime minister did not have the authority to appoint or dismiss cabinet members. It was possible, of course, if the minister involved could be persuaded and consented to resign. But there was no expectation that would be the case for Matsuoka, whose had made known his desire to become prime minister (Kido 1966, Vol. 2). The second Konoe cabinet resigned en masse on July 16; the following day Konoe received an imperial order to form a new cabinet. Established on July 18, the third Konoe cabinet was seen as possibly changing course to improve relations with the United States by welcoming Navy Admiral Toyoda Teijirō, a moderate, as the foreign minister. The situation radically changed, however, when Japan stationed troops in southern French Indochina, carried out immediately after the cabinet's creation. Washington moved to freeze all Japanese assets in the United States on July 25.

The firm US response came as a complete surprise. There had been some concern about whether stationing Japanese forces in southern French Indochina might worsen relations with the United States, as Chief of the Army General Staff Sugiyama Hajime explained at the July 2 Imperial Conference, yet the majority view was that the US reaction would probably be limited because Japan was only going so far as French Indochina and not touching Thailand (which shared a border with British Malaya, which had deep ties to Britain) (Sugiyama 1994).

The freeze order was not synonymous with an embargo. It was explained at US cabinet meeting on July 24 that US President Franklin D. Roosevelt may have frozen Japanese assets, but he did not impose a full embargo, because in fact oil export licenses were still being issued at present. The effect was, however, that not one more drop of oil flowed to Japan. Japanese domestic oil reserves stood at just 2 years-worth for peacetime consumption, and only a year and a half during wartime. The opinion emerged that Japan should seize natural resource zones through force of arms while it could still fight. It was the argument against a gradual decline. A crisis of "self-reliance and self-preservation," the Imperial Japanese Navy's prerequisite for war with the United States, had come to pass (Fig. 8.3).

Fig. 8.3 President Franklin
D. Roosevelt

Full Embargo and Japan-US Summit

Konoe, ever indecisive and irresolute, set out on a firm course of action at this time of crisis. He proposed a Japan-US summit meeting, hoping that a direct meeting with Roosevelt would lead to a breakthrough. There was no one who could directly oppose Konoe's extraordinary determination. Konoe sought to avoid any interference from domestic opposition, typified by the Imperial Japanese Army, by receiving the emperor's approval immediately after securing Roosevelt's agreement. To do so, he first had to elicit Roosevelt to Summit meeting. In response to Konoe's proposition, Roosevelt conveyed a favorable response on August 28 that referenced a meeting venue. The Japanese side hastily move on to selecting attendants to the leaders and preparing the ship for passage.

Outline for Executing the Imperial National Policy and the Fall of the Konoe Cabinet

There were growing fears within the IJA, especially the Army General Staff Office, that Konoe might impede the army by giving up too many concessions to the Americans. Whereas Imperial Japanese Navy officers in the middle and lower grades were swept up in the momentum of an armed southward advance, naval leadership was reluctant to go to war with the United States. Nonetheless, they were fully cognizant that a naval buildup was essential to prepare for a time of emergency. The navy had submitted its proposal for the national policy to the army, with completing preparations for war as its key provision. The intent of the upper-ranking officers was unclear on the topics of the use of force and the decision to go to war, even though their proposal contained the wording "resort to force" in the case that diplomacy failed (Daihon'ei, ibid.). The IJA, however, used this as its opportunity to drag the national policy toward going to war with the United States.

The Imperial Conference of September 6 determined the Guidelines for Implementing the Imperial National Policy: in the event there were no prospects for achieving Japanese demands by early October, it was resolved to go to war with the United States, Britain, and the Netherlands. The time limit for talks was established through a bit of reverse calculation: on top of estimates for decreases in oil reserves, operations in the south had to conclude by the following spring so that Japan could prepare to attack the Soviet Union. The conditions for the United States included the Army General Staff Office's demands to block the withdrawal of troops from China. At the Imperial Conference, Emperor Shōwa indicated his displeasure with the high-handed manner of the approach by reading a poem the Emperor Meiji had penned.[1] Thus, the government and the supreme command were required to demonstrate that they had exhausted diplomatic efforts first.

The issue was how far did they have to compromise until they could say they had exhausted diplomatic efforts? In fact, they decided at a liaison conference that it was possible to continue diplomatic efforts at the same time as the Army General Staff Office's demands. On those grounds, the proponents for carrying on with diplomacy sought to get around those demands.

Whether the United States would agree to the idea of a summit meeting, however, was the biggest hurdle. Anti-Japanese hardliners within the US government convinced Roosevelt that a summit meeting had no merit. (These hardliners, of course, had no idea that a cornered Japan would come attack the United States directly; they were concerned about public criticism of the administration if the summit produced no results.) So that is why the US side took the basic policy of fleshing out the preconditions to meet in detail. By so doing, the IJA's influence on the national policy could not be eradicated.

The US response arrived on October 3, rejecting the idea of a summit meeting. Konoe, Toyoda, and Navy Minister Oikawa Koshirō pushed to ease some of the conditions placed on the United States at the liaison conference held the following day, but Army Minister Tōjō refused. The IJA and IJN high commands also insisted on observing the time limit. If there had been any flaws in the determination of the September Imperial Conference, Tōjō asserted, all those responsible in the government and supreme command should resign. He publicly revealed this course of events in a cabinet meeting on October 14, too. The perception that Japan could not last long without its special interests on the continent is implied by Tōjō's comments, "the heart of the matter is the issue of troop withdrawals," and if that happened, then Japanese control over Manchuria and, by extension, Korea would be imperiled. It was the contemporary common sense of the Japanese people.

In the end, unable to admit a flaw or to make a decision for either war or diplomacy, Konoe abandoned his cabinet. The imperial order to form the next cabinet fell to Tōjō (Fig. 8.4).

---

[1] "All the seas in every quarter are as brothers to one another. Why, then, do the winds and waves of strife rage so turbulently throughout the world?" (Ike 1967, p. 151).

Fig. 8.4 The Tōjō Cabinet (18 October 1941). Front row from the left: Finance Minister Kaya Okinori, President of the Planning Bureau Suzuki Teiichi, Prime Minister Tōjō Hideki, and Navy Minister Shimada Shigetarō (*Mainichi Shimbun*)

Tōjō Cabinet and Reexamination of the National Policy

After ordering Tōjō to form a cabinet, the emperor ordered the army and navy Ministers to reexamine the national policy. Tōjō had been elevated, from being the representative for the institutional interests of the IJA, to a position steering the entire Japanese ship of state.

He immediately began the reexamination of national policy. The Army General Staff Office took the position that, as the imperial command for a reexamination had been directed to the government, the reexamination was unnecessary. Among the cabinet ministers, Foreign Minister Tōgō Shigenori and Finance Minister Kaya Okinori opposed going to war, and both Navy Minister Shimada Shigetarō and President of the Planning Board Suzuki Teiichi at first took the position of avoiding a war. As a result of the reexamination, which lasted from October 23 until the middle of the night of November 1, Shimada and Suzuki flipped their positions and now approved of starting a war, and ultimately even Kaya and Tōgō consented. Let us summarize the discussion that took place during the reexamination.

Japan had three options at the time. One, seize the natural resource belt of the Dutch East Indies through force. Two, reach an agreement through diplomatic negotiations for the United States and Britain to lift their embargos. Three, take no

Fig. 8.5 Chief of the Navy
General Staff Nagano
Osami

action and hope for a change in the situation (*gashin shōtan*, which means "enduring unspeakable hardships to achieve the objective").

The argument for option one could not hold water without prospects that the resources transported from the Dutch East Indies to Japan could sustain national power. The transport route's flank was exposed to the Philippines and Guam (US territories), so even if Japan tried to limit its war adversaries to Britain and the Netherlands, the strategic concept would all come to naught if the United States were to attack. Therefore, Japan was forced to fight all three countries. In addition, the biggest concern was whether Japan could sustain the tonnage of shipping required to transport the resources. In the end, an optimistic forecast was put forth that ship-building tonnage would increase, and tonnage lost would decrease after the second year. That led to the conclusion that the war might become a protracted conflict, which caused Shimada and Suzuki to now support this option.

The argument for option two was that there was no outlook for that unless Japan largely conceded on the issue of withdrawing its troops from China. Foreign Minister Tōgō Shigenori had compiled a plan (Plan A) that compromised to a greater degree than the previous cabinet had, yet even then compromise held out only thin hopes for a rather meager success. Out of necessity, he sought a breakthrough with a backup plan, a provisional concept of a Plan B (a barter: US lifting the trade embargo for withdrawing Japanese troops from southern French Indochina). However, diplomatic negotiations would adjust according to the other party's responses. This option, too, depended on wishful thinking (Moriyama 2012).

Of course, there was also option three, *gashin shōtan*. With Japan's oil stocks sure to run dry after 2 years, however, the country would be incapable of resisting a potential attack at that time. That is not to say that the United States would have come attacking for sure. A fierce debate unfolded between Nagano Osami, the chief of the IJN General Staff, and Tōgō and Kaya at the November 1 liaison conference. Nagano, though he could not speak with certainty about the probability of victory, repeatedly said that it would be better to go to war now than later. Pessimistic predictions fearing a war that may or may not occur, as it turned out, drew that war closer, making it imminent (Fig. 8.5).

Outlook on the War Situation and Rationale for the Choice

What was the IJN's outlook on the state of the war? Nagano explained that, should the war be protracted owing to the absence of a decisive battle (as had occurred in the Russo-Japanese War), the outcome would be determined by the international environment and the overall national power in physical and metaphysical terms (Sugiyama, ibid.). It was obvious that Japan was incapable of surpassing the United States physically, that is in material quantities, which meant it had to resort to spiritual power (metaphysical) and praying to the gods (a favorable change in the environment). Such an attitude for a head of high command staff is irresponsible, to say the least, and is no way to form a basis for a decision to secure an advantage in war. Just as Nagano had advocated, however, Japan plunged into starting the war. Why was that?

One reason is that the third option ("enduring hardships") lacked clear prospects for success; it was, in fact, associated with certainty of loss. Since we Japanese today know of the actual losses that defeat brought upon us, we can compare results and decide to choose the relatively better option of "enduring hardships." It is hard to assess this before the fact, however, since avoiding war by "enduring hardships" does not result in any losses. On the contrary, as the oil runs dry, you run the risk of being blamed, that you should have fought when you had the time. In contrast to that scenario, diplomacy and war were options that gave some hope, no matter how little. That, however, was grounded in wishful thinking of rather rosy predictions and falsified statistics.

In the course of the discussions, Nagano repeatedly stated that the outlook 3 years hence was uncertain (more precisely, the third year was 2 years later), and spoke no further regarding the outlook. In 3 years, one could easily imagine the United States coming for a counterstrike having prepared itself with overwhelming military might, even greater than at present. However, they stopped their conception right before that moment, locking themselves away in an imagined future that was to their liking. People who are anxious to avoid loss tend to take the far riskier, more speculative option for expected value, according to research results (Makino 2018). It is hard to simply attribute the decision to go to war against the United States as an idiotic choice taken by men who had ways of thinking different from our own.

Losing the War: Results and Lessons

Defeat meant Japan lost all its colonies and special interests on the continent that it had worked so hard to acquire since the Meiji period. In addition, China turning Communist meant that the lands supplying natural resources and markets that were developed with the support of Japanese capitalism disappeared on the other side of the "bamboo curtain" (the border dividing the Communist camp from the anti-Communist camp in Asia). Then numerous soldiers and civilians (approximately

6.6 million) returned to a devastated homeland. And yet, Japan later achieved miraculous economic growth even without colonies or special interests on the continent (Tanaka 2010).

Is this the hindsight of history? Not necessarily so. In the course of the reexamination of the national policy, Foreign Minister Tōgō insisted that if only the United States eased its conditions slightly and Japan accepted them, everything would take a turn for the better (Sugiyama, ibid.). There was no one, however, who would listen to him at that time. It was the understanding of everyone, aside from Tōgō, that Japan would become a third-rate country if it lost its continental interests. People who take the long view, being neither overly pessimistic nor optimistic— such people were in short supply at the center of Japanese policymaking. And what came of that? Many are the lessons that should be taken from the outcome of the war that cost an unimaginable number of victims.

Bibliography: For Further Reading

Daihon'ei rikugunbu sensō shidōhan. Gunjishi Gakkai hen (eds). 1998. *Daihon'ei rikugunbu sensō shidōhan: Kimitsu sensō nisshi. jōkan* (Imperial General Head- quarters, Army Division, War Guidance Section: Secret War Log [First Volume]). Tokyo: Kinseisha.

Department of State. 1943. Papers relating to the foreign relations of the United States, Japan, 1931–1941, Volume II. Washington, D.C.: US Government Printing Office. As referenced at: https://history.state.gov/historicaldocuments/frus1931-41 v02/d271

Ike, Nobutaka (trans., ed.). 1967. Japan's Decision for War: Records of the 1941 Policy Conferences. Stanford: Stanford University Press. [This reference, a transla- tion of the Liaison and Imperial Conference documents from 1941, was used for English wording.]

Kido, Kōichi. Oka, Yoshitake (eds). 1966. *Kido Kōichi nikki jōge-kan* (The Diary of Marquis Kido Kōichi, [Two Volumes]). Tokyo: The University of Tokyo Press.

Kotani, Ken. 2004. *Igirisu no jōhō gaikō: interijensu towa nanika* (British Intelligence and Diplomacy: What is Intelligence?). PHP Shinsho.

Moriyama, Atsushi. 2012. *Nihon wa naze kaisen ni humikitta ka: "ryōron heiki" to "hi kettei"* (Why Japan Decided to Enter the War with the United States). Tokyo: Shinchōsha.

An analysis of the characteristics of Japan's complicated policy-making system of the time: incorporating incompatible policy options and indecision. The book focuses on the period following the freezing of Japanese assets in the United States in late July 1941.

Moriyama, Atsushi. 2016. *Nichibei kaisen to jōhōsen* (Intelligence War before the Japan-US War). Kōdansha.

An analysis of the decision-making process in late 1940 for measures toward Thailand and French Indochina and the stationing troops in southern French

Indochina, centering on Matsuoka Yōsuke's role. In addition, the book sheds light empirically on the intelligence war between Japan and the United States over going to war.

Moriyama, Atsushi. 2017. *Matsuoka yōsuke: popyurisuto no gosan* ("Matsuoka Yōsuke: Miscalculations of a Populist") in Tsutsui, Kiyotada (eds). Shōwashi kōgi3 (Showa Lectures 3). Chikuma Shobō.

Nishiura, Susumu. 2013. *Shōwa sensōshi no shōgen: nihon rikugun shūen no shinjitsu* (Shōwa War History Testimonial: The Truth about the Final Days of the Imperial Japanese Army). Tokyo: Nikkei Bijinesujin Bunko.

Sugiyama, Hajime. Rikugun Sanbō Honbu-hen (eds). 1994. *Sugiyama memo. hukyū-ban, shinsō-ban* (The Sugiyama Memo [new, mass market edition]). Tokyo: Hara Shobō. (First published in 1967.)

Tanaka, Hiromi. 2010. *Fukuin, hikiage no kenkyū: kiseki no seikan to saisei e no michi* (Demobilization and Repatriation Studies: the Miraculous Survivors and their Road to Recovery). Tokyo: Shin Jinbutsu Ōraisha.

Additional Bibliography

Kitaoka, Shin'ichi. 2015. *Monko kaihō seisaku to nihon* (The Open Door Policy and Japan). Tokyo: The University of Tokyo Press.

In the concluding chapter, "The aims and points of dispute in the Pacific War," the author points out that conflict between Japan and the United States was over their principles only. It was not over concrete interests, and thus resolution through negotiation was difficult. This important study first appeared in print in Hosoya Chihiro et al (eds). 1993. *Taiheiyō sensō* (The Pacific War). Tokyo: The University of Tokyo Press.

Makino, Kuniaki. 2018. *Keizai gakushatachi no nichi-bei kaisen: akimaru kikan "maboroshi no hōkokusho" no nazo o toku* (Economists on the Start of the Pacific War: Solving the Mystery of the Akimaru Unit's "Illusory Report"). Tokyo: Shinchō sensho.

Why didn't the Akimaru Unit comprising Japan's leading economists prevent the war? An economist's high-level overview through the war's end that reveals the true aspects of the unit's "illusory report."

Chapter 9
US Policy for the Occupation of Japan and Changes to It

Ayako Kusunoki

Abstract US policy for the occupation of Japan following its defeat in World War II is the primary topic of this chapter. After an overview of the traits of the occupation of Japan by comparing with the Allied occupation of a divided Germany, it analyzes and broadly categorizes the various reforms to demilitarize and democratize Japan. The "reverse course" of US policy prioritizing Japan's economic revival, which coincided with the Cold War, is placed in a broader economic context.

Introduction

The George W. Bush administration, it is said, had imagined the occupation of Japan as a model for nation-building after prosecuting the war in Iraq. For the United States, the US occupation of Japan is a grand success story, transforming the erstwhile enemy, militaristic Japan, into a democratic, peaceful nation, as John Dower depicts in *Embracing Defeat* (Dower 1999). In contrast, whenever someone brings up the idea of "escaping from the postwar regime"[1] it is accompanied by an air of criticism, founded on the premise that the occupation distorted Japan's unique culture and tradition, as well as the shape the country would have had naturally. It appears that these two grand stories have constructed mutually exclusive, self-contained worlds.

On the other hand, underlying both narratives is the understanding that the Allied occupation lasting 6 years and 8 months, from the time of Japan's defeat to the moment the Treaty of Peace with Japan came into effect, brought about dramatic changes in the political, economic, and social systems that had made up the architecture of modern Japan. They merely differ in the perspective from which to consider those "changes" or how to place those changes within the discourse of

---

[1] The late Abe Shinzō's slogan.

A. Kusunoki
International Research Center for Japanese Studies, Kyoto, Japan

© The Author(s) 2023   111
M. Yamauchi, Y. Hosoya (eds.), *Modern Japan's Place in World History*,
https://doi.org/10.1007/978-981-19-9593-4_9

Japan's modern period. Before we return to the grand story of these "changes," let us retrace the picture of the occupation of Japan by focusing on the true nature and structural causes of these changes. I would like to offer three viewpoints in this chapter.

"American" Occupation

The start of the post-World War II international order brought with it the occupation of the Axis countries, Japan and Germany, as well as those countries and lands liberated from the Axis powers. The occupations of Japan and Germany, above all, were designated as the foundation for lasting peace and stability in the Allies' conception of the postwar world. Yet the methods used to implement occupation in the two countries greatly differed in two aspects.

First, whereas Germany was divided into four zones, placed under military governments, and administered by the United States, Britain, France, and the Soviet Union, respectively, Japan (except for Okinawa, the Ogasawara Islands, and the areas taken by the Soviet military) was placed under the authority of the General Headquarters of the Supreme Commander for the Allied Powers (GHQ/SCAP). US forces made up the majority of Allied troops deployed on the main islands. While the management of the occupation of Japan was under the multilateral framework, the US government retained the lead on occupation policy. The Far Eastern Commission (FEC), the highest decision-making body for the occupation of Japan, was established by the United States, Britain, the Soviet Union, the Republic of China, and a total of 11 major belligerents (increased to 13 in the autumn of 1949). The Allied Council for Japan (ACJ), made up of the United States, the British Commonwealth countries, the Soviet Union, and the Republic of China, was set up as SCAP's advisory body in Tokyo. Despite the constraints of these multilateral frameworks, the US government was able to achieve its policy aims by and large through exercising its veto power in the FEC or issuing directives (Interim Directive Authority) in emergency situations without waiting for the decision of the FEC.

In addition to the contrast between the European and Asia-Pacific fronts during World War II, the ground warfare waged with Allied forces resulted in Germany's collapse whereas in Japan's case, it surrendered by accepting the Potsdam Declaration before the US forces launched amphibious operations on the main islands, giving rise to the difference in form of each occupation. If Japan's acceptance of the terms of surrender had been delayed slightly, the Soviet army would have invaded the northern part of Japanese islands and Japan likely could not have avoided being physically divided during its occupation.

Germany became a nation divided, as the border between the occupation zones of the Soviet Union and other three countries solidified along with the eventual intensification of the Cold War. Moreover, despite the official agreement that the four occupying nations coordinated their policies in Germany, it was quite difficult in reality; from time to time, they each pursued separate occupation policies for their zone that reflected their own national interests. In Japan's case, in part because SCAP basically preserved Japanese administrative organs, it was possible for the United States to implement occupation policies uniformly through the Japanese government. Under the sole control of the United States virtually, Japan generally was able to maintain its integrity as a nation.

Second, all authority was concentrated in a single individual, General Douglas MacArthur, who by wearing the hats for SCAP and the Commander in Chief, US Army Forces in Pacific (CINCAFPAC) simultaneously, stood at the apex of both the administrative body for the occupation as well as the legal and military force supporting it. This is in stark contrast to the US occupation of Germany, which went without a clear division of roles between the military government overseeing administration of the occupation and US armed forces stationed in Germany, and the administration lacked a center for over 6 months.[2] Moreover, MacArthur had a strong sense of mission, as though appointed by God to remake militarist Japan into a democratic, peaceful country. He was also an exceedingly political soldier. The fact that he made the Japanese people understand, at an early stage, that he was the only power and authority standing atop the institutions ruling Japan, including the emperor, while he did treat Emperor Shōwa with respect, thoroughly attests to his keen political sensibilities. Though a man with many detractors, it is largely owing to MacArthur that the occupation of Japan was implemented without major turmoil.

Process of Occupation Reforms

In interstate warfare until World War II, the victors would often occupy part of the loser's territory to exact reparations or supervise its disarmament and demilitarization, but hardly ever did the thought occur to reorganize and reconstruct the defeated nation. The Hague Convention on Land Warfare (which entered into force in 1900 and was amended in 1907) stipulated the duty of the "occupant" to respect, unless absolutely necessary, the laws in force in the occupied country. That the occupying country would reorganize the body politic of an occupied country or force its transformation was a new phenomenon of the World War II era.

It is one of the inevitable outcomes of the Allied policy demanding the unconditional surrender of the Axis Powers. The Potsdam Declaration could be understood as the terms of surrender that the Allied Powers offered to Japan, which the Empire of Japan accepted without condition. Paragraph 7 of the Potsdam Declaration clearly states that "[u]ntil such a new order is established and until there is convincing proof that Japan's war-making power is destroyed, points in Japanese territory to be designated by the Allies shall be occupied to secure the achievement of the basic objectives we are here setting forth," and lays out the fundamental direction for

---

[2] On 1 July 1946, General Joseph T. McNarney finally took command over the Office of Military Government for Germany (US) (OMGUS) and US Forces, European Theater (USFET).

reforms starting in paragraph 8 (Potsdam Declaration 1945). The Potsdam Declaration can be seen as providing the legal grounds for occupation reforms.

One more thing we need to consider is the growing importance of ideology as a factor driving international politics. The Soviet Union established Communist regimes in all of the eastern European countries it liberated from Nazi Germany and in its occupation zone in Germany, as a result of deep-rooted anxiety and fear kindled by the experience of having European powers invade deeply within its own borders twice since the nineteenth century. US policy toward occupied Japan, beginning about halfway through, also prioritized rebuilding the country for fear that weakness made it vulnerable to Communism. The Allied occupation comprised one part of the Cold War struggle over the choice of political-economic national systems.

The Potsdam Declaration enumerated a menu of reforms: disarming Japanese military forces (paragraph 9), meting out stern justice to war criminals and establishing freedom of speech, of religion, and of thought, as well as respect for fundamental human rights (paragraph 10), abolishing industries enabling Japan to re-arm for war while permitting eventual Japanese participation in world trade relations (paragraph 11). Through such reforms to demilitarize and democratize the country, the US government intended to remake Japan's political, economic, and social systems that were premodern or even feudal from the US perspective as a liberal, democratic system while at the same time destroying Japan's ability to prosecute war so that it would never again challenge the international order. The Occupation started with the elimination of military elements—the disarmament and demobilization of Imperial Japanese forces which ended with the abolition of the Army and the Navy ministries in December 1945, the arrest of war criminals (starting in September 1945), and the purge of undesirables from public office (SCAP directive in January 1946)—with reforms focusing more on democratization following sometime thereafter.

It is possible to categorize the various occupation reforms to democratize Japan into three broad types according to the process in which they came about. The first type of reform is what the Japanese government achieved voluntarily, perhaps exemplified by revision of the Election Law (December 1945) that granted women's suffrage and the enactment of a Labor Union Law (December 1945) that was comparable to international standards.

The second type, in contrast, are the reforms GHQ compelled the Japanese government to make, for instance, dissolution of the *zaibatsu* (1945–1947), the Anti-Monopoly Law (April 1947), or the Law for the Elimination of Excessive Concentration of Economic Power (Deconcentration Law, December 1947). From the US perspective, the *zaibatsu*, business conglomerates centered around a family or a shareholding company, were the equivalent of absentee landowners in farming villages, symbols of Japan's feudalistic society. There was hardly anyone within the Japanese government who regarded the *zaibatsu* as an economic and societal problem, unlike the landlord-tenant system, the structural cause of the poverty of farming villages creating a bottleneck to economic growth in Japan overall, which at least some enlightened bureaucrats acknowledged as issues to resolve by curbing the power of landowners and improving the status of tenant farmers. It might also be possible to include among this second type the guarantee of religious freedom and abolition of State Shintō, as well as the reorganization of Shrine Shintō that ensued (Shintō directive, December 1945).

The third type falls between the other two: reforms the Japanese government started, either voluntarily or in response to the GHQ's wishes, that became more radical after the GHQ intervened mid-way through the process. Emblematic of this type is constitutional revision (the new constitution was promulgated in November 1946). Many reforms belong in the category of this third type: the Diet Law (promulgated in April 1947) that stipulated the primacy of the National Diet over administrative organs; agricultural land reforms (the law amending the Agricultural Land Adjustment Law and the Owner-Farmer Establishment and Special Measures Law promulgated in October 1946); local autonomy (Local Autonomy Law promulgated in April 1947) and decentralizing policing authority (Police Law, December 1947) that led to the ultimate breakup of the Ministry of Home Affairs; and educational reform (Law for Fundamental Education and School Education Law promulgated and implemented in March 1947).

Continuity/discontinuity of modern Japanese history has been always an issue on the occupation studies. When thinking about Japan's modernity, occupation reforms perhaps take on a sense of completion by redressing distortions in that modernity. Focusing on the fact that changes in the economic and social systems had proceeded apace under Japan's total war system shows that there are arguments to be made that Japan did not change all that much under the US occupation's democratizing reforms, or that these sorts of reforms would have happened even without the US occupation of Japan. These arguments, constructed on the research achievements of Japanese modern history, are very suggestive, for they consider the significance of occupation reforms from a longer-term perspective. On the other hand, reforms to demilitarize and democratize Japan made unsteady progress, and their power to disrupt varied from area to area. Even if you grant that the orientation for systemic reform was inherent in Japanese society, we must not disregard the hard truth: the fact that reforms were accomplished in that period and in that way is what made postwar Japan's political, social, and economic reality, a reality made possible by the Allied occupation of Japan.

"Reverse Course"?

The occupation period for 6-year and 8-months can be devided in two, with 1947–1948 as the turning point. The first half is the period when the pursuit of demilitarization and democratization reforms was heavily emphasized; major reforms were intensively implemented in roughly these 2 years. The second half, in contrast, was a period when priority was placed on stabilizing and reconstructing the Japanese economy, which eventually led to making peace and recovering independence.

The occupation policy's evolution away from the direction of demilitarization and democratization has frequently been called the "reverse course." The expression connotes a criticism, that the program for rebuilding the Japanese economy accompanied the strengthening of the state's power, which ended up making the democratization reforms unfinished. The change in occupation policy is generally understood as being a process that was integrated with the process for incorporating Japan into the Western bloc, because it coincided with the deepening of the tension between East and West. The "reverse course" theory inevitably gives rise to the view that Japan's subordinate relationship to the United States was firmly established, and that Japan became the junior partner strategically in the Cold War, through the Peace Treaty with Japan and the U.S.-Japan Security Treaty.

An examination of the late occupation period from the context of US policy toward Japan suggests that the characterization of the "reverse course" is not entirely appropriate. First, the US government had conceived the shift from demilitarization and democratization toward economic reconstruction during the war, at the stage it began drawing up plans for the occupation of Japan. I would also remind the reader that paragraph 11 of the Potsdam Declaration clearly states that "[e]ventual Japanese participation in world trade relations shall be permitted." Because the key reforms to demilitarize and democratize Japan had completed by the end of 1947, the United States would have changed course to stabilize and revive the country's economy, even if the Cold War had never happened.

Also at work were demands to reduce the burden on the US taxpayer. Even though US ground forces deployed in Japan stood at 100,000 men in 1948—a reduction to about one-quarter of the initial figure—outlays on the occupation were not an insignificant burden to the US government. It is only natural that policy moved in a direction to promote Japan's economic independence. There is practically no ideological meaning to be found here.

Still, it is a fact that the change in occupation policy coincided with the period that the Cold War intensified in Europe and in Asia. And the US government's policy for Japan underlying the change (National Security Council (NSC) Report 13/2, approved October 1948) is, beyond a doubt, the very product of the US Cold War strategy of containment. For that reason, the shift in occupation policy is colored by an ideological significance and thus is understood as part of the Cold War in Asia.

The policy of containment promoted by George F. Kennan, the US State Department's Soviet expert, was predicated on the idea that conciliation with Communist powers was not possible. Even as it argued the need to oppose the Communist military threat with force, the policy held as its core concept the goal of driving the Soviet Union into dialogue with the West and the collapse from within over the long term, by means of maintaining healthy societies based on liberal and democratic values among the Western countries. In that conception, Japan was designated together with Western Europe as regions where the spread of Communism must be prevented. In addition to its strategic location in the Asia Pacific region, forming a part of the island chains from the Aleutian Islands to the Philippines, Japan's potential industrial power was believed to pose a grave threat to the United States if it might fall into Soviet Communist hands. Accordingly, the creation of a politically, socially, and economically stable Japan that was not vulnerable to Communism was emphasized as the policy that the United States should pursue in the Cold War. Starting in the summer of 1947 and throughout the following year, the State Department reexamined the existing policies toward Japan focused on demilitarization and democratization from such a perspective.

In keeping with the resultant NSC 13/2, the US government issued a nine-point economic stabilization plan in December 1948 that featured a balanced budget, price controls, and wage stability. In February 1949, it dispatched a chairman of the Detroit Bank, Joseph M. Dodge, who instructed the Yoshida Shigeru cabinet to implement policy measures to stabilize the economy. The budget for fiscal year 1949 was planned to balance the overall budget, starting with the general accounts, the special accounts, and government-related institutions, by abolishing and reducing subsidies and price supports, and minimizing expenditures for public works or unemployment compensation. Following these inflation-fighting measures, a single exchange rate at 360 Japanese yen to one US dollar was introduced. Inflation, which had plagued Japan since the defeat of the war, rapidly returned to normal through this series of policies that were called the Dodge Line. Taking a scalpel to the economic system which had been comfortably protected by various forms of subsidies, public lending through government financial institutions, and a doubling and tripling of the exchange rate, facilitated restoration of fiscal health, the elimination of inflationary factors, and the rationalization of industry to achieve international competitiveness.

Measures to promote the reconstruction of the Japanese economy and foster an environment for the country's independent economic management were also put into effect over the course of 1947–1949. The US government had relented on reparation policies that had aimed at minimizing Japan's productive capabilities, with the final declaration on the termination of the raparation program in May 1949. It started the flow of GARIOA (Government Aid and Relief in Occupied Areas) and EROA (Economic Rehabilitation in Occupied Areas) assistance that focused on heavy industrial materials and machinery, in addition to relief products such as foodstuffs and medicines. Finally, it permitted a limited restart of private trade, as well as amended the anti-monopoly law and relaxed policies aimed at deconcentrating businesses that had been the core of economic democratization policies. The basic policy on easing reparations was ultimately reflected in the Peace Treaty which did not obligate Japan to make reparations, except for Allied powers so desiring, whose present territories had been occupied by Japanese forces and damaged by Japan, by making available the services of the Japanese people in production, salvaging, and other work for those countries. Various US assistance measures, beginning with GARIOA and EROA, were indispensable elements that supported the Japanese economy throughout the 1950s.

It is widely known that the Dodge Line immediately contained inflation and even gave rise to a stabilization crisis. Social instability grew in the summer and autumn of 1949, with mysteries such as the Shimoyama incident[3] coupled with the large-scale typhoons hitting the mainland. For the Japanese economy to escape from deflation and enjoy a temporary recovery, it would have to wait for a special procurement boom brought by the Korean War (*Chosen tokujū*). The problem of a weak Japanese economy would continue to constrain US policy toward Japan even after the occupation was concluded, for it was in the latter part of the 1950s when the economy finally embarked on a stable growth path. The shift of US occupation policy would require time until the objective of Japanese economic stability was achieved.

The fact that the Yoshida Shigeru cabinet braved the Dodge Line's surgical treatment is thought to have held important significance for US policies toward Japan. Economic stabilization policies, while necessary for Japan's economy in the long term, were to nobody's advantage in the short term; in fact, these measures brought disadvantages to a large number of people. The unwavering will and ability of the Yoshida cabinet to carry out such unpopular policies that could precipitate political instability, even if it was able to count on the absolute power of the GHQ/SCAP if necessary, was certain proof from the US standpoint that Japan had the potential to resist Communism. It was in the latter half of the occupation period that it became clear: Japanese political powers brought up under a democratic political system were capable of sustaining the US long-term objective to foster Japan as a member of the Western bloc.

Assessing the Occupation of Japan

During the peace negotiations in 1951, Yoshida and his staff occasionally expressed their aversion to laws and institutions established under the Occupation, in particular internal security, economic, and labor fields, being made permanent by the peace treaty. The Yoshida cabinet also seemed eager to amend policies that were not suited to Japan's customs and mores based on the work of the cabinet ordinance consultative committee to reexamine every law and ordinance stemming from the occupation. The Reform Party (founded in February 1952), Hatoyama Ichirō's faction, and other conservative anti-Yoshida forces advocated a policy to comprehensively reexamine institutions forced by the Allied powers, which they generally considered to be incompatible with Japanese tradition and culture, after the Peace Treaty was signed in September 1951.

As restoration of sovereignty meant that Japan could no longer depend on the absolute power of GHQ/SCAP, the Japanese government recognized an importance to strengthen its authority necessary for economic reconstruction or maintaining public order. In addition, for conservative forces, notably those designated as war criminals or purged from public office as undesirables, it was unbearable to

---

[3]The disappearance and death of Shimoyama Sadanori, the first president of Japanese National Railways (JNR), who was put in charge of drastic cutbacks at JNR under the Dodge Line.

accept the various institutions introduced during the occupation period as a new reality, and they believed that inappropriate or excessive reforms were supposed to be corrected as soon as possible so that Japan could restore its true independence. The most important political issue for them was revising the constitution. The fact that Japan was able to survive only under the aegis of the United States in terms of the economy and national security even after peace was established gave further impetus to seek for breaking the fetters of occupation reforms. That is why the expressions "genuine independence" and "autonomous independence" had so much allure in the political space in the 1950s.

Yet no fundamental changes were made to the overall direction set by the reforms that democratized and demilitarized Japan. Occupation reforms, together with the Treaty of Peace with Japan and the Treaty of Mutual Cooperation and Security between Japan and the United States of America (Japan-US Security Treaty), constituted the basic framework for Japan's domestic and foreign policies from the 1950s onward. Why had they become institutionalized?

First and foremost, many people benefitted from these liberal and democratic reforms. Occupation reforms, on the whole, had the effect of advancing equality by compelling a redress of wealth disparities while they also raised the degree of freedom in politics, society, and the economy. The achievement of freedom and equality unmistakably boosted the legitimacy for governance and the resilience of the society in the long term. Moreover, demilitarization and democratization reforms changed the rule of political games. Not only those who supported the vast array of the GHQ's occupation policies, but also those who were at the mercy of and opposed to them, had, in the course of the daily struggle for their own and for Japan's survival, turned into a new class with vested interests, which internalized the norms and rules that occupation reforms had created. As for the people who had not been permitted to enter the political arena during the Occupation and held no loyalty to the product of those reforms, they, too, had to adapt to the new rules in order to participate in the game, the struggle for power.

Bibliography: For Further Reading

Dower, John W. 1999. *Embracing Defeat: Japan in the Wake of World War II.* New York: W.W. Norton & Co. (Iwanami Shoten published the first edition translated into Japanese in 2001).

National Security Council. 1948. *Report by the National Security Council on Recommendations With Respect to United States Policy Toward Japan (NSC 13/2).* Referenced at https://history.state.gov/historicaldocuments/frus1948v06/d588.

Potsdam Declaration. 1945. Referenced at https://www.ndl.go.jp/constitution/e/etc/c06.html.

Additional Bibliography

Amamiya, Shōichi. 2008. *Shirīzu nihon kingendaishi, 7 Senryō to kaikaku* (Japan's Modern History Series, Vol. 7: Occupation and Reforms). Tokyo: Iwanami Shinsho.
  The author's treatise on occupation reform based on his research of the "system" throughout the wartime to postwar periods. It emphasizes the seeds of reform found within the total-war system.
  Fukunaga, Fumio. 2014. *Nihon senryōshi 1945–1952: tōkyō, washington, okinawa* (The Occupation of Japan, 1945–1952: Tokyo, Washington, and Okinawa). Tokyo: Chūkō Shinsho. [Published in English as: Fukunaga, Fumio. The Japan Institute of International Affairs (trans). 2021. *The Occupation of Japan, 1945–1952: Tokyo, Washington, and Okinawa*. Tokyo: Japan Publishing Industry Foundation for Culture.]
  This book lays out the process resulting in peace, as demilitarization and democratization reforms were eventually altered under the "reverse course," replaced with policies to foster Japan as an anti-Communist, pro-American state amid the Cold War. It features new points from Okinawa's perspective.
  Iokibe, Makoto. 1997. *Senryōki: shushōtachi no shin Nihon* (Occupation Period: The Prime Ministers and their New Japan). Tokyo: Yomiuri Shinbunsha, 1997.
  Defeat, occupation, making peace—how did the Japanese government respond when presented with these critical scenarios? An examination, centering on the five Japanese prime ministers of the occupation period.
  Itabashi, Takumi. 2014. *Adenauā: gendai doitsu o tsukutta seijika* (Adenauer: the Politician who Made Modern Germany). Tokyo: Chūkō Shinsho.
  This book sheds light on the domestic and foreign policies of Konrad Adenauer, "the man seeming responsible for all of the roles played in Japan by Yoshida Shigeru, Hatoyama Ichirō, Kishi Nobusuke, and Ikeda Hayato." The author offers a perspective for considering an international comparison to Japan's occupation and postwar eras.
  Kusunoki, Ayako. 2013. *Gendai nihon seijishi. 1, Senryō kara dokuritsu e, 1945–1952* (History of Modern Japanese Politics, Vol. 1: From Occupation to Independence, 1945–1952). Tokyo: Yoshikawa Kōbunkan.
  This book depicts how Japan's political powers-that-be responded to US-led occupation reforms, economic crisis, the Cold War, and making peace, and how that shaped Japan's postwar political system.

Chapter 10
Law and Politics in the Tokyo Trial

Yoshinobu Higurashi

Abstract This chapter provides a detailed examination of the legal and political aspects of the International Military Tribunal of the Far East of May 1946–November 1948, more commonly known as the Tokyo war crimes trial. It reviews the legal origins of the three classes of war crimes, assesses the perspectives of the Allied prosecutors, and traces the process whereby judgments and sentences were reached. The chapter concludes with how international policy developments (peace and independence of Japan) affected the fates of those convicted and poses questions about the judicial process itself.

What Are Class A War Criminals?

The Tokyo Trial (officially, the International Military Tribunal for the Far East; May 3, 1946 to November 12, 1948) was a war crimes tribunal held after World War II had ended, in which 11 victorious Allied powers (the United States, the United Kingdom, the Republic of China, the Soviet Union, France, the Netherlands, Canada, Australia, New Zealand, India, and the Philippines) prosecuted and tried 28 leaders of the defeated Japan. Its precedent was the Nuremberg Trial in Germany (the International Military Tribunal; November 20, 1945 to October 1, 1946), where four Allied powers (the United States, the United Kingdom, the Soviet Union, and France) sat in judgment on Nazi leaders.

The Tokyo Trial was the concluding point of the wars of the Shōwa period as well as the starting point for postwar thought. For that very reason, there has long been a dispute between two diametrically opposed views concerning the trial. One is the affirmative argument: the school of thought that the Trial was "civilization's justice," and that it was only natural to sit in judgment on the barbaric Japanese militarists responsible for perpetrating a war of aggression and atrocities. Then, there is the

Y. Higurashi
Faculty of Law, Teikyo University, Tokyo, Japan

© The Author(s) 2023
M. Yamauchi, Y. Hosoya (eds.), *Modern Japan's Place in World History*,
https://doi.org/10.1007/978-981-19-9593-4_10

negative argument: the theory that the tribunal was "victors' justice," vindictive in terms of fairness and the grounds for punishment.

Both arguments are attractive, being plain, simple, and easy to understand, though which is more compelling varies according to whether you see Japan or the Allies as being in the right. Each theory directly confronts the other, as you can trace in the arguments put forth by the prosecution and the defense. The 1978 enshrinement of the 14 Class A war criminals together with the other souls in Yasukuni Shrine was a sort of spiritual measure that served as a complete rejection of the Tokyo Trial. It remains very difficult to discuss the Tokyo Trial calmly and rationally.

With that as a brief background, I have tended to endorse the view that takes the Tokyo Trial as a policy of international politics, combining aspects of both civilization's justice and victors' justice, deeming it a mistake to see it as either one or the other exclusively. So, it is from such an angle that I would like to use this chapter to make a political history examination of several points related to the Trial.

First, let us start by defining what Class A war criminals were. The term "war criminals" used by today's mass media means those responsible for defeat and the mistakes leading to it in sporting events and corporate governance. The original meaning, however, is different. Officially, the Nuremberg and Tokyo International Military Tribunals had jurisdiction over three types of war crimes. First, "crimes against peace" are international crimes of planning, preparation, initiation or waging of a war of aggression (Class A crimes). Second, "war crimes" are violations of the traditional laws or customs of war (Class B crimes). And third, "crimes against humanity" are international crimes for inhumane acts against any civilian population or persecutions on political, racial, or religious grounds (Class C crimes). Those indicted for crimes against the peace were called Class A war criminals. Moreover, indictment for crimes against the peace was an essential condition at the Tokyo Trial, so simply put, a Class A war criminal meant the same as being a defendant in the Tokyo Trial. (The designation of Class A war criminal was not used in Germany.)

The Establishment of New War Crimes

Of the three types, punishment for the second (conventional war crimes) was traditionally recognized and accepted. But the first and third (crimes against peace and crimes against humanity) were crimes newly defined in the later stages of World War II; in other words, they are ex post facto laws. Just how were international military tribunals established on the basis of laws created after the fact?

In the Atlantic Charter they issued on August 14, 1941, US President Franklin D. Roosevelt and British Prime Minister Winston Churchill revealed their concept for post-war, the "final destruction of Nazi tyranny." It was to remake the German state.

Two months later, Churchill also endorsed the punishment of war criminals who committed "Nazi atrocities" as an Allied objective of the war, which gained the support of other Allied powers. By eliminating the Nazi leadership, Roosevelt and other Allied leaders thought to remake Germany as a peaceful country. In this way, punishing war criminals after the end of World War II became something on a much larger scale, leading to the intermingling of Allied occupation reforms with the drive to remake the states of the defeated.

Nazi atrocities, not starting a war, were subject to punishment at that time. Further, how exactly to try these crimes was left vague. It was only in the autumn of 1944 that things became more specific.

The United States began planning in earnest for the postwar settlement after the Normandy landings of June 1944, when Allied victory seemed more certain. US Treasury Secretary Henry Morgenthau, Jr. insisted that Nazi leaders be summarily executed; they were to be shot dead immediately after confirmation by the witnesses themselves. Though it seems like an unreasonable approach from today's perspective, Roosevelt had indicated a degree of understanding at the time.

Morgenthau's summary execution proposal borrowed from British ideas. Britain, opposed to a trial, thought to resolve the issue of war criminals expeditiously by summary executions, as Attorney General David Maxwell-Fyfe spoke plainly: "There are two things to avoid—one is Nazi propaganda; the other is the trial of the actions of the countries of the prosecutors" (Department of State 1949).

However, Secretary of War Henry L. Stimson severely chastised Morgenthau and criticized summary execution as a barbaric, feudal method. The "thorough apprehension, investigation, and trial of all the Nazi leaders" (i.e., employing the civilized method of a trial) that would leave a public record is how we can demonstrate to the German people the evil of the Nazi crimes, he stated (Department of State 1972). Civilization's justice was, above all, a rejection of summary executions.

In the end, Stimson's argument won out and became US national policy. Decision makers in the War Department under Stimson's command created the framework for the International Military Tribunal. In the course of their work, the range of acts subject to punishment expanded beyond atrocities to include planning and starting a war of aggression.

As for the grounds for punishing the act of starting a war, attention focused on the 1928 Pact of Paris (officially, the General Treaty for Renunciation of War as an Instrument of National Policy). Although this treaty outlawed wars of aggression, it did not stipulate punishment for violators. Regardless, the War Department highhandedly reinterpreted the treaty, making it the legal grounds to criminalize such acts, thereby enabling the punishment of individuals, too, an interpretation that was then employed at the International Military Tribunal.

Britain, the Soviet Union, and France agreed with the US approach, and lawyers and jurists from the four countries debated the concepts for the International Military Tribunal at the London Conference (June 26–August 8, 1945). Their final agreement, the London Agreement dated August 8, and its basic laws, the annexed Charter of the International Military Tribunal, established the "crimes against peace" and "crimes against humanity."

Activities of the Allied Prosecutors

The aforementioned policy approach for the punishment of German war criminals was then applied to Japan. The Potsdam Declaration that the United States, Britain, and the Republic of China issued on July 26, 1945 clearly laid out the basic policy for punishing war criminals in the case of Japan. Paragraph 10 states: "stern justice shall be meted out to all war criminals, including those who have visited cruelties upon our prisoners."

The defense at the Tokyo Trial appealed that "war criminals" of the Declaration were those who violated the traditional laws or customs of war, and that it did not include the retroactive laws of "crimes against peace" and "crimes against humanity." Although their arguments were persuasive, the Allies' aim lay elsewhere. The London Conference had not yet reached its conclusions when the Potsdam Declaration was issued, which is why it used the expression "all war criminals."

Japan accepted the Potsdam Declaration and surrendered on August 14. That means Japan had accepted that the Allies would carry out war crimes trials and that the Japanese government had a duty to cooperate with it.

The US prosecutorial team led by Joseph B. Keenan arrived in Japan in December 1945. They were confronted with the unexpected situation of a dearth of evidence, however, because the Japanese side had systematically destroyed a large quantity of records and documentation at the time of the country's defeat, so the team had to collect information through interrogations and questioning of the accused and other related parties. Other written materials began to turn up after a little time had passed, including secret documents and Lord Keeper of the Privy Seal Kido Kōichi's diary. Thus, quite a bit of material was gathered in the end. We can say this collection was one significance of the Tokyo Trial.

Along with gathering information and evidence, the prosecution also examined who to indict. The team became more international after February 1946 with the addition of participants hailing from countries other than the United States. There were four criteria for selecting defendants: (1) they could be indicted for crimes against the peace; (2) they represented an event or organization; (3) there was firm evidence of their guilt; and (4) they either participated actively in, or at least did not oppose, the conspiracy for a war of aggression.

We should perhaps pay special notice to the second point. The level of international notoriety of Japanese leaders was remarkably low, unlike their counterparts in Germany, and many people did not know who was responsible, Tōjō Hideki aside. Members of the prosecutorial team for the most part did not know much about Japanese politics, diplomacy, economics, or culture. And so, they found it efficient to select representatives in high-level posts at the time of the Manchurian Incident and other incidents during the Pacific War.

At a meeting of associate prosecutors on April 8, 1946, they removed Ishiwara Kanji, Masaki Jinzaburō, and Tamura Hiroshi as potential candidates for prosecution and settled on 26 men as defendants. But, owing to a proposal from the Soviet associate prosecutor who had arrived late to Japan, Shigemitsu Mamoru and Umezu

Yoshijirō were added, increasing the number of defendants in the Tokyo Trial to 28. (There were 24 defendants at the Nuremberg Trial, as well as *Die Schutzstaffel* (the SS) and five other groups indicted as criminal organizations.)

The Process for Drafting Judgments

Let us next look at the process for how the group of justices drafted their judgments. The International Military Tribunals in Japan and in Germany consisted of only judges representing Allied countries; there were no jurists from neutral nations. On this point, Stimson's right-hand man, John J. McCloy, the former assistant secretary of war, later remarked that "[d]uring the last war we had failed to get any neutral support on the war criminal problem," admitting that they had not even considered getting a judge from a neutral country (Department of State 1983). A "victors' court" was an outcome of the war.

The Tokyo Trial opened on May 3, 1946 at Ichigayadai Heights, in the building of the former Ministry of the Army and the former Imperial Army General Staff. The defense filed a motion on May 13 challenging the jurisdiction of the court. It argued that, since crimes against peace and crimes against humanity did not exist as war crimes at the time the Potsdam Declaration was issued, these crimes were outside of the court's jurisdiction.

In response, the justices engaged in fierce discussion behind closed doors of the judges' chambers. They decided to dismiss the defense's motion for the time being but delayed announcing their reasons for doing so, owing to a lack of consensus among the judges regarding jurisdiction.

The first judge to express his doubts about crimes against peace was actually Chief Justice William F. Webb, the representative from Australia. Although, unlike Indian judge Radhabinod Pal, he lacked a clear argument against the court's jurisdiction, Webb did question whether they should, once again, carefully consider the question of the criminality of wars of aggression under international law.

The judges from the other Commonwealth countries (Britain, Canada, New Zealand) protested vociferously, insisting that their duty as judges was to try the defendants under the condition that the criminality of war was a given. There was no consensus of opinion among the other justices.

The rift among the judges deepened with every passing day. Alvary Douglas Frederick Gascoigne, head of the United Kingdom Liaison Mission in Japan (UKLIM), reported the following information to the British Foreign Office in London on April 25, 1947. According to British Justice William Donald Patrick, reaching a unanimous judgment would be impossible. Webb was writing his own "judgment" using his own legal grounds that did not accord with the judgments at Nuremberg (October 1, 1946) that recognized the criminality of war. He believed that Pal and Dutch Justice B. V. A. Röling would probably not agree to guilty verdicts (Lord Chancellor Office 1945).

The British government responded by exploring various options, but after realizing all were problematic, concluded that they would have to hope for the best and leave it up to Patrick to shape the majority. Around the spring of 1948, a majority group among the justices was established, comprising the seven judges from Britain, Canada, New Zealand, the United States, the Soviet Union, the Republic of China, and the Philippines, over the point of affirming the criminality of war using the same rationale as Nuremberg.

This majority wrote the legal theory and finding of facts for the judgment—the reason why the judgment of the Tokyo Trial is called the "majority judgment" and the "majority opinion"—and they excluded the four justices who did not agree with the principle set by Nuremberg from drafting the judgment. Through such maneuvers, the justices kept the process from falling apart.

Meanwhile, the four judges who had been excluded each submitted a separate opinion. French Justice Henri Bernard's dissent laid bare the inner workings of the process. "The part of the judgment relating to the finding of facts was drafted entirely by the majority drafting committee. . . and copies of this draft were distributed to the other four justices. The 11 justices were never called to meet to discuss orally a part or in its entirety this part of the judgments. Only the individual cases of the draft were discussed orally" (Asahi 1962).

Then, the judgment of the majority (1445 pages in English) was read aloud in the courtroom from November 4 to 12, 1948. The legal theory of the judgment was the following. "The Charter [of the Tribunal] is . . . the expression of international law existing at the time of its creation. . . . With the foregoing opinions of the Nuremberg Tribunal and the reasoning by which they are reached this Tribunal is in complete accord. . . . Aggressive war was a crime at international law long prior to the date of the Declaration of Potsdam . . ." (Nitta 1968).

What Were the Grounds for a Death Sentence?

Over the course of the hearings in opening court, Ōkawa Shūmei was excluded from the Trial due to mental illness, and Matsuoka Yōsuke and Nagano Osami died of illness. Thus, there were only 25 defendants at the time the judgment was rendered. Chief Justice Webb pronounced their verdicts and sentences on November 12, 1948. All were guilty. Seven were given death by hanging: Dohihara Kenji, Hirota Kōki, Itagaki Seishirō, Kimura Heitarō, Matsui Iwane, Mutō Akira, and Tōjō Hideki. Shigemitsu Mamoru was sentenced to 7 years' imprisonment, Tōgō Shigenori to 20 years', and the remaining 16 men were given life sentences. Incidentally, of the 22 defendants at Nuremberg, 12 were sentenced to death by hanging, four sentenced to prison terms, three to life imprisonment, and three were found not guilty.

And so, what were the grounds for the death sentences? While nothing definitive has yet been discovered that clearly explains the reasoning, we can understand from examining several documents available to us now that the United States and Britain decided long before the tribunals that the grounds for any death sentence should be found in atrocities committed (violations of the laws or customs of war). They reasoned it was dangerous for the Allies to seek death sentences based on crimes against peace, which some regarded with grave doubt as ex post facto law. And so, the US Justice Myron C. Cramer said the following to Webb in June 1948: "There is no specific statute in international law saying that those responsible for planning or waging aggressive war shall be sentenced to death." The tribunal, however, does have the authority to impose a death sentence for incidents that violate the laws of war (Higurashi 2002). In summary, the basis for the death sentence was grave atrocities that violated the laws or customs of war (Class B war crimes). For crimes against peace, those found guilty received a maximum of life in prison.

Judged from this angle, mistreatment of prisoners of war was linked to the political administration of the Ministry of the Army in charge of dealing with prisoners of war as well as the army commanders in the field. The seven men sentenced to death by the Tokyo Trial were found guilty of grave atrocities, which formed the basis for their punishment.

Even Tōjō (prime minister, army minister, and home minister) received a death sentence for the "barbarous treatment of prisoners [of war] and internees" at home and abroad related to the Bataan Death March and the construction of the Taimen Railway (between Burma and Thailand, then called Siam). According to the judgment, "He took no adequate steps to punish offenders and to prevent the commission of similar offences in the future. His attitude towards the Bataan Death March gives the key to his conduct towards these captives. . . . Thus the head of the Government of Japan knowingly and wilfully [sic] refused to perform the duty which lay upon that Government of enforcing performance of the Laws of War. . . . he advised that prisoners of war should be used in the construction of the Burma-Siam Railway . . . The Tribunal finds Tōjō guilty under Count 54 [related to the laws or customs of war]" (Nitta 1968).

In the cases of Matsui Iwane and Hirota Kōki, the sole civilian to get a death sentence, the reason for their sentences was the Nanjing Incident during the Second Sino-Japanese War. Of particular note, Matsui was found completely not guilty in relation to a war of aggression, and yet he received a death penalty for being the commander of the Central China Area Army at the time of the Nanjing Incident. Irrespective of this seeming imbalance, it appears that it was necessary to find someone responsible for the Nanjing Incident that shocked the world.

Meanwhile, that not a single member of the Imperial Japanese Navy received a death sentence is explained by the fact that there was insufficient evidence to convict Oka Takasumi and Shimada Shigetarō on charges of committing atrocities; the judges sentenced both of them to life imprisonment.

The San Francisco Peace Treaty and Release of the War Criminals

After the close of the Tokyo Trial, the General Headquarters (GHQ) began moving on a system of clemency, reducing sentences and paroling prisoners in March 1950. This was a natural part of normal judicial proceedings under civilization's justice, not related to the so-called reverse course. The review for parole was extremely rigorous.

The Japanese side had hoped that peace would bring a general amnesty for all Class A war criminals and all Class B and C war criminals related to atrocities. However, the Allied powers, especially the United States, would not allow it, in order to uphold the righteousness of civilization's justice. They believed it to their advantage to maintain the sentences (i.e., justice) that they imposed.

Article 11 of the peace Treaty of San Francisco, signed on September 8, 1951, reads as follows: "Japan accepts the judgments of the International Military Tribunal for the Far East and of other Allied War Crimes Courts both within and outside Japan, and will carry out the sentences imposed thereby upon Japanese nationals imprisoned in Japan. The power to grant clemency, to reduce sentences and to parole with respect to such prisoners may not be exercised except on the decision of the Government or Governments which imposed the sentence in each instance, and on the recommendation of Japan" (The Peace Treaty with Japan 1951).

That means Japan had the obligation to carry out the sentences of convicted war criminals even after its sovereignty was restored. As for reducing sentences or parole, Japan had the authority to recommend but the authority to grant them rested in the country that made the judgment. Even after regaining its independence, Japan was not permitted to simply release the prisoners and rescind the judgments.

Concerning the oft-debated phrase "Japan accepts (*judaku*) the judgments," the Japanese Ministry of Foreign Affairs (MOFA) acknowledged and did not oppose the judgments. It is useful to reference a March 1953 document from the Third Division of the Foreign Ministry's Treaties Bureau: "'acceptance (*judaku*)' means that Japan does not dispute . . . the legality of the trials under international law . . . or, in the case of the Allied Nations continuing those sentences and carrying them out, the legality of doing so. In other words, Japan is obligated by Article 11 [of the Treaty] not to object to the claim that these are crimes under international law" (Ministry of Foreign Affairs 2013).

This is not a narrative of actively approving and "deeming the judgments to be appropriate" but rather one passively acknowledging that Japan "would not oppose the legality of the judgments under international law." A result naturally arising out of the Potsdam Declaration and the peace treaty, the Japanese government and MOFA had no other alternative from the perspective of international trust.

In fact, MOFA sought to find a solution in negotiations for releasing war criminals after the peace treaty. During the Allied occupation, 892 prisoners including Class A criminal Shigemitsu were paroled. As of April 28, 1952, when Japan regained its sovereignty, there were 1244 convicted war criminals imprisoned, including those serving time overseas and, as of September that year, 12 Class A war criminals imprisoned in Sugamo Prison (former prime minister Hiranuma Kiichirō passed away in August). For Japan, the convicted war criminals were nothing more than the "remnants of the occupation", thought to be an injustice unbecoming of an independent country. Even both wings of the Japan Socialist Party agreed on the release of the Class B and C criminals. The era was steeped in such an atmosphere. It was in this context that the Japanese government actively recommended the parole of the remaining war criminals.

Talks were difficult, but the solidarity of the West was viewed quite seriously during this period of the Cold War. With the parole of Satō Kenryō on March 31, 1956, all Class A prisoners had been paroled. On May 30, 1958, at the time of Kishi Nobusuke's cabinet, the remaining Class B and C convicts were also paroled, and all effectively had their sentences reduced as their terms were considered served in full as of December 29, 1958.

The final aspect to consider is the actual political settlement. Until the very end, however, the United States maintained the public fiction that the paroles and reduced sentences were by judicial settlement, in order to maintain the righteousness of "civilization's justice."

Meanwhile, Japan came through the occupation a nation based firmly on an axis of cooperation with the United States. It might be said that the Tokyo Trial, which was the contemporary hurdle to settling accounts for war responsibility, facilitated the shift toward cooperation with the United States.

Bibliography: For Further Reading

Asahi Shimbun Hōtei Kishadan. 1962. *Tōkyō saiban. gekan* (The Tokyo Trial [Vol. 3]). Tokyo: Tokyo Saiban Kankōkai.

Department of State. 1949. *Report of Robert H. Jackson United States Representative to the international Conference on Military Trials*. Washington, D.C.: US Government Printing Office.

Department of State. 1972. *Foreign Relations of the United States, Conference at Quebec, 1944*. Washington, D.C.: US Government Printing Office. Also referenced at: https://history.state.gov/historicaldocuments/frus1944Quebec/d85

Department of State. 1983. *Foreign Relations of the United States, 1952–1954, Western European Security, Vol. V, Pt. 1*. Washington, D.C.: US Government Printing Office. As referenced at: https://history.state.gov/historicaldocuments/frus1952-54v05p1/d36

Higurashi, Yoshinobu. 2002. *Tōkyō saiban no kokusai kankei: kokusai seiji ni okeru kenryoku to kihan* (The Tokyo Trial and International Relations: Power and Norms in International Politics). Tokyo: Bokutakusha.

Lord Chancellor Office (LCO) Papers. 1945. LCO 2/2992. Kew, London: National Archives of the UK.

Ministry of Foreign Affairs. 2013. *Gaiko Kiroku* (Diplomatic Records). Tokyo: Diplomatic Archive of the Ministry of Foreign Affairs.

Nitta, Mitsuo (ed). 1968. *Kyokutō kokusai gunji saiban sokkiroku. dai-10kan* (Stenographic Record of the International Military Tribunal of the Far East [Vol. 10]). Tokyo: Yūshōdō Shoten. [English taken from the Judgment referenced at: http://www.worldcourts.com/imtfe/eng/decisions/1948.11.04_IMTFE_Judgment. htm, https://werle.rewi.hu-berlin.de/tokio.pdf]

The Peace Treaty with Japan (Treaty of San Francisco). Signed on September 8, 1951. As referenced: https://treaties.un.org/doc/publication/unts/volume%20136/ volume-136-i-1832-english.pdf

Additional Bibliography

Awaya, Kentarō. 2013. *Tōkyō saiban e no michi* (The Road to the Tokyo Trial). Tokyo: Kōdansha Gakujutsu Bunko.

This careful analysis of the interrogations of Japanese charged with war crimes and their associates based especially on materials from the International Prosecution Section is groundbreaking historical research that clarified the various issues before the trial opened.

Higurashi, Yoshinobu. 2008. *Tōkyō saiban* (The Tokyo Trial). Tokyo: Kōdansha Gendai Shinsho. [Published in English as: Higurashi, Yoshinobu. Japan Institute for International Affairs (trans). 2022. *The Tokyo Trial: War Criminals and Japan's Postwar International Relations*. Tokyo: Japan Publishing Industry Foundation for Culture.]

Research of political history that takes the Tokyo Trial as a policy of international politics, and empirically analyzes the political process from World War I through the release of war criminals in the 1950s.

Minear, Richard H. Andō, Nisuke (tr.). 1998. *Tōkyō saiban: shōsha no sabaki shinsōban* (Tokyo Trial: Victors' Justice [Special Edition]). Tokyo: Fukumura Shuppan. (First Japanese Edition 1972). [Originally published as: Minear, Richard H. 1971. *Victors' Justice: The Tokyo War Crimes Trial*. Princeton: Princeton University Press.]

Historical research that set a new era disseminating the school of thought rejecting the Tokyo Trial, excising problematic points of the Tokyo Trial from the viewpoint of an American historical scholar's critical examination of his own country's foreign policies.

Chapter 11
Japanese Colonial Rule and the Issue of Perceptions of History

Kan Kimura

Abstract This chapter takes up the question of whether, and in what ways, Japanese colonial rule was an exception to the colonial rule of other imperial powers. It seeks to define what a colony is and to tackle oversimplifications in historical interpretations. It closes with a discussion of some of the issues still affecting relations between Japan and the Korean Peninsula today.

Was Japanese Colonial Rule an Exception?

There has been an active and ongoing debate over Japan's rule of its colonies that has also seeped into its diplomatic relations with South Korea and Taiwan. This debate, unfortunately, fails to reflect the present views of historical research to a sufficient degree, frequently containing egregious errors. It is not possible to address all these shortcomings in a brief chapter, of course, but my goal is to address the major errors to provide an aid to the understanding of colonial rule.

So, let us start with one of the typical arguments concerning Japan's colonies, which might be summed up as: Japanese colonial rule was an exception. In other words, Japan's control and administration over the Korean Peninsula, Taiwan, and its other Asian colonies differed from that of other countries over their colonies.

We can divide this argument broadly into two categories. The first argues and emphasizes the differences between Japan's rule of Korea and Taiwan and the Western Great Powers' rule of their colonies from the affirmative standpoint. Occasionally this argument stresses that, unlike the colonial rule of the West, which was vicious, Japan's was something good, bringing great benefits to the local population. Furthermore, this argument is often linked to the claim that Japanese rule over the Korean Peninsula and Taiwan was, in fact, not colonial rule at all.

K. Kimura
Graduate School of International Cooperation Studies, Kobe University, Kobe, Japan

M. Yamauchi, Y. Hosoya (eds.), *Modern Japan's Place in World History*,
https://doi.org/10.1007/978-981-19-9593-4_11

135

In contrast, the second argues and emphasizes the differences between Japanese and Western colonial rule from the negative standpoint. It stresses that Japanese rule was vicious compared to that of the Western Great Powers, focusing particularly on the later period of Japanese colonial rule with the mobilization of labor and "comfort women" and the compulsion to adopt Japanese names and worship at Shintō shrines.

So, we can see that both arguments, affirmative and negative, contain a comparison with the colonial rule of the Western Great Powers. That being the case, do they have an accurate understanding of Western colonial rule?

The Errors in Both the Affirmative and Negative Schools of Thought

For instance, the Korean Peninsula and Taiwan under Japanese rule showed economic growth and colonial finances that were in deficit, facts that are highlighted and form the basis for the affirmative view of the difference between Japanese and Western colonial rule. The underlying premise seems to be based on an understanding that colonial rule by the Western Great Powers thoroughly exploited and impoverished local societies.

The actual condition of Western colonial rule, however, was quite different from such a stereotyped understanding. During the sixteenth century, the Age of Discovery, the Spanish and Portuguese rule in the American continents was cruel, and well-known is the significant decline in native populations, in part owing to the impact of communicable diseases from the Old World. But comparing the situation of Japanese rule of Korea and Taiwan between the late nineteenth to early twentieth centuries to that of the Western colonial rule from an era over 300 years earlier is, to put it mildly, a bit unfair.

So, what about Western Great Power colonial rule contemporaneous with Japanese colonial rule in the late nineteenth/early twentieth centuries? The important fact to note is that Britain, France, and the Western Great Powers at this moment in time had already entered an age where their mother countries all had democratic political systems. So naturally, that means economic developments greatly influenced elections.

One concern for a colony was its economic situation; especially for someone making investments in the colony, the issue of the colony's economic situation was tied to one's own economic interests. Therefore, the governments of the Western Great Powers undertook enormous investments in order to maintain favorable conditions in the economies of their colonies. It was an age when railroads and ports were built and school education was started thanks to the mother country's investments.

Increased fiscal investment from the home country resulted in fiscal deficits for the home country in relation to its colony contemporaneously with the rapid development of the colony's economy. Rapid population growth was one sign of such colonial economic development. In other words, growing fiscal deficits from the home country to its colonies in exchange for their economic development was a situation universally apparent for colonial rule of the time rather than something special seen only in Japan's rule of its colonies.

We can also discuss the many errors in the argument emphasizing the distinctiveness of Japanese colonial rule from the negative standpoint. For instance, it is well known that, especially at the start and in the early stages of Japanese colonial rule, there were many deaths and casualties that resulted from the suppression of people engaged in powerful movements protesting that rule. Notably, the number of Taiwanese victims was disturbingly large: it is estimated that the number of deaths greatly exceeded 10,000 in a few short years from the start of Japanese colonial rule there.

Yet, it is not so simple to conclude that the number of victims arising from Japanese colonial rule was especially greater than that in other colonies. For instance, in the Philippines, where the United States began its colonial rule slightly after Japan in Taiwan, it is widely known that the suppression of independence movements resulted in many victims.

Also, the mobilization of labor and troops from colonies during World War II was a phenomenon evident not only in Japan's colonies. In order to support total war twice, in World War I and World War II, Britain and France mobilized vast human resources from their colonies, also a well-known fact. This is also true for policies of assimilation. For instance, France had carried out measures similar to Japan's change of name policy at a considerably earlier stage.

To a certain extent, it is quite obvious and natural that it would be so. Japan after the Meiji Restoration pursued modernization modeled after the Western Great Powers, so it would be natural for political leaders of the time to reference Western colonial policies when faced with the matter of colonial rule over the Korean Peninsula and Taiwan. To rephrase the idea, it would be impossible to even consider that the Japanese government before World War II would choose policies that were completely different from those of the Western Great Powers, especially only in the realm of colonial rule.

What Is a Colony?

A thorough investigation of the problems with the arguments surrounding Japan's colonial rule reveals these errors are caused by a lack of sufficient consideration of their premises. Thus, these arguments are swept up in the popularly held image of Japan's colonial rule. And it is there, in their points based on this ill-defined image, that we can see rather clearly the deficiency of thought given to the main premise underlying all these arguments: what is a colony?

For instance, some proponents of the exceptionalism of Japanese colonial rule school insist that Japan's administration of Korea and Taiwan was not colonial rule. Needless to say, to correctly make this argument, one must clarify the matter of what colonial rule is before getting into the substance of Japanese colonial rule itself. And almost no one making this argument does so after explaining what colonial rule is first.

Once again, the reason is simple. Proponents of the argument believe that colonial rule is–in their vague conception of the matter—the sort of governance that the Western Great Powers carried out in Asia and Africa. Most likely, they have an image of an oppressive system where white men suppressed the colored races, discriminated against them, and exploited them.

The shapes that colonies took, however, were more varied. For instance, British rule of Canada and Australia are examples of colonial rule. Obviously, the majorities in these colonies were not the indigenous peoples who lived there long before colonization, but the people who moved there from all parts of Europe and other regions under Western rule. In short, what existed there was not an oppressive system where whites from the home country suppressed, discriminated against, and exploited the native inhabitants of color but a system of people sharing similar culture and skin color, where some were on the ruling side as home country nationals and others were on the ruled side as colonials. And we call this an example of a colony, much like Canada or Australia.

To delve a bit deeper, there was not just one type of system for colonial rule in Asia and Africa where home country nationals, who were white, ruled the native populace, who were colored. There were regions, such as parts of Algeria which were ruled almost as extensions of the French mainland; regions directly managed by the sovereign country and regions indirectly administered through native or princely states or protectorates; and even regions where administration was carried out by colonial corporations, epitomized by the "East India Companies" that Britain and the Netherlands created. In summary, it is not possible, in fact, to give a response to the question of what the typical form of colonial rule was.

Yet, this does not mean there was no commonality among the diverse range of colonial rule types. To give the reader a hint: a colony is a place, not a people or a society. To put it another way, when we call some region a colony, it means that some sort of condition must exist at that place, in common with other colonies, and that is different from the home country.

There is only one such trait. It is that the laws applied in that region are different from the laws applied in the sovereign country. By being such a place, it means that the region experiences a condition in which the relationship of rights and duties of the local inhabitants is inferior to that relationship enjoyed by citizens in the mother country, particularly arising from the differences in the laws. Incidentally, a region where local inhabitants have a relationship of rights and duties more favorable than that in the mother country should be called a type of special zone, rather than a colony.

To elaborate a bit more, it is also important to note that the situation where the relationship of rights and duties changed according to the type or class of "people" also varied with the colonial rule even in the same region. For instance, there were situations where racial and/or gender discrimination existed. But such situations were present even in home countries that were not colonies, as was distinctively evident in the United States or South Africa until a certain period. So, we must decouple the fact that a region has discrimination problems from the discussion of whether or not it is a colony.

The archetype of the relationship of rights and duties being inferior in the colony versus the mother country is enfranchisement (as a right), especially whether one has the right to vote in national elections, and conscription (as a duty). In fact, inhabitants in almost all colonies were not given the right to vote in national politics; even in those cases where they were, the scope was different from that of the sovereign country. The same was true for conscription: even where the sovereign country had a system of military conscription, many times conscription was not implemented in the colony.

So, in keeping with this matter of "what is a colony," what is clear when looking at the Japanese rule on the Korean Peninsula and in Taiwan is the fact that the laws implemented in both regions were very different than those applied in the Japanese mainland. For instance, in Korea and Taiwan, they never held an election for the House of Representatives by war's end (one had been scheduled for 1946), but they implemented military conscription finally in 1944. It is not widely known that a system of voluntary military service was not implemented until 1938 in Korea and 1942 in Taiwan, so it was extremely difficult for people in Taiwan and Korea to enter the military so long as they continued to live in the colonies, leaving aside a small group of exceptions such as a handful of people granted permission to go to the Imperial Japanese Army Academy, members of a privileged class such as the Korean royal family (the former imperial family of the Korean Empire (1897–1910) who received special treatment equivalent to the Japanese imperial family), and people who were already in the Korean military at the time of Japan's annexation of Korea in 1910.

Not even the Constitution of the Empire of Japan was implemented in Korea or Taiwan at first, nor were the laws enacted by the Imperial Diet immediately applied locally. In other words, the laws implemented in these regions differed from those in the mother country, and the relationship of rights and duties of those inhabitants were inferior to the residents of the sovereign country. Thus, we can say that, by definition, Korean and Taiwan were clearly colonies.

The Simplification of Regional Differences and Era Differences

These are not the only problems with the arguments related to colonial rule by Japan, of course. One more is the excessively simplified understanding of it, notwithstanding the diversity of conditions that existed within Japanese colonial rule. There are two broad types of oversimplification.

The first ignores the regional differences among the Korean Peninsula, Taiwan, Southern Karafuto (Sakhalin), the Guandong Leased Territory, and the South Sea

Islands.[1] Guandong was territory leased from China that came about in the Treaty of Portsmouth (1905) and the South Sea Islands were "Class C Mandate territories," which the League of Nations entrusted Japan with administering after World War I. So, by a strict definition, neither were territory under the Japanese Constitution. Given that the majority of residents in Southern Karafuto comprised migrants from the Japanese mainland, some villages and towns were self-governed, and conscription was introduced after 1924, and so the relationship of rights and duties of residents was quite close to that of the mainland. In Korea and Taiwan, a governor-general who was the emperor's representative reigned, administering legislative, judicial, and executive authorities, and whose rule essentially fell outside the control of the cabinet or the Imperial Diet. That meant each colony had its own set of laws that its governor-general enacted, executed, and adjudicated on that basis.

The second oversimplification is to overlook the changes that occurred over time. Colonial rule began in Taiwan in 1895; the Annexation of Korea was in 1910. So each rule lasted a long time of 50 and 35 years, respectively. As we can immediately discern by reflecting on the times that we ourselves have lived through, it cannot be the case that policy measures toward the colonies remained unchanged over the course of events during this long period of time. Furthermore, there were large political changes occurring within Japan during this period. In short, the period in which Japan ruled its colonies corresponds to a period in which the *genro* (elder statesmen) politicians who had wielded absolute power in the Meiji period lost their authority, to be replaced by political party cabinets, and later those same party cabinets lost power, changing to the system of imperial rule assistance. Economically, this period was marked by startling changes from the "Great War Boom" of the World War I known for its *nouveaux riches*, to a postwar recession when the war ended, transitioning through favorable economic conditions of the short-lived interwar period, then experiencing the Great Depression, and finally moving to a system of total mobilization.

Such changes in Japanese domestic conditions naturally had an impact on the shape of Japan's colonial administration. For instance, the Japanese government restricted the immigration of labor from Taiwan and the Korean Peninsula in the 1920s, strictly enforcing this restriction. Party politicians of the era were loath to let an influx of colonial residents drive a rise in unemployment on the main islands and thereby result in increased voter dissatisfaction. Contemporary conditions in the colonies were the polar opposite of the commonly held image of "the Japanese rulers mobilizing labor from the colonies."

The situation completely changed, however, after the onset of the Second Sino-Japanese War when Japan began mobilizing a large number of soldiers and laborers. As human resources on the mainland became inadequate under the total war system, Japan started to systematically mobilize the labor force from the colonies. The shortage of mainland human resources eventually spread to the military, leading to the mobilization of soldiers and civilians working for the military from its colonies,

---

[1] Today part of Palau, the Marshall Islands, Micronesia, and the Northern Mariana Islands.

too. The Japanese government, forced to rely on human resources from its colonies, began to compel "Japanification" of the colonial populace at the same time. Maintaining wartime institutions would become very difficult unless colonial inhabitants had the same way of living, customs, and sense of values as mainland Japanese. Therefore, education in the local language was abolished, worshipping at Shintō shrines was made compulsory, and individuals were forced to change their names to make them Japanese.

It means that most of the problems raised as emblematic of Japanese colonial rule actually appeared bunched up in the last five or so years of the long period of colonial rule that lasted 50 or 35 years. As a matter of course, it would be a mistake to make an argument about Japanese colonial rule based only on the understanding of conditions during this short period of time. This error of taking up just one part of the variety types of colonial rule in a diversity of regions is common among all of these arguments.

The Issues Left Over from Colonial Rule

Well, let us now consider the issues left over after Japanese colonial rule. As I just laid out, the majority of phenomena often discussed as constituting the image of Japanese colonial rule occurred in the period under a total war system, and thus they are the developments of only a short interval within Japan's long period of colonial rule. And yet, there are two reasons why the developments from this short period had a decisive influence shaping the image of Japan's colonial rule. First and foremost, colonial rule ended right after this period of total war; the second is that Japan's large-scale interference in its colonies' societies during this total war period continued to have significant impacts on these regions long after it ended. In summary, Japan made significant interventions in the way it ruled its colonies to prosecute the war, doing so in a concentrated fashion toward the end of its rule, so that when colonial rule ended suddenly under these conditions, the result was to leave this as the popular image of the "Japanese model of colonial rule."

Therefore, the impression of Japan's colonial rule was very negative immediately after Japan's defeat, not only on the Korean Peninsula but also in Taiwan (it was later that a reappraisal of Japanese colonial rule happened in Taiwan). And yet, this fact does not mean the disputes over colonial rule between Japan and its neighbors that we see today began in this period.

Let us look at the example of the relations between Japan and the Republic of Korea (ROK or South Korea) on this point. The important point is, as formal state-to-state relations did not exist between the two countries from 1945 to 1965, it was not actually possible for people on the Korean Peninsula to raise problems directly with the Japanese government or Japanese corporations (setting aside the matter of the *zainichi* ethnic Koreans who stayed in Japan). And so, the Japanese and ROK governments, as representatives of their own citizens, engaged in talks that finally resulted in the Treaty on Basic Relations Between Japan and the Republic of Korea

(1965) and the series of ancillary agreements. In the treaty, as you know, the ROK government received economic cooperation assistance of total value equivalent to $500 million: $300 million in grants (non-repayable basis) and $200 million in soft loans. In exchange, Japan and the ROK both confirmed that the "problem concerning property, rights and interests of the two Contracting Parties and their nationals . . . is settled completely and finally" (Agreement 3 1965).

The troublesome thing, however, is that when the ROK government accepted the economic assistance under the treaty, it did not adequately compensate its citizens who had been mobilized as soldiers or civilians employed by the military or laborers and "comfort women" during the period of Japanese colonial rule. Consequently, the people's lingering discontent eventually emerged as protest movements.

Yet, such movements were unable to achieve much under a succession of authoritarian regimes from Park Chung-hee to Chun Doo-hwan. There is a backstory to this: between the late 1960s and the 1980s, South Korea was a poor, divided country situated on the frontline of the Cold War between the two superpowers, the United States and the Soviet Union, and whose economy was largely dependent on Japan. Raising a dispute over colonial rule of the past in the midst of this situation would create obstacles in bilateral economic relations with Japan and have tremendous implications for the ROK economy, so Seoul's political and economic elite worked hard to avoid aggravating the issue.

This situation changed significantly in the 1990s for two reasons. First, pro-democracy movements brought about the collapse of the authoritarian regime, which reinvigorated South Korean civil society. In this new environment, the Korean people began an active push for compensation for the period of colonial rule.

A more important reason was the shift in economic relations between Japan and South Korea. This change resulted from three phenomena that made progress during this period: the collapse of the Cold War system, growth of the ROK economy, and the advance of globalization. The change created a new situation in which the ROK economy's degree of dependence on Japan dropped rapidly. As Fig. 11.1 clearly demonstrates, Japan's share of South Korea's total trade (exports and imports), which had topped 40% in the early 1970s, had fallen below 10% in the 2010s. In terms of the movement of goods, at least, the importance of the Japanese economy to South Korea's economy had shrunk to less than one-fifth of what it had once been.

In this new situation, the former mechanism fell into dysfunction: when issues linked to colonial rule were stirred up, the elite no longer calmed the situation out of consideration for the importance of economic relations. The situation in South Korea had changed; as President Lee Myung-bak flatly stated in 2012, "Japan's influence is not like it once was."

This situation naturally showed itself in both the frequency and the prolongation of the issues over colonial rule cropping up in bilateral relations. The latter is particularly important. Japan and South Korea held different perceptions of history concerning colonial rule right from the beginning, as became readily apparent in the two governments' differing interpretations of the sentence ". . . all treaties or agreements . . . [including that concerning colonial rule] . . . are already null and void" in Article 2 of the 1965 Basic Treaty. (Treaty on Basic Relations 1965).

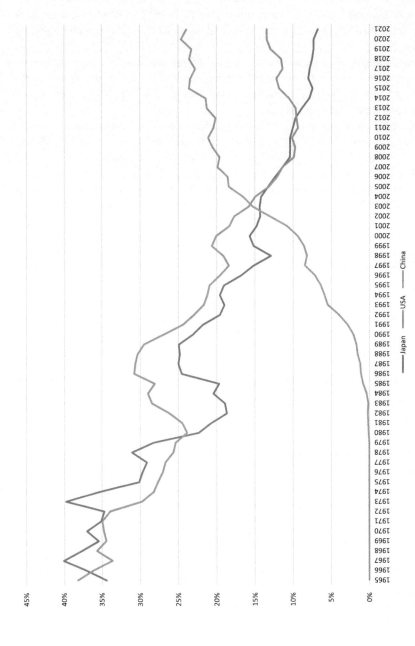

Fig. 11.1 Changes in key countries' share of South Korean exports and imports. (Source: STATISTICS-KOREA)

Regardless, the reason these differences had not been a major political problem before is because both governments, especially the ROK elite, made sure to nip it in the bud. For instance, ROK media lambasted Prime Minister Nakasone Yasuhiro right after his official visit to Yasukuni Shrine in 1985. The ROK media situation was suppressed after a few days, however, and Japan-ROK relations soon returned to normal.

In the bilateral relationship of today, however, no one is brave enough to pull the chestnuts out of the fire by settling the perceptions of history issue. The reason is simple: the risk in doing so far outweighs the reward. The dispute gets more heated as the situation becomes prolonged.

In October 2018, the Supreme Court of Korea (the nation's highest court) handed down a decision seeking compensation from Japanese corporations for former civilian workers from the Korean Peninsula. The Japanese and ROK governments have been slow to react to settle the matter; public opinion in both countries has inflamed the dispute. It seems that the era has not yet arrived when the history of Japan's colonial rule of the past is, in the true sense of the word, in the past.

Bibliography: For Further Reading

Agreement 3 On the Settlement of Problems Concerning Property and Claims and on Economic Co-operation between Japan and the Republic of Korea. 22 June 1965. As referenced at: https://treaties.un.org/doc/Publication/UNTS/Volume%20583/volume-583-I-8473-English.pdf

Treaty on Basic Relations Between Japan and the Republic of Korea. 22 June 1965. As referenced at: https://treaties.un.org/doc/Publication/UNTS/Volume%20583/volume-583-I-8471-English.pdf

Additional Bibliography

Asano, Toyomi. 2008. *Teikoku nihon no shokuminchi hōsei: hōiki tōgō to teikoku chitsujo* (Japanese Empire in the Nation State System by Legal Analysis). Nagoya: Nagoya University Press.

To understand the diversity of colonial rule types and the differences among countries, one must understand what sort of laws were initially applied in each region and how they changed over time. Though the contents are somewhat academic, it is a good book for tracing how the legal systems related to Japanese colonial rule changed up to the end of the war.

Kimura, Mitsuhiko. 2018. *Nihon tochika no Chōsen: Tōkei to jisshō kenkyū wa nani o kataruka* (Korea under Japanese Rule: What do Statistics and Empirical Research Tell Us?). Tokyo: Chūkō shinsho. [Published in English as: Kimura, Mitsuhiko. The Japan Institute of International Affairs (trans). 2021. *The Economics of Colonialism in Korea: Rethinking Japanese Rule and Aftermath.* Tokyo: Japan Publishing Industry Foundation for Culture.]

Regarding the economic conditions in the colonies, we are often presented with conflicting opinions from the affirmative and negative sides of Japanese colonial rule. However, as much reliable statistical data does exist on economic conditions of the colonial period, we can statistically recreate quite a large portion of it. This volume takes pains to show those related to the Korean Peninsula.

Peattie, Mark R. Asano, Toyomi (trans). 2012. *Shokuminchi—20-seiki nihon: teikoku 50nen no kōbō* (Twentieth Century Japan: Colonies—Fifty Years of the Empire's Rise and Fall). Tokyo: Jigakusha Shuppan. [Originally published as: Peattie, Mark R. 1983. *The Japanese Colonial Empire, 1895–1945.* Princeton: Princeton University Press.]

Though an older one (originally published by Yomiuri Shimbun in 1996), still the best book for getting an overview of Japanese colonial rule in one volume. The author is an American who writes with the perspective of the differences with European and US colonial rule in mind. A must-have work for considering colonial rule by Japan.

Chapter 12
Postwar Japan-China Relations

Masaya Inoue

Abstract Postwar relations between Japan and China is the subject of this lengthy chapter, from the process of normalizing relations, through a period of Sino-Japanese "amity" toward special relations, and then again to ongoing issues of "perceptions of history" in the post-Cold War era. Taiwan figures as an important factor, and there is a danger of amity between the two nations turning again to enmity.

The Path to Normalizing Relations

"Abnormal" Japan-China Relations

Mainland China was a constant subject of interest for Japanese policymakers throughout the history of early modern Japan. This remained the case after World War II, too. Founded in 1949, the People's Republic of China (PRC; hereafter, China) was a country with a political system that differed from Japan's, possessing an expansive territory, and having the world's largest population. An important task for the Japanese government was how to construct a relationship of some kind with its vast neighbor, a developing economy then led by a dictator intent on revolution.

Japan and China did not have formal state-to-state relations until 1972. The Cold War structure in Asia prevented a rapprochement between the two countries. Immediately after its founding, China became quite close to the Soviet Union, giving rise to a vast Communist bloc on the Eurasian continent. The Korean War breaking out in June 1950 decisively established Sino-US confrontation in Asia.

The outbreak of the Korean War spurred a dramatic rise in the strategic value of the Japanese archipelago in America's eyes. In tandem with that, Washington started the move to make peace with Japan, then under the occupation of Allied forces. To guarantee Japan's national security after independence, the Yoshida Shigeru

M. Inoue
Faculty of Law, Keio University, Tokyo, Japan

administration signed the Treaty of Mutual Cooperation and Security between the Japan and the United States (the Japan-US Security Treaty) at the same time it signed the peace Treaty of San Francisco. The security treaty determined that US forces would remain stationed on the Japanese mainland after Japan regained its independence.

In addition, the Yoshida administration concluded the Treaty of Peace between the Republic of China (ROC) and Japan in April 1952 with the Nationalist government of Chiang Kai-shek, which fled to Taiwan after its defeat in the Chinese Civil War. Japan concluded a peace treaty with the Nationalist government in Taiwan and not with the Chinese government at the request of John Foster Dulles, then the Consultant to the Secretary of State, who wanted to impede a Japanese rapprochement with Beijing.

The Chinese reaction was extremely negative to the choice that Japan had made. In April 1952 when the Treaty of San Francisco came into force and the Japan-ROC peace treaty was concluded, the Chinese government further hardened its firm opposition to both treaties. The period of the "abnormal state of affairs" between Japan and China had commenced.

Security Treaty Issue and the Taiwan Question

What were the points of dispute in postwar Japan-China relations? For China, the Japan-US Security Treaty was the most problematic. The US military bases situated on the Japanese mainland under the treaty were, to China, a military threat to its own existence. In order to have these US military bases removed from Japan, it would be necessary to separate Japan from the United States and make it neutral. To that end, China emphasized that it was a "peaceful power" that did not welcome war, increased pro-China forces led by revolutionaries inside of Japan, and tried to drive a wedge between Japan and the United States.

The Chinese side emphasized the role of private interactions and exchanges as a means to achieve its objectives. It sought to strengthen solidarity between the people of the two countries with a campaign of diplomatic invitations to members in all sectors of Japanese society. It attempted to expand its relations with Japan in practical aspects, by moving forward to conclude private agreements on trade and fisheries. This policy called *yimin cuguan* (private sector leading the public) became China's basic policy line for its diplomacy toward Japan in the period before diplomatic relations were normalized (Ō 2013).

For its part, the United States was concerned about the wedge China was trying to drive into the Japan-US relationship. Washington severely restricted Japan-China trade in an attempt to hinder a political rapprochement between Tokyo and Beijing. The Japanese government, bolstered by public opinion favoring a reopening of trade with China, was considering its genuine desire for relations with China. It was not possible for Japan to draw closer to a China that was seeking to nullify the Japan-US security treaty, which Japan had made the cornerstone of its diplomacy. Japan thus found itself caught between the United States and China.

One issue troubling Japan, in addition to the security treaty with the United States, was the relationship Japan had with the ROC in Taiwan. After the end of World War II, the Nationalist government of Chiang Kai-shek and the Communist Party of China led by Mao Zedong plunged into civil war, and as mentioned above, the defeated Chiang fled to Taiwan. Yet, the United States provided assistance to Taiwan, and the Nationalist government, which had lost the Chinese mainland, retained its seat in the United Nations. Until 1971, the "China" that was a permanent member of the UN Security Council was the ROC in Taiwan.

Having concluded a peace treaty with the ROC, Japan had to grapple with the issue of "two Chinas" (also known as the Taiwan question), or how to construct relations with China while continuing to have treaty relations with the Nationalist government. To thread this needle, Japan's basic policy stance was *seikei bunri* (the separation of politics and economics), which promoted private trade and cultural exchanges without maintaining relations with the government of China, a desperate measure taken out of necessity.

The Nationalist government, however, was critical of this approach. When Ikeda Hayato's administration decided to grant approval for a Japanese public financial institution to finance the export of a synthetic fiber plant to China, Taiwan strongly protested, making it a large diplomatic problem. In contrast, when the Satō Eisaku administration appeared ready to strengthen Japan-Taiwan ties, it was China this time that went on to fiercely attack the Satō government. Troubles arising from this "two Chinas" dilemma always beset Japanese policymakers up until the normalization of Japan-China diplomatic relations.

Normalization of Japan-China Relations

Rapid changes in the international situation in the early 1970s had a significant impact on Japan-China relations. The first of these was the Sino-Soviet split. What began as an ideological argument gradually worsened throughout the 1960s until erupting into armed skirmishes on the Sino-Soviet border in March 1969. For China, the Soviet Union had supplanted the United States as its greatest military threat.

Sino-Soviet skirmishes proved to be a key turning point for the United States, which was looking for a way to extricate itself from the Vietnam War. The Richard M. Nixon administration took the bold move of improving relations with China in order to gain strategic advantage over the Soviet Union. Sino-US Rapprochement in July 1971, which took place without Washington consulting Tokyo, is called the "Nixon shock" for the impact it had within Japan.

Sino-Soviet confrontation and Sino-US conciliation prompted a dramatic shift in China's strategy toward Japan. China began to adopt a strategy of containing the Soviet Union, teaming up with the United States and other key countries in a single policy line (*yitiao xian*). Thus, incorporating Japan into this net encircling the Soviet Union became a more important diplomatic task than the issue of the Japan-US security treaty or the Taiwan question (Masuo 2010).

The situation began to move in Japan in response to the Nixon shock. There were a series of visits to China by Japanese business interests and the Japanese public was swept up in a "China boom." In October 1971, the ROC withdrew from the United Nations and the People's Republic of China became a member. In reaction, there were growing calls within the Japanese government supporting the normalization of relations with China, predicated on severing ties with Taiwan.

The Chinese side took the lead on normalization talks from start to finish. By the time the Tanaka Kakuei administration was established in July 1972 after the resignation of the Satō cabinet, the Chinese side had already started preparations for normalization. It took a soft position on the issues of the security treaty and Taiwan which had been key points of disputes until then. It also publicly indicated for the first time that it would formally waive its claims for war reparations. By limiting what it demanded from Japan to just cutting ties with Taiwan, China stimulated the Japanese side's resolve to normalize diplomatic relations.

Prime Minister Tanaka and Foreign Minister Ōhira Masayoshi, having learned of Beijing's intentions through Kōmeitō Chairman Takeiri Yoshikatsu's visit to China, overcame the opposition of the pro-Taiwan factions within in their Liberal Democratic Party (LDP) and made the decision to normalize relations with China. First, Tanaka attended the Japan-US summit in Hawai'i in late August. After obtaining US understanding, Tanaka and his delegation flew to Beijing and entered normalization talks with China. The Joint Communique of the Government of Japan and the Government of the People's Republic of China was issued, and diplomatic relations normalized, on September 29, 1972.

That normalization talks were effectively settled in an unusually short period of 4 days suggests that the expectations of both countries were largely in alignment. The Chinese side hurried the talks, worried that the Soviet Union would attempt to draw closer to Japan. As for Japan, Tanaka sought to achieve normalization all at once, so as to not give the LDP's pro-Taiwan factions an opportunity to unravel the progress made.

There were also aspects of sharp disagreement in the negotiations on normalization, such as when the war ended, the legal issues concerning war reparations, and the legal status of Taiwan. But the two parties ultimately decided to tailor the wording of the joint communique so that it showed the position of both sides.

On the Taiwan question, they agreed that Foreign Minister Ōhira would make a statement concerning the "termination" of the Japan-ROC peace treaty after the signing of the joint communique. The Two Chinas issue that had troubled Japan was now settled, and the separation of politics and economics that hitherto had been applied to Japan-China ties was now used to maintain private relations with Taiwan, transformed by the termination of the Japan-ROC peace treaty.

The Era of Japan-China Amity

From Revolution to Economic Development

The 1972 normalization of diplomatic relations meant the establishment of an agreed framework concerning the issues that had long been contentious between Japan and China: the Japan-US security treaty and Taiwan. Yet, the sources of conflict had not been extinguished. In place of these issues, the new issue of the Soviet Union rose to the forefront. In the negotiations for a bilateral peace and friendship treaty that started with the normalization of ties, the Chinese side sought to include an anti-hegemony clause in the treaty notionally aimed at the Soviet Union. Negotiations lasted longer than expected because the Japanese side refused to include the clause. After the Tanaka administration stepped down, the administration of Miki Takeo that followed continued negotiations, but talks were suspended in part owing to confusion in the Chinese political situation with the deaths of Zhou Enlai and Mao Zedong, and the arrests of the Gang of Four.

It was after the rehabilitation of Deng Xiaoping in July 1977 that both countries began to move toward signing a treaty of peace and friendship. Deng, who aimed to modernize China, hurried to introduce technologies and obtain economic cooperation from the West, beginning with Japan. Prime Minister Fukuda Takeo was in agreement with this push by the Chinese, and so the Treaty of Peace and Friendship between Japan and the People's Republic of China was signed on August 12, 1978.

The year 1978 was a landmark in Japan-China relations. After having declared the Great Proletarian Cultural Revolution officially over the previous year, China's highest leadership began to turn its interest toward developing the economy. Believing Deng's modernization line to be their chance to expand into the Chinese market, Japanese business interests viewed the peace and friendship treaty as providing the institutional backing for a genuine advance into the Chinese economy.

Japan-China relations thus entered its most favorable era since the war. The period from the late 1970s into the 1980s was one where both countries had for the first time found a shared national goal of economic development. Foreign Minister Ōhira announced the first Yen Loans that would be provided to China during his visit there in December 1979. The major goal of Japan's Official Development Assistance (ODA) to China was to firmly tie Beijing's cooperative relationships with the Western world by assisting Chinese development under its modernization line. In contrast, even though there was a dispute over the line around economic policies within China, the introduction of the latest equipment and technologies from Japan meant that China was actively following a policy of opening to the outside world.

The international environment also provided tailwinds for expanding the Japan-China economic relationship. Fukuda tried to maintain ties with both China and the Soviet Union under his slogan, "omnidirectional peace diplomacy." The succeeding Ōhira Masayoshi administration, however, made clear its position as a member of the West as the rise of the Soviet military precipitated the remarkable evidence of a renewed Cold War. After the Soviet invasion of Afghanistan in late 1979, the Ōhira administration imposed economic sanctions against Moscow, acting in concert with the United States. This gave rise to a situation in Asia that could be called a quasi-alliance between Japan, the United States, and China.

With this stronger encirclement of the Soviet Union, China found itself in a favorable position that facilitated the receipt of assistance from the West targeting its economic development. Japan, the first among Western countries to start ODA to China, provided over 3.6 trillion yen ($32.4 billion) in total over the course of 40 years, making it the world's top provider of assistance to China.

Formation of Special Relations Between Japan and China

Another important point when considering Japan-China relations in this period is the existence of favorable Japanese public opinion toward China. Many Japanese then were eager to contribute to the modernization of China, in part owing to feelings of wanting to atone for the war. There were many pro-China groups, too, within Japanese politics and business that developed through the private exchanges that had continued since the 1950s.

The pro-China LDP factions came about during the time of the Kishi Nobusuke administration, fueled by Chinese maneuvers to invite the anti-mainstream factions within the party to visit China. Ishibashi Tanzan and Matsumura Kenzō visited China at Beijing's invitation; upon returning home, they began claiming within the party that they had achieved a breakthrough in Japan-China relations. Also, Takasaki Tatsunosuke, who before the war had served as the president of Manchurian Industrial Development Company, met with Premier Zhou Enlai, his first meeting with a sitting Japanese cabinet minister, at the First Asian-African Conference (the Bandung Conference) held in 1955. Takasaki was also working for a breakthrough in Japan-China relations during the same time.

The fruit born of the efforts of Matsumura and Takasaki was LT Trade.[1] LT trade was a system of trade, nominally viewed as private, that was actually half-government, half-private, as it had Ministry of Trade and Industry (MITI) support in terms of human and financial resources. Tokyo and Beijing established liaison offices in each other's capitals and permitted the exchange of newspaper reporters, both of which played important roles in promoting private-level exchanges during an era without formal diplomatic ties.

Okazaki Kaheita, the president of All Nippon Airways, was the man in charge of the practical aspects of LT trade. LT trade was distinguished from other Japan-China friendship groups because it sought to maintain its stance of separating politics from economics by keeping a distance from the Chinese side's political tenets. Okazaki

---

[1]The letters L and T derive from the names of Liao Chengzhi and Takasaki Tatsunosuke, the men who signed the comprehensive trade agreement.

and others involved in the trade were placed in a difficult situation by the radicalization of China under the Cultural Revolution in the latter half of the 1960s. But they earned an immense degree of trust from the Chinese side because they maintained Japan-China trade, refusing to allow the flame of exchange to die out. Even after diplomatic normalization, Okazaki continued to act as a key conduit between China and the Japanese business world as an advisor to the Japan-China Economic Association.

In addition to these men who "dug the well" before diplomatic normalization, the Chinese government also had great respect for the new LDP pro-China faction members who emerged on the stage at the time of normalization: Tanaka and Ōhira. These men were leaders of mainstream factions, the Tanaka faction (*nanoka-kai*) and the Kōchi-kai, respectively, in contrast to the pro-China politicians until then who had weak bases within the party. Tanaka withdrew from the center stage of politics after the Lockheed scandal, and Ōhira died in 1980, but their factions' connections to China were carried on by influential politicians, Gotōda Masaharu and Itō Masayoshi (Inoue 2016).

The Chinese side made active use of these friendly personages whom they held in great esteem. Every time some conflict arose in bilateral relations, Beijing would seek to resolve the issue through behind-the-scenes negotiations with the business interests or influential LDP factions, separate from the formal diplomatic avenue. While such special relations between Japan and China contributed to the stable development of bilateral ties, they also retarded the institutionalization of Japan-China relations, unable to free itself from being forever reliant on a limited set of people.

The Issue of Perceptions of History

The Origin of the Perceptions of History Issue

Perceptions of history emerged as a new point of contention in relations between Japan and China beginning in the 1980s. The issue of how to perceive the past war had already appeared during the normalization of diplomatic ties. One famous episode indicating the divergence in perceptions of history of both parties in the normalization talks may be Prime Minister Tanaka's speech where he used the expression, "[Japan] caused the people of China much trouble (*tianle mafan*, in Chinese)" to refer to their past history. For the Chinese, who had suffered an enormous degree of damage and loss from the war, the decision to renounce demands for war reparations at the time of normalization was not taken lightly. In fact, the Chinese government held meetings throughout the country ahead of Tanaka's visit to soften the people's discontent about normalizing ties with Japan. That is why the Chinese side reacted so negatively to Tanaka's casual use of the expression "*meiwaku*" (trouble or inconvenience) for Japan's war responsibility (NHK 1993).

A thorough investigation of the Chinese government's position indicated that its magnanimous stance toward the damage from the past war such as waiving reparations was taken as a package with Japan's soul-searching reflection and remorse (*hansei*) for its war of aggression. Underlying the Chinese thinking was *erfenlun* (militarist/people dichotomy), a concept which divided the Japanese people in two groups, making a distinction between a group of militarists and the general populace, and concluded that the Japanese populace should not be forced to bear responsibility for the war. The opening paragraphs of their Joint Communique even emphasized that Japan was aware of and "deeply reproaches itself" for its "responsibility" for the "serious damage" it caused to the Chinese people through the war. Moreover, wording was added that the Chinese government, "in the interest of the friendship between the Chinese and the Japanese peoples" renounced its demands for war reparations from Japan.

It is hard to say that this same logic was shared by the Chinese and Japanese peoples to a sufficient degree at the time of normalization, however. Many Japanese were unaware that the Chinese people's displeasure toward Japan had been suppressed. A general accounting for the past war was supposed to be the most important point of the normalization talks. Regardless, the two sides failed to adequately close the gap between their perceptions, which was left vague amid the subsequent atmosphere of Japan-China amity. China's waiving of reparations contributed to a large improvement in Japanese public opinion of China in the short-term, whereas in the long term it left kinks in the two countries' perceptions of history.

This malalignment in their perceptions of history surfaced in the 1980s. The first problem to occur was the first history textbook issue in 1982 surrounding the approval of a history textbook for Japanese high schoolers. Then, in reaction to the official visit by Prime Minister Nakasone Yasuhiro to the Yasukuni Shrine in 1985, student protests erupted all over China in opposition to "the revival of Japanese militarism."

The Chinese domestic political situation of the time was a related factor behind the Chinese side starting a flap over the history issue. As recent research has made clear, the Chinese government pursued a "patriotic united front" to foster patriots to defend socialism even as it aimed to develop its economy. The goal was to lay the foundation for a national unity-centered nationalism in the wake of the Cultural Revolution. For China, the history of the "Anti-Japanese War of Resistance" was a source of national unity. In addition, aspects of criticizing Japan over its perception of history have been used as a means to increase Chinese patriotism (Etō 2014).

Yet, both Japan and China have tried to keep the history issue from decisively harming the bilateral relationship. Regarding the first textbook issue, Chief Cabinet Secretary Miyazawa Kiichi issued a statement on history textbooks, and a "neighboring countries clause" was later added as a criterion for textbook approval. Regarding the issue of Yasukuni visits, Nakasone voluntarily refrained from paying a visit to the shrine the following August. It is said that Nakasone canceled his visit because he feared it would weaken the domestic position of General Secretary Hu Yaobang, with whom he had been building a close partnership (Hattori 2015).

Japan-China Relations in the Post-Cold War Era

The favorable period in relations between Japan and China reached its zenith with the Japanese emperor's visit to China in October 1992. The Chinese side had been pushing strongly for a visit from the emperor since the 1970s, and the Japanese side had hoped the visit would help to bring the history issue to a close.

Contrary to expectations, the dispute over perceptions of history became more severe in the 1990s. The collapse of the 1955 system caused by the LDP's breakup in 1993 brought about new changes in the Japanese government's position on the history issue. In a press conference after assuming office, Prime Minister Hosokawa Morihiro, head of a non-LDP coalition government, became the first in a succession of prime ministers to publicly use the term "war of aggression" in a press conference. Prime Minister Murayama Tomiichi of the Japan Socialist Party issued the "Murayama Statement" in August 1995, "on the occasion of the 50th anniversary of the war's end," in which he expressed his "heartfelt apology" concerning Japan's past "colonial rule and aggression" (Murayama 1995).

However, this series of corrections of Japan's perception of history generated a backlash from conservative forces. Feeling increasingly beleaguered, the Japan War-Bereaved Families Association, a vote-gathering organization for the LDP, began protest movements through its nationwide branches and its ties to LDP Diet members. Around the same time, cabinet members in the coalition government made a string of inappropriate remarks concerning the history issue. The disappearance of the confrontation between conservatives and progressives brought about by the Cold War's conclusion paradoxically served to sharpen the ideological claims within the conservative camp (Hatano 2011).

Meanwhile, China under Jiang Zemin, who took up his post as the head of state in 1993, was moving forward with patriotic education aimed at preventing a recurrence of the Tiananmen Incident. Consequently, the Chinese side, appearing very alarmed at Japanese conduct that clouded its stance on war responsibility, took a posture firmly seeking Japan to "draw lessons from history and repent deeply the acts of aggression it committed." And so Japan-China relations fell into a vicious circle, with Chinese criticism of Japan over its perception of history inciting a backlash from Japan against this criticism (Shimizu 2003).

Added to the history issue, concerns over the rise of China's military were stoked by the Third Taiwan Straits Crisis in 1995–1996. The dispute surfaced once more within the LDP over its policy line regarding the Taiwan question. Conservative pundits emerged, arguing the "China threat" and objecting publicly to Tokyo's long-standing policy of providing economic assistance to China. It was almost as if these critics had stepped up to replace the key people, whose numbers were now dwindling, who had constructed amicable ties with China since diplomatic normalization.

Thus, the agreed framework for Japan-China relations established by normalization of diplomatic ties started to show signs of strain from the 1990s onward. As a shadow enveloped the slogan of Japan-China friendship, a major shift occurred in the general attitude of each nation's people toward bilateral relations, turning from amity toward enmity.

Bibliography: For Further Reading

Etō, Nahoko. 2014. *Chūgoku nashonarizumu no nihon: "aikoku shugi" no hen'yō to rekishi ninshiki monda*i (Japan in the Context of Chinese Nationalism: The Transformation of "Patriotism" and the Issue of Differing Historical Perspectives). Tokyo: Keisō Shobo.

Hatano, Sumio. 2011. *Kokka to rekishi: sengo nihon no rekishi mondai* (The State and History: Postwar Japan's History Problem). Tokyo: Chūkō Shinsho.

Hattori, Ryūji. 2015. *Gaikō dokyumento, rekishi ninshiki* (Diplomatic Documents: Historical Understanding). Tokyo: Iwanami Shinsho. [Published in English as: Hattori, Ryūji. Cannon, Tara (trans). 2019. *Understanding History in Asia: What Diplomatic Documents Reveal.* Tokyo: Japan Publishing Industry Foundation for Culture.]

Inoue, Masaya. 2016. "Nitchū kankei: habatsu seiji no hen'yō to taigai seisaku (Japan-China Relations: Foreign Policy and The Transformation of Factional Politics)" in Ōyane, Satoshi and Ōnishi, Yutaka (eds). *FTA/TPP no seijigaku: bōeki jiyūka to anzen hosho/shakai hosho* (The Politics of FTAs and the TPP: Securitization of Trade Policy). Tokyo: Yūhikaku.

Masuo, Chisako. 2010. *Chūgoku seiji gaikō no tenkanten: kaikaku kaihō to "dokuritsu jishu no taigai seisaku"* (A Turning Point in Chinese Politics and Diplomacy: Reform, Opening Up, and "Foreign Policy of Self-Reliance"). Tokyo: Tokyo University Press.

Murayama, Tomiichi. 1995. Statement by Prime Minister Tomiichi Murayama "On the occasion of the 50th anniversary of the war's end (15 August 1995)" As referenced at: https://www.mofa.go.jp/announce/press/pm/murayama/9508.html

NHK Shuzaihan. 1993. *Shū Onrai no ketsudan: nitchū kokkō seijōka wa kōshite jitsugen shita* (Zhou Enlai's Decision: This was how Normalization of Japan-China Relations was Achieved). Tokyo: NHK Shuppan Kyōkai.

Ō, Setsuhyo [Wang, Xueping] (ed). 2013. *Sengo nitchukankei to ryo shoshi* (Liao Chengzhi and Postwar Japan-China Relations). Tokyo: Keio University Press.

Shimizu, Yoshikazu. 2003. *Chūgoku wa naze "hannichi" ni natta ka* (Why did China become "anti-Japanese"?). Tokyo: Bungei Shinsho.

Additional Bibliography

Inoue, Masaya. 2010. *Nitchū kokkō seijōka no seijishi* (A Political History of Sino-Japanese Normalization). Nagoya: The University of Nagoya Press.

Diplomatic historical research that analyzes Japan's policies toward China leading to normalization of relations. It describes in detail the reciprocal ties between LDP factional politics and Japan-China relations.

Kokubun, Ryōsei; Soeya, Yoshihide; Takahara, Akio; Kawashima, Shin. 2013. *Nitchū kankeishi* (Japan-China Relations in the Modern Era). Tokyo: Yūhikaku.

[Published in English with new final chapter as: Kokubun, Ryōsei; Soeya, Yoshihide; Takahara, Akio; Kawashima, Shin. Krulak, Keith (trans). 2017. *Japan-China Relations in the Modern Era*. London: Routledge Taylor & Francis Group.]

A general history of postwar Japan-China relations based on the latest research. A compact and well-balanced presentation, primarily from the political viewpoint, of Japan-China relations after the foundation of the People's Republic of China.

Mōri Kazuko. 2006. *Nitchū kankei—sengo kara shinjidai e* (Sino-Japanese Relations: from the Postwar to a New Era). Tokyo: Iwanami Shinsho.

General historical research by a leading figure in China studies. While considering significant structural shifts in both Japan and China, it describes in detail the issue of historical understanding and China's policies toward Japan.

Takahara, Akio; Hattori, Ryūji (eds). 2012. *Nitchū kankeishi, 1972–2012 I. seiji* (A History of Japan-China Relations, 1972–2012. I Politics). Tokyo: The University of Tokyo Press.

A general history addressing in detail the key topics in Japan-China relations from diplomatic normalization through the period of the Democratic Party of Japan government. It analyzes the domestic situation and international conditions that were the key factors shaping Japan-China relations.

Chapter 13
The Issue of Historical Perspective from the Post-Heisei Era: Looking Back at Meiji from the Postwar Period, and Looking Ahead

Hiroshi Nakanishi

Abstract This chapter presents a high-level, historical retrospective from modern-day Japan, looking back at the Meiji period with which the book began, through the immediate postwar period and into the 1960s and Japan's rise as an economic power. It then looks at Japan's "meanderings" following the end of the Cold War and the collapse of its bubble economy, before taking a speculative look at what might lie ahead for the nation in the new era of Reiwa. The author posits a need to supplant the popular "Shiba view of history" with a perspective more appropriate to the present changing postwar order and that reevaluates the successes of the Meiji period.

What Is Meant by Historical Perspective

In this chapter, instead of addressing any particular issues in the modern history of Japan, I would like to discuss the topic from the angle of historical perspective. To the question "What is history?" there can be various replies, such as the famous one by E.H. Carr in his classic work, *What is History?*: "an unending dialogue between the present and the past" (Carr 1962). My reply here is to take history as a "map on the axis of time." A regular map is drawn out on a spatial axis, but when a map is drawn on a time axis or timeline, we call it history. In this analogy of history as a map, the monographs undertaken by expert history researchers are comparable to the work of drawing an accurate map, through the collection of basic data and by measuring the landscape using precise, scientific methods. These days, the principal aim of academic historical research that is usually called empirical history in Japan is to reconstruct an accurate past based on historical materials that have been scrutinized rigorously as historical evidence. Though other standards to evaluate quality of research such as narrative clarity can be included, in principle, the rigor with which

H. Nakanishi
The Graduate School of Law, Kyoto University, Kyoto, Japan

© The Author(s) 2023
M. Yamauchi, Y. Hosoya (eds.), *Modern Japan's Place in World History*,
https://doi.org/10.1007/978-981-19-9593-4_13

the historical materials are investigated forms the framework for the system of knowledge called empirical history.

However, greater detail and precision does not necessarily make for a better map. Too fine a map sometimes becomes impractical. If I wish to go 100 m in front of me, a map with the scale of 1 cm, or even 1 mm, safe to say, is not more helpful than one with a scale of 1 m. The duty of a map, is to give a sense of spatial direction, so it may be handier to have an easy-to-understand outline drawing that simplifies away the precise details of survey measurements. You can say the same thing about history. It is often difficult to grasp a broad sense of direction from historical research that focuses on the details. What we desire from a "bird's-eye view from 30,000 feet" is not every detail on the ground down to the last centimeter; likewise, what we expect from a bird's-eye historical perspective is an omission of minor facts that are too trivial: we want a sense of direction from the present to the future. What I describe here is similar to what Mutsu Munemitsu, a highly esteemed Meiji-period diplomat, wrote in the preface to his memoir *Kenkenroku*, making a contrast between a survey map, whose measurements derived from official archives and records, and a bird's-eye view painting drawn from life, and then characterizes his book as the latter sort (Mutsu 2015).

Not many historians of the present day, however, involve themselves often with such broad overviews; they cannot, in fact, for fear that colleagues in their line of work will criticize them for sketching out some perfunctory sort of map when, being an expert in the field, they should be drawing highly detailed maps. In *What is History?*, Carr disdainfully mocked German historian Oswald Spengler and British historian Arnold Toynbee for preaching the history of mankind from a perspective of the rise and fall of civilizations.

Meanwhile, every society holds the desire for a general overview map of its own history. Therefore, the writing of such a map more often falls to novelists and general historians than academic researchers. Oftentimes these broad maps are sloppy, having no clear connection to detailed surveys of historical research. "Deduction from above" was how author and literary critic Takeyama Michio[1] once criticized Marxist-influenced histories written in the 1950s. This does not pertain only to Marxism; any history that cherry-picks facts and historical evidence to support its predetermined conclusion runs the risk of being drafted as a good-looking overview. Just as an attractive map drawn without reference to proper measurements cannot help you find your way to your destination, a simplistic and clear-cut view of history that is not based in fact will deceive the public, leading them astray into dogmatism. What is needed in these cases is a well-drawn overview that is mindful of the trade-offs between precise detail and intellectual utility. In this chapter I plan to look back over postwar history by focusing on the issue of how a "historical view" or "historical perspective" was created as a series of bird's-eye view maps of the Japanese postwar period.

---

[1] Active in the Shōwa period he is famous for his novel *Harp of Burma*. In criticizing historical materialism, Takeyama wrote in his *Shōwa no seishinshi*: "When interpreting history, it is a mistake to establish a principle that serves as a major premise first, and then proceed on that basis to explain specific phenomena. 'Deduction from above' always leads to wrong conclusions."

Selecting the Regime in the Immediate Postwar

The era from Japan's defeat in 1945 to 1960 was a busy one, as the country and people responded to the many changes that defeat and the occupation brought about. It was an era when people were too busy making history rather than thinking about historical perspectives.

Selecting a regime, a form of government, was the most important task in the immediate postwar period. "Preserving the national polity" was the sitting Suzuki Kantarō administration's objective at the time of Japan's surrender, so the process of enacting the Constitution of Japan throughout 1946–1947 meant carrying out the most fundamental selection of a system in that environment. The greatest concern of Japan's leadership was to avoid the fate that had befallen Germany. Subjected to the harsh peace imposed on it under the Treaty of Versailles after World War I, Germany found itself divided and occupied by four major powers at the end of World War II. Japan's request to preserve the national polity was tied to the mindset wishing to escape such a fate. As is well known, when the Supreme Commander for the Allied Powers (SCAP/GHQ) presented them with the draft constitution, the administrations of Shidehara Kijūrō and Yoshida Shigeru, which followed, had to accept it. It is likely that for Supreme Commander General Douglas MacArthur revising the constitution was the means rather than the objective, because he had a strong interest in preventing any interference in the Occupation of Japan from the Far Eastern Commission (which also included the Soviet Union, Australia, [the Republic of] China, and other Allies). At the same time, the Japanese government welcomed the draft because the new constitution guaranteed the status of the emperor, albeit as a symbol, and thereby did preserve the national polity.

Several "cons" weighed against this "pro": the "no-war clause" of Article 9 paragraph 2 was finalized at this very early stage of the postwar period, and the constitution overall had been drafted rather hastily. Ironically, because the Cold War was intensifying, the issue of Japan's security reached a key turning point as the Constitution of Japan was going into effect in May 1947. Here, too, there was a balance of merits. It was a major advantage to Japan that, under a strategy to strengthen Japan as an ally in the Cold War, the US-led Western bloc had adopted a basic policy linked to a generous peace. But it was detrimental for Japanese politics that Japan rearmed itself while keeping Article 9's stipulations intact, because constitutional revision became impossible with the nation split politically under the Cold War.

The start of the Korean War in June 1950 precipitated a head-on confrontation between the United States (as a member of the United Nations' forces) and the People's Republic of China (with its "People's Volunteer Army"). The war resulted in a US security commitment to the Korean Peninsula by, among others, US military stationing in South Korea, a positive for Japan's own national security. But the attendant divisions of China, Taiwan and the Korean peninsula complicated the post-World War II settlement as well as Japan's efforts to form its own ties with these countries, a negative for Japan. Yoshida Shigeru was especially eager to build relations with China after Britain recognized the People's Republic of China (hereafter, China), which was in control of the mainland, as early as January 1950. But out of consideration for US wishes (the United States and China had become belligerent adversaries), Yoshida could only secure a peace treaty with the Republic of China (hereafter, Taiwan), which left Japan's relations with China in an unsettled state.

As for Japan's domestic regime, what came to be called the "1955 regime" was established as political party system in 1955 when the Liberal Democratic Party (LDP) was formed, the left and right wings of the Japan Socialist Party were reunified, and the Japan Communist Party abandoned its armed struggle line. The government's economic white paper issued the following year contained the phrase "the postwar period is already over." Yet at this stage, the anti-Yoshida forces leading the LDP were pushing to revise the constitution and rearm the country; the progressive left, meanwhile, fiercely opposed rearmament and the Japan-US Security Treaty system; and there were several foreign policy issues outstanding. The riots over the 1960 revision of the security treaty brought a temporary resolution to these issues. Under Kishi Nobusuke's administration, the LDP, which had been split between the Yoshida and anti-Yoshida factions, decided to accept the US-centric policy line that Yoshida had created as its general framework, and to prioritize the revision of the Japan-US Security Treaty thereby pushing off constitutional revision. Consistent with this choice, the LDP expressed its basic policy that Japan would not become involved in military conflict outside of its own territory by stating that, "the exercise of the right of collective self-defense [for Japan to participate in another country's conflict overseas] ... is not permissible under the Constitution." As a result, the Japanese people chose a balance in general elections from the end of the 1950s, entrusting the LDP with the power and authority to rule yet giving the opposition parties over one-third of seats, thereby preventing revision of the constitution.

Formation of the "Postwar" Consciousness in the 1960s

Japanese people could not view the "postwar" year from a historical perspective until the start of the 1960s, when the issue of the political regime had been settled. This point itself is easily understandable. Yet, it must be noted that the postwar social consciousness formed in the 1960s had the following two features.

First, the postwar consciousness created in the 1960s has survived the 70 years since the war's end largely unchanged. This partly stems from the fact that during this interval Japan has not encountered any momentous changes, such as a world war. The historical consciousness of the 1960s still strongly shapes the politics and society of today's Japan, over half a century later—this point is perhaps one feature of "postwar Japan" on the axis of time.

Second, the postwar consciousness formed in the 1960s is deeply connected to the historical consciousness of how to view modern Japan since Meiji, something that had existed well before World War II. We must distinguish this point from the historical consciousness that the great reforms of the Meiji period, the Meiji Restoration, ushered Japan into a new era. Though 1945 was the origin of the "postwar" era, it is a "beginning" only in a moderate sense; in fact, in a chronological sense, it is seen as a second starting point since the Meiji. To put it another way, the postwar consciousness had been shaped and taken hold as a corollary to the consciousness of modern Japan since Meiji.

Already in the 1950s there were debates within intelligentia stretching from the prewar period among the Marxists over the Meiji Restoration or the failed modernization school of thought of progressive scholars, epitomized by Maruyama Masao. But they were strongly characterized by what Takeyama Michio criticized as "deduction from above," mentioned previously. In contrast to these arguments, a new way of looking at Japan's modern history emerged—on the one hand, rooted in more empirical historical research and, on the other, influenced by modernization theory that had been a growing school of thought within the West since the latter half of the 1950s. This new approach, based on its understanding that Japan since Meiji was an exemplar of successful modernization, took the wars of the Showa Period as a deviation from its success. For instance, Ueyama Shunpei's *The Significance of the Greater East Asian War*, Hayashi Fusao's *The Affirmative Thesis on the Greater East Asian War*, and *Asianism* edited by Takauchi Yoshimi are books published in the early 1960s that construct a historical consciousness, laid along a continuous timeline from the Meiji period onward, that states the task of postwar Japan is to recover from the temporary mistake of veering off into war and return to work vigorously on its path of modernization. What grabbed the public's attention in this trend of thought was Shiba Ryōtarō's *Ryōma ga yuku* (published as a serialized article in the newspaper from June 1962 to May 1966).[2] Sakamoto Ryōma, a figure known by all Japanese today, was all but forgotten for a time after a brief rise to prominence in the Meiji/Taishō periods. Through his serialized novel featuring Ryōma as its heroic protagonist, Shiba tied the spirit of the Meiji Restoration to the Japan of the 1960s.

Around the same period, international political scholar Kōsaka Masataka of Kyoto University made his debut as a public intellectual, publishing his theses *Prime Minister Yoshida Shigeru* and *Concept of Japan as a Maritime State*. These theses, written as essentially current policy affair writings, laid out an appraisal of Yoshida Shigeru and the proper form of Japanese diplomacy, and both were linked to an assessment of the Meiji state. These works characterized Yoshida—before the war, a diplomat in the camp favoring Anglo-American cooperation who came into conflict with the military and was later suppressed; after the war, a prime minister— as choosing a policy line that prioritized economic recovery through commerce, light military armament, and the Japan-US security alliance. Depending on how you see it, this approach can be understood as an attempt to position Yoshida's postwar choice as an extension of "*senchū hassaku*," an eight-point program that Ryōma

---

[2] Published in English as *Ryōma! The Life of Sakamota Ryōma: Japanese Swordsman and Visionary*, a four volume set.

conceptualized around the end of Edo period for the restoration and foundation for a new government.

Concept of Japan as a Maritime State is a relatively long essay, patterned after Watsuji Tetsurō's *Sakoku: Japan's Tragedy* (published in 1950), that starts with a comparison of Japan and Britain in the seventeenth century. According to this article, Britain by that period had become a maritime state under the reign of Elizabeth I, whereas Japan, which had once been open to trade and interaction with the world at large, had made the choice to become an island country under the *sakoku* policy of self-imposed national isolation. Watsuji had called that "Japan's tragedy," a sense that Kōsaka embraced, asserting that postwar Japan should become a maritime state by adopting policies for open commerce and by investing in natural resources to make full use of the oceans.

Thus, a historical perspective was formed, particularly in the early 1960s, that overlay that time with the Meiji period, asserting that postwar Japan must recreate itself as a maritime state, a claim rooted in the belief that despite having the potential to develop as a maritime state, Meiji Japan had erred at some point in time by deciding to use military force in an effort to become a continental state. The fact that they held the Tokyo Olympics and started operating the Tōkaidō Shinkansen in 1964 at exactly that time underpinned the social consciousness that they were not only recovering from the devastation of war but creating a new Japan in terms of having learned from mistakes in its modern history.

As we come to the later part of the decade, however, the consciousness of the issues slightly shifted. Though high-speed economic growth had entered its peak, Japan also entered a political season at home and abroad. The United States was bogged down in the quagmire of the Vietnam War; China was feeling the full devastating force of the Cultural Revolution; and in Japan, student protests had become so radicalized that the University of Tokyo cancelled its entrance examinations. It was in these conditions that the first state funeral in the postwar period was held, for Yoshida Shigeru who died in 1967, and that the 100th anniversary of the Meiji Restoration was celebrated as a government-initiated program the following year. This meant an even greater awareness of the continuity with Meiji. With the growing awareness Japan's postwar economic achievements, interest shifted to the sequence of events linking Meiji's successes to Shōwa's failures, and interest in how to avoid repeating the mistakes of the past came to the fore.

To cite an extreme example of this, Mishima Yukio, the most conspicuous of postwar pundits, wrote a short essay for the *Sankei Shimbun* that smacked of a suicide note: "If things continue at this rate, Japan will disappear... perhaps leaving behind an economic powerhouse in a corner of the Far East that is inorganic, empty, neutral, neutral-colored, affluent, and shrewd. I no longer have any interest in speaking to people who think that such a development is alright." His dramatic suicide in November 1970 can be interpreted as a man of letters with such acute sensibilities expressing his irritability and the sense of unease which he held toward postwar Japan.

Even as their consciousness of the issues overlapped with Mishima's, Shiba Ryōtarō and Kōsaka Masataka actively tried to avoid the solution which Mishima had hoped for, a revival of nationalist sentiment stemming from the traditional spirit to revere the emperor. To begin with, aspects of what Mishima hoped for miss the mark. Mishima's spirit of revering the emperor in truth is not something traditional, but a modern product of the Meiji period, a fact pointed out by Hashikawa Bunzō that even Mishima could not help but acknowledge.

Shiba's *Clouds above the Hill*[3] began its serialized run in the *Sankei Shimbun* newspaper in April 1968. A long novel that was started clearly influenced by the Meiji centennial, this work of historical fiction depicting the era from the Shogunate's close and the Meiji Restoration weaves its narrative through parallel storylines focusing on several characters, rather than centering on a single protagonist. As is well-known, the story at first begins as a *bildungsroman* of three young men, the Akiyama brothers (Yoshifuru and Saneyuki) and Masaoka Shiki. But Shiki dies in the third volume of the complete set of eight, and the Akiyama brothers become lost within the military historical description of the Russo-Japanese War. The main theme of the latter half of the story is that of Japanese leaders barely managing to keep in check the dangers brought about by irrational spiritualism, which Shiba ascribed to Nogi Maresuke,[4] to lead the country to victory in the war. As has been widely noted, Shiba's depiction of Nogi is undeserved, and major parts of the bitter fighting that was the Russo-Japanese War originated in the inhumanity of war in an industrial age that, with World War I, became obvious war. Be that as it may, Shiba's motive was to imply that after the Russo-Japanese War, Meiji's modernization success gave way to the path toward irrational spiritualism, precipitating the mistakes of Shōwa, a caution for postwar Japan against falling into Mishimaesque spiritualism.

Kōsaka, too, planned a symposium titled, "Illusion of 'a Powerless State'" (hosted by the Japan Cultural Congress) in 1969, where he argued the dangers of Japan disregarding the importance of political concepts as it achieved its economic successes. Kōsaka was laying out his maritime state concept as not something conceived simply from an economic viewpoint, but as the political objectives for which postwar Japan should be aiming.

Success and Challenges of an Economic Power

This resulted, however, in half-accepting and half-ignoring the recommendation for realism that Shiba and Kōsaka offered. For sure, there was no revival of spiritualism or Mishimaesque ideology. Yet Japan of the 1970s increasingly defined its identity as an economic power, falling into a habit of making light of politics.

---

[3] Translated into English as *Clouds above the Hill: A Historical Novel of the Russo-Japanese War*, published in four volumes.

[4] A national hero in Imperial Japan, General Nogi captured Port Arthur (Lüshun) in the Russo-Japanese War at the cost of many lives; he committed *seppuku* on the day of Emperor Meiji's funeral, an act that simultaneously marked the end of an era, influenced contemporary writers, and made him a public symbol of loyalty and sacrifice.

It is just a historical "what-if" exercise, but what if this era had held an opportunity for Japan to make a serious diplomatic decision, how would that have changed Japan thereafter? For instance, if Japan had been able to engage China on establishing diplomatic normalization before US Secretary of State Henry Kissinger's July 1971 visit to Beijing, it may have been able to combine a policy of Japan-China diplomatic ties co-existing with Japan-Taiwan relations with the US reversion of administrative control over Okinawa, and if so, subsequent history may have changed. Of course, given the international environment of the time, it would have been extremely challenging to make this move, but there may be some value in simply considering the possibility at least.

In the event, Sino-US rapprochement went forward, and the Tanaka Kakuei administration played catch-up to achieve a restoration of diplomatic ties with China. By then, there were growing trade frictions between Japan and the United States evidenced in the bilateral textile negotiations held in the later days of the Satō Eisaku administration. In addition, Japan was forced to respond to yen appreciation resulting from the Nixon shocks related to the economy.[5] Subsequently, Japanese society experienced a major panic with the first oil shock in 1973. Japan's self-perception as an economic power had taken hold firmly before the country surmounted this chain of crises in the mid-1970s. A summit was held in 1975, at France's overture, by the leaders of the advanced industrial economies (which became the G7 the following year); afterwards, Japan was recognized as a leading economic power, by itself and others, becoming one corner of the triangular relationship among Japan-US-Europe.

Japanese diplomacy as an economic power certainly scored some successes in the 1970s and 1980s. Firstly, Japan took the initiative to focus Asian regional international relations on economics by using terms like "Pacific Rim" and "Asia-Pacific." The activities of the Association of Southeast Asian Nations (ASEAN), the fundamental regional mechanism, increased starting with its leaders' summit in 1976; thus, Prime Minister Fukuda Takeo announced his "Fukuda Doctrine" in Manila in 1977. Through Japan-Australian cooperation, Prime Minister Ōhira Masayoshi called for a Pacific Economic Cooperation Council (PECC), which became the basis for Asia-Pacific Economic Cooperation (APEC) that started in 1989. In addition, as China's Deng Xiaoping changed course toward reform and opening in 1978, a shift supported by Japan and the United States, Japan pursued a diplomatic strategy to avoid splitting Asia and the Western world that combined free trade and economic cooperation/development assistance.

Secondly, Japan contributed to international cooperation, particularly on the economic front, as the first advanced industrial nation in the non-Western world to be included in the G7. One praiseworthy success of Japanese diplomacy was its very adoption of the basic policy that "international order is a public good, and an

---

[5] A series of anti-inflationary economic measures the Nixon administration took in 1971, including wage and price controls, surcharges on imports, and the ending of the gold convertibility of the US dollar.

economic power must bear its proportional share to maintain it," something that was communicated in the concept of "comprehensive security" formalized by the Ōhira administration.

However, just because you have economic power does not make politics unnecessary. First, economic tensions deepened with Europe and the United States as Japan's economic power grew relative to theirs, and they increased pressure on Tokyo to open its markets and restrict its export abilities. The situation became so serious in the 1980s that the revisionist school of thought, which claimed the threat that Japan was trying to control the world through its economic power, had an influence on politics.

Second, an assessment of Japan's modern history became an international political problem. The historical debate over the war into the 1970s had always focused on relations between Japan on the one hand with the United States and other Western countries on the other, and criticisms of the International Military Tribunal of the Far East were asserted from the viewpoint that Japan's modern history was that of confronting Western imperialism (epitomized by Hayashi Fusao's *The Affirmative Thesis on the Great East Asian War*). The enshrinement of the Class A war criminals in Yasukuni Shrine in 1978 took place in the context of such debates.

Beginning in the 1980s, however, political frictions began to aggravate the history issues with Asian countries that had been dealt with until then on the basis of economic cooperation. Part of the background for this change is the growth of nationalism that accompanied economic growth in these Asian countries; an anti-Japanese posture was used as an excuse to criticize the ruling authorities and in political struggles for power. But the fundamental problem was that the historical perspective of modernization established in the 1960s had no clear response to the questions of how to characterize relations with Asian countries in Japan's modern history since Meiji, and how to evaluate these relations historically. Moreover, before Japan could address these questions head on, the Cold War ended, which roiled Japan's postwar identity.

Post-Cold War Meanderings

Though Japan and the other countries from the West naturally greeted the Cold War's sudden demise with cries of delight, they did not inquire too deeply why the Cold War ended so abruptly and peacefully. It was accepted relatively simply as the victory of liberal democracy and market economics.

So, it was hoped that the Cold War would similarly end in Asia. Though the forces pushing for political reform in China were suppressed in the Tiananmen Square Incident in 1989, it was hoped that reform and opening even under the Communist Party's leadership would ultimately promote liberalization, faced with the overwhelming impression of the collapse of the Soviet Union and its Eastern European bloc. The same held true for the socialist countries of North Korea and

Vietnam. It is with these expectations that Japan struggled to find an amicable settlement of history with China, South Korea, and North Korea.

The Japanese emperor's visit to China in 1992 and South Korean President Kim Dae-jung's visit to Japan in 1998 marked breaks in their respective history issues and the visits had been planned as a means to construct future-oriented relations. In the same manner, the Japanese side expressed its apologies regarding the comfort women issues and responsibility for the war through government statements: the Kōno, Hosokawa, and Murayama statements (*tanwa*). Japan and North Korea seemed to pursue normalization of diplomatic relations, kicked off by the dispatch of a supra-partisan group of Japanese lawmakers to North Korea in 1990. Even the 1998 state visit to Japan by Chinese President Jiang Zemin, who sought to press Japan on its historical responsibility, was seen at the time as bearing diplomatic results in the joint declaration both sides issued.

The collapse of Japan's bubble economy and the First Gulf War that occurred contemporaneous with the end of the Cold War shook Japan's postwar identity. Under the 1955 system built on the premise of the Cold War structure, postwar Japan had made its identity the pursuit of pacifism and economic prosperity as a means to overcome military disputes, after reflecting on its history of militarization since the closing days of the Meiji period. However, the collapse of the bubble laid bare the weaknesses of the Japanese capitalist economy; the Gulf War exposed the contradiction between its basic policy of nonparticipation in international conflicts and its contributions to the UN-led order, a contradiction that during the Cold War had been completely unforeseen, leaving Japan concerned about international criticism and scorn. Naturally, Japan's primary task in the 1990s became its response to these shocks.

Generally speaking, the 1990s was a chaotic period for Japan, notwithstanding certain changes that occurred, such as domestic political administrative reforms and Japanese participation in UN Peacekeeping Operations. First among the factors for this was that Japan was pressed to respond to two overlapping tasks simultaneously: the political task of selecting a post-Cold War political system and diplomatic policy line as well as the economic task of clearing the bad debts of the bubble and transforming the structure of the economic system to better match a shrinking labor population and the increasing role of information technology. Economic reforms were nigh impossible without political stability, but economic turmoil caused political reforms to lose their sense of direction. Political chaos forced putting off measures for the economy, giving rise to a vicious circle resulting in a feeling of stagnation and ever deeper discontent toward politics.

The second factor was that Japan was influenced by the excessive optimism the rest of the world felt toward the shape of the post-Cold War order. In recent years there have been assertions that throughout the postwar period the international order was a liberal one. But the international order during the Cold War should be viewed as combining liberal and illiberal elements, with liberalism becoming predominant only after the end of the Cold War. At the end of the 1990s, globalization came to be touted as the world standard, as the BRICs (Brazil, Russia, India, China) and other emerging market economies joined the US-led new liberal global marketplace.

Japan's attempt to rapidly introduce global standards despite the weakness of its political and economic systems precipitated a drop in its international influence. International cooperation in the Asia-Pacific was in retreat with the 1995 APEC (Asia-Pacific Economic Cooperation) Osaka Summit, and at the time of the 1997 Asian Financial Crisis, Japan was unable to demonstrate its international leadership, beset by its own financial system crisis, leaving China, the future economic power, an opportunity to boost its presence.

A temporary halt to this situation came with Koizumi Jun'ichirō, who rose to prominence and bolstered his popularity by calling for reforms within the LDP; by following a structural reform policy line, he achieved his aims of reducing public works spending and reforming the postal system. Internationally, on the one hand, Japan-US relations became even closer in the wake of the 9/11 terrorist attacks in 2001 and the ensuing war on terror, with the dispatch of Japan Self-Defense Forces to the Indian Ocean region. In Asia, on the other hand, frictions with China and South Korea increased because of Koizumi's Yasukuni Shrine visits, and diplomatic normalization talks with North Korea stalled because of Pyongyang's admission that it had abducted Japanese citizens and its nuclear program developments. Also, radical liberalism emphasizing global standards provided impetus for insisting on pursuing the issue of individual suffering from war politically. This trend especially aggravated the territorial issue and historical debate over the responsibility for colonial rule between Japan and South Korea, issues the governments had dealt with through a series of political compromises.

Despite Koizumi's reforms, the LDP government lacked the ability to respond to developing domestic structural problems: an aging society and declining birthrate as well as expanding inequalities between Tokyo and the municipalities at home; and international problems such as decline of American influence amid the chaos in its postwar administrations of Afghanistan and Iraq and in the wake of its 2008 financial crisis sparked by the collapse of Lehman Brothers; global economic recession; and the growing assertiveness of China and other emerging market economies. After the Koizumi administration, criticisms of the LDP grew so loud that the Democratic Party of Japan (DPJ) won a landslide victory in the August 2009 general election. At first, the public had high hopes for the DPJ administration, but confusion increased owing to intra-administration conflict over the direction of reforms. In particular, the Japan-US alliance and China's hardline stance surrounding the Senkaku Islands, as well as the 2011 Great East Japan Earthquake all heightened the Japanese public's sense of crisis and increased its disillusionment toward not only the DPJ government but the path of reform itself.

The second Abe Shinzō administration took the stage, its slogan "Take back Japan" matching the popular sentiment of the time. The three arrows of his Abenomics plan also struck a favorable impression with the people: the first arrow of unconventional monetary easing by the central bank would be painless, with the possibility for a second arrow of fiscal spending and a third arrow of structural reform. Interstate competition and conflict drew greater attention in the 2010s, as the world entered a period of reassessing the optimistic theory of a "Liberal International Order." It was in this context that the Abe administration, which valued geopolitical strategic concepts, strengthened the Japan-US alliance and bolstered Japan's diplomatic presence, fully grasping the mood of the times in terms of diplomacy, too.

And yet, it remained rather nebulous whether the Abe administration was seeking to escape from the postwar system or aiming to revive the earlier good old postwar years. The matter became murkier when it was decided that the 2020 Olympics would be held in Tokyo, easily harkening back to the image of the 1960s: would the Olympic Games be used to revive the good postwar years or to move on from them? This vagueness was reflected in Abe's statement on the 70th anniversary of the end of the war issued in 2015. The statement elicited sympathy with its use of a historical perspective commonly called the "Shiba view of history." The Abe statement neatly applied the Shiba perspective which considered post-Meiji Japan a successful example of modernization that absorbed the modern order of the West, thus it deemed the period from the Manchurian Incident in 1931 through the end of the Pacific War an aberration. This framing also underscored the opportunity for *Meiji 150* in 2018, as if to relive the experience of the 100th anniversary of Meiji (in 1968).

The Task of a Historical Perspective Looking to the Future

Amid the deepening turmoil in the world at present (2019), it is quite natural that the Japanese people seek stability from something like a "Shiba view of history." However, Shiba Ryōtarō himself rejected such an expression and, lest we forget, he insisted that history is that which is built on the accumulation of small facts. Shiba's thinking may be inferred from the fact that, before he died, he never granted his permission for *Clouds above the Hill*, his representative work treating the Meiji period to be made into a movie.

All the same, "Shiba view of history" expression gained currency among the population because the "postwar identity" formed during the Shōwa 30s (1955–1964), which characterized postwar Japan as an extension of the narrative of Meiji Japan as successful Western-style modernization, is so comfortable to the Japanese even today.

However, the Japanese people cannot stay with, if not outrightly reject, the Shiba view of history now, when the postwar order is undergoing significant transformation. I believe that we need a new historical perspective that comprises three mutually overlapping issues. First is to move beyond regarding Meiji as the sole starting point and consider how to incorporate the experiences of the prior Edo period. A nation under self-imposed isolation from the world (*sakoku*) is the perception of Japan born at the end of the Edo period. But it has become common historical knowledge nowadays that during the Edo period Japan communicated and had relations with the Qing (China), the Joseon (Korea), the Ryūkyū (Okinawa), and the Ezo (in Hokkaido). We need to find a perspective for a comprehensive understanding of the process of melding this experience into the modern Western order after Meiji. For instance, the background to the enormous domestic political and foreign policy problems that the *Seikanron* (plan for a punitive expedition to Korea) generated right at the start of the Meiji Restoration should be understood in the context of a process of transformation from the Edo international system to the Meiji international system.

Second is Japan's relations with the countries on the continent. The process of modernization since Meiji has greatly depended on cooperative relations and the alliances with Britain from Meiji through the Taishō period, then with the United States after World War II. This undoubtedly was a choice suited to the nature of Japan, as a maritime country surrounded by the seas. Then again, as an island nation not far from the continent, Japan cannot just make do without having relations with the countries on the continent: China, Russia, and the Korean Peninsula. Modern Britain, in fact, established a role for itself as the balancer of power on the European continent while simultaneously being a maritime country. Japan has not yet defined its own role that it should play on the continent. We should inquire once more of Japan's modern history as to the reasons and consequence for that.

Third is the understanding that the rapidity of modernization since Meiji is belied by its shallowness. This was something perceptive Japan's intelligentsia were keenly aware of when they viewed their country after the Russo-Japanese War. "Under Reconstruction," a short story that Mori Ōgai wrote in the waning days of Meiji, ends with the protagonist coolly responding to a former lover who has come from Germany to see him that "Japan is still under reconstruction." This story can be interpreted as a work satirizing the thin veneer of civilization that Japan hurriedly donned following Western models as "under reconstruction." Around the same time, Ōgai advocated the need for an organization for knowledge that understood both Western and Eastern knowledge, as represented in his expression "the two legs of knowledge." This task remains unfinished still to this day.

In his short essay "My Sōseki," Shiba Ryōtarō remarked that "One of the reasons Japanese are bad at foreign languages is because the Japanese language became established as a written language in the last days of Meiji." Japan is the only late-stage development country that made textbooks for physics, chemistry, and mathematics all in Japanese. And the man who perfected such written Japanese was Natsume Sōseki, according to Shiba (2006). In other writings, Shiba also remarked that it was in the Shōwa 30s that written Japanese became something for the masses, along with the spread of weekly magazines (Shiba 2000). These days Shiba's novels are called "national literature," but Shiba's writing itself might be called the crystallization of a postwar Japanese language that popularized the written Japanese style Sōseki had perfected. This way of writing Japanese spread among the general populace, so that it could perhaps even be called the cultural identity of the present-day people of Japan. This useful Japanese language itself, however, has also become an unintentional barrier opening a large knowledge gap with the world. The average Japanese is likely unaware that the term for the Japanese (*kokugo*) used as the language by Japanese at their places of learning and work is distinguished from the term for Japanese (*Nihongo*) used for the language foreigners learn. What the sages of Shōwa would expect from the Japanese of Reiwa is not that they live contentedly with the memories and historical perceptions of the past successes Japan experienced from Meiji through Shōwa, but that they construct new expressions and historical perspectives, wouldn't they?

Bibliography: For Further Reading

Carr, E.H. Shimizu Ikutarō (trans). 1962. *Rekishi to wa nanika* (What is History?). Tokyo: Iwanami Shinsho. (Published in English by London: Macmillan and Co. 1961.)

Mutsu, Munemitsu. 2015. *Kenkenroku.* Tokyo: Chūkō Classics. [Published in English as: Mutsu, Munemitsu. Gordon Mark Berger (trans). 1982. *Kenkenroku* (Kenkenroku: a Diplomatic Record of the Sino-Japanese War, 1894–95). Princeton: Princeton University Press.]

Shiba, Ryōtarō. 2000. "Gengo ni tsuite no kansō (Thoughts on Language)" in *Kono kuni no katachi 6* (The Shape of this Country, Vol. 6). Tokyo: Bunshun Bunko.

Shiba, Ryōtarō. 2006. "Watakushi no sōseki (My Sōseki)" in *Shiba ryōtarō ga kangaeta koto 15* (Things that Shiba Ryōtarō Thought, Vol. 15). Tokyo: Shinchō Bunko.

Additional Bibliography

Hattori, Ryūji. 2018. *Kōsaka Masataka: sengo nihon to genjitsu shugi* (Kōsaka Masataka: Postwar Japan and Realism). Tokyo: Chūkō Shinsho.

As an international political scholar, Kōsaka Masataka had a significant impact on postwar Japanese diplomacy as well as its historical consciousness; this biography carefully traces his footsteps. For a collection of Kōsaka's essays treating the various aspects of his achievements, I would recommend Iokibe, Makoto; Nakanishi, Hiroshi (eds). 2016. *Kōsaka masataka to sengo nihon* (Kōsaka Masataka and Postwar Japan). Tokyo: Chūō Kōron Shinsha.

Iokibe, Makoto. 2014. *Sengo nihon gaikōshi dai-3ban hochōban* (Postwar Japan's Diplomatic History [Third Revised Edition]). Tokyo: Yūhikaku.

I would recommend this as a textbook, patterned on academic analysis, which depicts how postwar history unfolded, though mainly through the lens of Japanese diplomatic history.

Saitō, Shinji (ed). 1996. *Shiba ryōtarō no seiki* (Shiba Ryōtarō's Century). Tokyo: Asahi Shuppansha.

Shiba Ryōtarō is a permanent presence in any discussion of the historical consciousness in the postwar period. However, it is difficult to know where to start, as there are voluminous writing and critiques regarding Shiba. This book is a trustworthy introduction to Shiba.

Watanabe, Akio; Katō, Yōko; Amamiya, Shoichi; Kage, Rieko; Muramatsu, Michio; Ōtake, Hideo. Fukunaga Fumio; and Kōno Yasuko (eds). 2014. *Sengo to wa nani ka: seijigaku to rekishigaku no taiwa. jōgekan* (What was the Postwar?: a Dialogue between Political Science and History). Tokyo: Maruzen Shuppan.

A record of a study group and questions-and-answers on the theme of the evolution of political science and history studies in the postwar years. Though a collection of essays targeted at researchers interested in academic history, it is valuable for understanding how shifts in academia were situated during postwar history.

Correction to: The First Sino-Japanese War and East Asia

Takashi Okamoto

Correction to:
Chapter 2 in: M. Yamauchi, Y. Hosoya (eds.),
Modern Japan's Place in World History,
https://doi.org/10.1007/978-981-19-9593-4_2

The original version of this chapter was inadvertently published with the following errors in figure captions, which have been corrected now as follows:

Fig. 2.1: "Toyotomi Hideyoshi's dispatch of troops to Korea (Bunroku War, 1592)" has been changed to "First Sino-Japanese War (1894–1895)".

Fig. 2.2: "The Korean War (1950–1953 Armistice)" has been changed to "Toyotomi Hideyoshi's dispatch of troops to Korea (Bunroku War, 1592)".

Fig. 2.3: "First Sino-Japanese War (1894–1895)" has been changed to "The Korean War (1950–1953 Armistice)".

The updated original version of this chapter can be found at
https://doi.org/10.1007/978-981-19-9593-4_2

Afterword

Japan's Modern History: A Reiwa Era Perspective—From the Malice of Herodotus to the Impartiality of Liu Zhiji

Masayuki Yamauchi
Institute for Global Affairs, Musashino University, Tokyo, Japan

The Structure of Change: History and Time

> Alas! how quicker far to mortals' ears
> Do ill news travel than the news of good! (from Plutarch's *Moralia* Plutarch 2000)

The year 2015 marked 70 years since the conclusion of World War II and Japan's defeat. The figure 70 years holds no special meaning in terms of contemplating history. And 2018 was 100 years since the end of World War I. The people of Japan may not intend to differentiate the two world wars, associating one with "bad news" and the other more with "good news." Yet, they have only a faint knowledge of World War I, whereas each of them is weighed down by an inability to forget completely the experience of having lost World War II.

The basic material of history is time. When we regard time as an issue in history, two "advances" or features are intimately connected with history. One is essential: the definition of a chronological starting point, a historical fact such as Japan's defeat (or the birth of Jesus, the Hegira, etc.), that seeks significance from the stream of political, diplomatic, societal, and cultural happenings. The other may carry meaning: the search for "periodization" (the creation of equal, measurable units of time, i.e.: the 24-h day, the 100-year century, etc.), to use the term coined by French historian Jacques Le Goff (2011), that constructively captures the passage of history with symbolical measurements, such as the figures "70 years" and "100 years" used above.

A periodization, such as 70 or 100 years since the war, gains greater validity in cases where it captures the time innate in history within the context of these advances. This is because the passage of time in history tends to be tied to some characteristic of that era, in some sense, to a predominant world view and "perceptions of history," not only to the memories of individuals. On that point, the time segments that elapsed in the 70 and 100 years after the 2 world wars express periodization in a different sense: the advent and development of pacifism and spirit of international cooperation that had failed under Taishō democracy, stemming from the start of a new *Nihon-koku*[1] and linked to the collapse of the Empire of Japan, which left a legacy and memories of loss both at home and abroad.

Turning our attention to world history, 2015 marked 100 years since the "Great Catastrophe" of the Armenian people at the hands of the Turkish (Ottoman) Empire during World War I. Claiming that the Turks slaughtered 1.5 million of their countrymen, the Armenians demand an apology and compensation from the people and government of the Republic of Turkey. Thus, it has given rise to a complex problem where the present-day politics and diplomacy of Turkey and Armenia are entangled with their differing perceptions of history, a situation not unlike the one in East Asia between Japan, China, and Korea. The Armenian people held a ceremony on April 24, 2015 in the capital, Yerevan, to mourn the victims of the genocide their people suffered. Russian President Vladimir Putin and French President François Hollande were in attendance.

Meanwhile, Turkey held a ceremony on April 25, a day after Armenia remembered its Great Catastrophe, to mourn the British and ANZAC (Australia and New Zealand) forces that gallantly fought and lost the final battle on the Gallipoli peninsula during World War I. In attendance were Britain's Prince Charles, Australian Prime Minister Tony Abbott, and New Zealand Prime Minister John Key. President Recep Tayyip Erdoğan scored a diplomatic victory by having the Commonwealth leaders participate in the memorial ceremony, offsetting Armenian criticism over the genocide issue. In September 2018, I had the opportunity to visit the Gallipoli shore where ANZAC troops came ashore amid heavy fighting. There, on the silent beaches, waves noiselessly crept up on the shore and quietly withdrew, as if casually reproaching us for our atrophying memories. Deeply moving are the words of Mustafa Kemal Atatürk, the Republic of Turkey's first president, visible on the memorial tablet on the seashore:

> *Those heroes that shed their blood and lost their lives... You are now lying in the soil of a friendly country. Therefore, rest in peace. There is no difference between the Johnnies and the Mehmets to us where they lie side by side here in this country of ours... You, the mothers, who sent their sons from far away countries, wipe away your tears; your sons are now lying in our bosom and are in peace. After having lost their lives on this land they have become our sons as well. (1934)*

---

[1] Japan's official name since 1947.

For Armenians, however, Atatürk is one of the men responsible for the Great Catastrophe. Words of condolence befitting the victims, foreign and domestic, of a fierce battle with the West are unacceptable to the descendants of the Armenians in Anatolia in the East whose fates were changed by force. The troubling thing is, the Turkish people today believe it is unwarranted that they are asked to take responsibility for an atrocity they never admitted actually took place.

How to evaluate periodizations such as 70 or 100 years varies according to the viewer's standpoint and angle of view—that is, does the viewer use it while remaining fixed on the past, or by gazing into the future, using it to sublate history, preserving yet changing it? That is the difficulty with perceptions of history. As you can appreciate by looking at Japan's relations with China and the Republic of Korea (ROK), perceptions of history do not simply concern the past. Above and beyond the past, perceptions of history are about the issues that mattered to the people living in those eras, and that being the case, these issues are an intricate, complex reflection of the conditions of those eras (Kimura 2014).

Issues of perceptions of history are not limited to pre-World War II issues such as war crimes and colonial rule, but include issues related to the treatment and interpretation of the postwar collapse of empire and decolonization. To rephrase my point, perceptions of history do not exist just because there is history. Indeed, there is no way for history to exist without first having a perception of history from a certain point of view.

I participated in a joint historical research project between Japan and China on the Nanjing Incident. The Japanese members, without bias or partiality, introduced various scholarly arguments with estimates for the number killed in the incident at 20,000 or 40,000 victims, but we decided to set an upper bound of 200,000. The Chinese participants, meanwhile, consistently determined that the victims numbered well over 300,000 and remained inflexible.

To continually remember and criticize only specific incidents is an effect of the way the flash of a perception of history illuminates only part of the subject, resulting in the same pattern of highlights and shadows. Not only does a diplomacy conscious of national unity and public opinion, with every change of political leadership, make ever stronger claims pertaining to those points illuminated by the flash, it can also make new allegations regarding areas where the light had not fallen. You might consider ROK President Moon Jae-in's perception of history to be an example of this phenomenon. Rather than a sound academic research of history, it is a mechanism, which makes the relationship between the victim's investigation and the perpetrator's responsibility constant, that begins self-movement.[2] What then becomes important is forcing your opponent to capitulate diplomatically on the basis of political arguments, not historical facts.

Meanwhile, the Chinese government and Chinese Communist Party have not even tried to acknowledge that Japan's achievements as a nation of peace in the 70 years postwar and the contribution of its Official Development Assistance (ODA)

---

[2] *Selbstbewegung.*

to China's prosperity are a humble expression of Japan's remorse and apology. As an aside, though it is estimated that 15 million Chinese starved to death during the Great Leap Forward (30 million according to some foreign demographic scholars) and another 4 million deaths and 100 million victims occurred under the Cultural Revolution, Chinese authorities have yet to publish any official figures. There are some estimates that 10,000 people died in Beijing and 20,000 died in other major cities during the Tiananmen Square Incident. The reason a country that withholds the facts and figures related to the sad fate of its own countrymen in history clearly shows the figures related to certain historic events such as the Nanjing Incident is because it considers history to be of a political nature, not historical fact.

A "1000-Year Grudge" and the Perfect Omelet

At a March 1, 2013 ceremony marking the March First Independence Movement, former President Park Geun-hye remarked, "The historic dynamic of one party being a perpetrator and the other party a victim will remain unchanged even after a thousand years have passed." Those obsessed with the study of history as a discipline about time would probably wish to inquire as to the starting point for this 1000-year history. Is it the Annexation of Korea in 1910 (Meiji 43)? Or does it start from this 2013 statement? Or was the span of 1000 years chosen based on feeling and conviction alone? Whatever the case may be, so long as the South Korean position seems like a 1000-year grudge, political and diplomatic negotiation and compromise are, for all intents and purposes, impossible, and no matter the efforts made to see eye-to-eye on perceptions of history, it will be nothing more than a superficial ceremony of reconciliation. On April 3, 2015, a senior ROK foreign ministry official reportedly said on the topic of the history issue with Japan, "shouldn't the one who caused offense apologize (to the victim) even if it is 100 times? The number (of apologies) doesn't matter" (Yonhap News 2015). However, when the administration changes, the next South Korean government will also inherit anti-Japanese popular sentiment and may not be satisfied with even 100 apologies. No doubt, it will say that 1000 or even 10,000 apologies are not enough.

South Korea is fixated on perceptions of history because it has seized on this historical framework of emphasizing the perpetrator's responsibility and apology rather than examining the historical facts with precision, wanting to reserve the right to employ this political/diplomatic tool against Japanese counterparts in the future. In fact, Moon Hee-sang, speaker of the ROK National Assembly, said February 7, 2019 that resolution of the comfort women issue would require an apology from Japanese Emperor Akihito, since Moon declared that he is "the son of the main culprit of war crimes." On the 11th, responding to Japanese criticism, he retorted, "Japan says that it has apologized dozens of times, but that's not true." Though President Moon Jae-in and Speaker Moon, both, are political rivals of former President Park Geun-hye, they have no differences insofar as it pertains to the position considering the perpetrator/victim relationship as unchanging.

Even if you can find relative meaning in a periodization of history and its significance, identifying an absolute truth is difficult, if not impossible. In 1967 when I was a second-year university student, the young generation was transfixed by special reports in all the magazines on the 50th anniversary of the Russian Revolution and was reading Isaac Deutscher's newly translated and published *The Unfinished Revolution: Russia 1917–1967*. In sharp contrast, the attitude of pundits and the media in Japan and the world (including Russia, no less) toward the Russian Revolution's centennial in 2017 could be summed up as largely disinterested. Put in stark terms, the reason for ignoring programs on the Russian Revolution's 100th anniversary, perhaps to forget its chronology justifying the Stalinist view of history, was because they caused people to remember the unsavory history that was completely out of step with the fundamental factors of history: liberty and progress.

Isaiah Berlin, a British political thinker, remarked: ". . . to make mankind just and happy and creative and harmonious forever—what could be too high a price to pay for that? To make such a [perfect] omelet, there is surely no limit to the number of eggs that should be broken—that was the fate of Lenin, of Trotsky, of Mao, and for all I know, of Pol Pot." If he had lived, Berlin surely would have added Kim Jong Un as well as his father and grandfather to this list (Berlin et al. 1993).

Any logic that can justify sacrificing people for the ideals of a revolution or state-building, like a chef infatuated with his own recipes, is unacceptable to modern citizens unless they are egotistical revolutionaries and ultranationalists. If there is an exception, it would have to be North Korea. The rule of three generations of the Kim family, blending Stalinism with Juche ideology, employs the periodization of the Juche calendar, which counts 1912 (the year of Kim Il Sung's birth) as year one, to carve out its own rhythm of history.

History surely does not move forward in a straight line. It zigs and zags, often through a process of trial and error. On New Year's Day 2012, Arabnews.com proclaimed that 2011, which begat the Arab Spring, was "the year that changed the world" and a "truly game-changing year" for the Arab people in the Middle East. It was also a year that brought people hopes out of "the darkness of a dying year." The news site predicted that in history, 2012 "promises to be anything but dull." However, it now seems as though the brutal civil wars that spread rampantly from Syria and Iraq to Libya and Egypt have shattered these expectations to make history. Nevertheless, the fact that Arab citizens destroyed their long-lived dictatorial and autocratic regimes is unlikely to lose its significance as a new historical point of departure.

Where Is the Starting Point for Japan 1.0?

You can find many misinterpretations in readings of modern history. One is the sadly mistaken impression that Japan has never had a national strategy and the Japanese lack strategic thinking. This prejudice remains quite pervasive among the Japanese public itself. Many of them innately dislike the word strategy (two characters in

Japanese: *senryaku*). I once served as the chairperson of a certain ministry's expert panel discussion on cultural strategy. On that occasion, someone argued that it was an inappropriate name for a cultural discussion because the first character, "sen," came from war (*sensō*) and the second, "ryaku," came from the word for invasion/ aggression (*shinryaku*). I was flabbergasted. Of course, the use of the term strategy is not limited to the military sphere.[3] The concept of strategy also refers to a variety of scenarios worked out by various organizations, such as government ministries, business corporations, and universities, to manage long-term plans and achieve certain goals for the future of a nation and its people. Edward Luttwak, an expert on strategies, argues that the Japanese people have never been bad at strategy building; rather, they have been at the forefront of employing a very advanced "strategy culture" (Luttwak and Okuyama 2018). Reviewing Japan's history of development through three phases—the Edo, Meiji, and post-World War II periods—he thinks the Japanese have kept a "perfect strategic system" in place for about 400 years while occasionally updating it as required.

In his book *Nihon 4.0*, he refers to the Edo period (1603–1867)—the early modern era of shogunate rule launched by Tokugawa Ieyasu (1543–1616)—as "Japan 1.0," or the starting point of Japan's peace and prosperity, not the Meiji Restoration of Imperial rule that marked the outset of the country's modernization. In this respect, I praise Luttwak for his historical acumen. In excavating and uncovering the foundations and bases for the lectures on the modern history of Japan, it is critical to identify the continuities between Japan's early modern and modern periods rather than simply emphasizing the breaks and changes.

Setting up a shogunate government in Edo (now Tokyo), Ieyasu imposed "gun control" nationwide to bring a complete end to a period of civil war waged by feudal warlords. He also successfully developed an Edo system, the best possible "alliance strategy" that led to the complete elimination of enemies by forcing *daimyo* feudal lords to follow a variety of acts of obedience set forth by the Tokugawa regime and enforcing rigid control over them. Truly, the first shogun was a "strategist of genius" who was well-versed in the logic of alliance formation. He restored peace and stability to Japan, which had been torn apart by conflict throughout the Warring States Period, then again by Toyotomi Hideyoshi's invasions of Korea (1592–1598). He built a composite state that consolidated the 270 domains under the central control of his shogunate.

We can be proud of this peaceful and stable Edo system, which remained in effect for nearly 300 years, a continuous period of peace and prosperity in world history that should be dubbed *Pax Tokugawa*. Visiting Dejima in 1775 (An'ei 4), Swedish natural historian Carl Thunberg found the shogunate system of government so intriguing, he advised his king to create such a system. If Gustav III, intrigued with the idea, had not been assassinated and been able to implement this system for

---

[3]The rest of this chapter's English translation borrows heavily from Yamauchi, Masayuki. 2018. "Rethink postwar system from view of past," The Japan News by *The Yomiuri Shimbun,* October 22, 2018, Edition S, p. 5.

controlling the *daimyo*, certainly "European history would have become a bit more interesting," as Donald Keene quipped (Keene 2000).

Luttwak's emphatic assessment of Tokugawa Ieyasu as one of the "highest-level strategists" is similar to my viewpoint on the first shogun. In the February 2018 issue of *Bungei Shunju* magazine, I appreciated Ieyasu for the all-around capability he had developed as a rare military politician. Ieyasu was, in my view, more successful as a ruler than Julius Caesar and Napoleon Bonaparte in terms of maintaining both prudence and boldness and losing neither appetite for knowledge nor originality, whether in war or peace or diplomacy. Ieyasu was not involved in bloody purges at home and did not feel compelled to undertake military adventures and aggression abroad, unlike Caesar, betrayed by friends and colleagues and dying violently, or Napoleon, who drove his own countrymen and countless other Europeans into despair and death. As strategists, Takeda Shingen (1521–1573), a *daimyo* who exiled his father and killed his first-born son, and Uesugi Kenshin (1530–1578), a *daimyo* who led his brothers into misfortune, could be comparable to Saladin (1138–1193), who led Muslim forces during the Third Crusade. But, in terms of competence, the three men do not even come close to Ieyasu, who realized a multidimensional and composite state that was based on the separation of the authority of the emperor and the power of the shogunate (Yamauchi 2018).

Emperor Akihito (the emperor of the Heisei era) abdicated on April 30, 2019 (Heisei 31) and the new emperor was enthroned May 1. "Reiwa," the name chosen for the new era, derives from a line in the preface to 32 poems about plum blossoms in the *Man'yōshū*, Japan's oldest poetry anthology: "In this <u>auspicious</u> (*rei*) month of early spring, the weather is fine and the wind <u>gentle</u> (*wa*). The plum blossoms open like powder before a mirror while the orchids give off the sweet scent of a sachet."[4]

The new emperor of the Reiwa Era will declare the 2020 Tokyo Olympics open.[5] There is also a chronology hidden within 2020: it is 420 years after the Battle of Sekigahara and the 430th year since Tokugawa Ieyasu made his triumphal entry into Edo on the auspicious *Hassaku* festival (August 1 in the old lunar calendar). After that event, the might of the Tokugawa shogunate grew the cold little village that was Edo into a major city with a million inhabitants in just a century. In comparison, London's population around the same period was 460,000, Paris' was 550,000 at the turn of the nineteenth century, and Berlin's was about 150,000. It was called *Ō-Edo*, an appellation evoking an image of prosperity for this enormous consumer city that was the country's administrative center. Ieyasu's urban planning and civil construction projects, such as land reclamation and water and sewerage systems, arguably built the foundations of modern Tokyo.

Moreover, Edo dominated the others with its good public safety and cutting-edge public sanitation. The leaders of the Meiji Restoration installed the new government in Edo because they had drawn up a 100-year plan to avoid bankruptcies and

---

[4] English translation taken from the April 1, 2019 Statement by Prime Minister Shinzo Abe, "In the New Era Name 'Reiwa', https://japan.kantei.go.jp/98_abe/statement/201904/_00001.html.
[5] On July 23, 2021—postponed a year by the COVID-19 epidemic.

unemployment in this enormous consumption area by converting daimyo residences into government offices to cut wasteful spending and establishing new administrative bureaucracies and corporate headquarters to enhance the functionality of the modern capital.

Pax Tokugawa and Japan 1.0

The Edo castle that Ieyasu built was turned as-is into the Imperial Palace, bestowing upon the citizens almost 430 years later an oasis of green tranquility at the heart of the capital. Also, through his creation of a stable country without war for 270 years under "Pax Tokugawa," Ieyasu had put an end to the chaos of Japan's Middle Ages that bred unrest and civil wars like the Ōnin War (1467–1477). So, we ought to credit Ieyasu's leadership for creating Japan's early modern era that, having fostered early-stage and proto-industrialization domestically, quietly prepared the country for its modern era, when it had to respond to pressures to open to foreign interaction and to the Industrial Revolution.

Ieyasu's achievements were at risk of being forgotten at the start of 2018, the 150th anniversary of the Meiji Restoration. A reappraisal of the abilities and talents of this man who built Japan's distinctive national system, constructing stable relationships between emperor and shogun, and imperial court and shogunate, underscores the historical significance of Emperor Akihito's abdication, the first in 200 years since the Emperor Kōkaku in the late Edo period. Ieyasu's true nature as a world-class politician has been distorted by the impression of him as an "old silver-haired badger," how he is portrayed in the *bunraku* puppet theater piece *Eight Battle Arrays to Protect Honjō Castle*.

Ieyasu's high caliber can be expressed using classical Greek poet Archilochus' parable, "The fox knows many things, but the hedgehog knows one big thing": Ieyasu's abilities comprised both aspects. Separated for life from his mother at age 3 and remaining a hostage of the *daimyo* Oda Nobuhide and Imagawa Yoshimoto from 6 to 18, his early life was full of hardships. Yet the richness of these experiences nourished a tactical precision and ability to conceptualize strategy necessary in a military commander and political leader. While sworn to serve Oda Nobunaga and Toyotomi Hideyoshi, Ieyasu concealed his hedgehog shrewdness and ingenuity and he learned various tricks and schemes like a fox, talents he cautiously hid. No matter how well he concealed his abilities, they were destined to be revealed, for as the saying goes, the drill will always poke through the bag. His victory at the Battle of Sekigahara (1600) and subsequent designation as *Seii Taishōgun* (1603)—the unifying great general—that occurred over 420 years ago must certainly be the moment his drill pierced through, putting his abilities on full display. Ieyasu's perseverance and decisiveness, which enabled him to transform ideals into reality, is epitomized by his resolve that "I, alone, should die by suicide to save the people," when allegedly Hideyoshi pressed him to come to Kyoto to become his vassal. By which he meant, if refraining from engaging Hideyoshi's forces would save many lives, Ieyasu would not balk at sacrificing himself. This type of long view is a necessary quality in executive leaders, past and present. It cannot be learned from experience only; it must be gained through a daily habit of reading philosophy and history diligently.

Though not endowed with anything special, Ieyasu was blessed with a literary training that would have enabled him to participate in poetry and prose contests. During the Siege of Osaka (1614–1615), hearing of a tufted *ashi* reed in a village nearby, he ordered that some be brought to him, but his grandson Ikeda Tadatsugu[6] offered an unsolicited commentary that the reeds in the area were not *ashi* but *ogi*, a different variety. Ieyasu immediately cautioned his grandson, asking if he knew of the saying "Naniwa's reeds are Ise's rushes" (Zeami).[7] How very like Ieyasu to chide nonchalantly while providing a key lesson: as a leader, you must learn that the names of things, customs, and mores all vary with the land (Hotta and Kawakami 1915, Vol. 14). While he was not fond of composing Chinese-style or Japanese *waka* and *renga* poetry unrelated to politics and military matters, Ieyasu enjoyed Confucianism, history, Chinese books on military science, the *Engi-Shiki* (a set of ancient Japanese governmental regulations), and *Azuma-kagami* (written chronicles of the Kamakura shogunate). He was not the writer Caesar was with his *Gallic Wars*, and he could not think up *bon mots* on the spot *a là* Napoleon.

Even so, Ieyasu knew enough to acquaint himself with science and knowledge so that he could overcome any political challenges by consulting with experts, a lesson that can also be found in the teachings of the *Al-Fakhri*, the Islamic treatise on governance. Around the time he made the *Kinchu narabini kuge shohatto*[8] which laid out his intentions toward the emperor's role in affairs of state, Ieyasu had copies made of all the books treasured and handed down by the imperial court and the nobles; many classic works and documents survive today, spared from fire, thanks to this undertaking. Even though he did not know of the teachings of Mu'awiya, the first caliph of the Umayyad Caliphate, who said "it is not good for a man who is king to delve too deeply in any given area of knowledge," Ieyasu was true to the knowledge and experiences of a ruler.

Unlike Hideyoshi, Ieyasu did not engage in superfluous construction of shrines and temples or spend on extravagances. While not miserly, he was tight with a budget. For his daily repasts, he made do with fish pickled in sake lees and *Hama-natto* (dried fermented soybeans). Compared to the Imperial Palace under Emperor Go-Yōzei and Emperor Go-Mizunoo, who enjoyed partaking of sake and red seabream starting in the morning, Ieyasu's meals were positively meager. In part thanks to such efforts, when Ieyasu retired to Sunpu, he left his son Hidetada, successor as shogun, a reserve of 30,000 pieces of gold and 13,000 *kan* of silver,

---

[6] One of his daughter's sons who was then the teenage lord of Okayama Castle.

[7] From the Noh drama *Ashigari* [*The Reed Cutter*] attributed to Zeami. *Naniwa no ashi wa Ise no hamaogi:* Naniwa is the former name for Osaka.

[8] A 1615 law that provided the grounds for the shogunate to regulate the imperial court and defined the relationship between the court and the shogunate.

in preparation for extraordinary expenses such as fires and natural disasters. In addition, he distributed money to the 3 branches of the Tokugawa family—300,000 *ryō* each to the Owari and Kii clans and 100,000 *ryō* to the Mito clan—from the roughly 3 million *ryō* in gold and silver of the wealth he brought with him to Sunpu, and further lent the 3 clans 230,000 *ryō*. Though the primary sources of his revenues were gold and silver mines and foreign trade, they say such wealth would not have been possible without Ieyasu's sense of economy and thrift (Ōno 1996).

Good luck is also indispensable for a leader to have. Ieyasu managed to do without having to dispatch any troops overseas, like Hideyoshi did in the Bunroku-Keichō War (1592–1598) (in Korean, the Imjin and Chongyu disturbances). His good fortune of getting by as military commander without any bloodshed lost fighting unjust wars, later allowed him to approach normalizing relations somewhat with China and Korea, ties of amity that Hideyoshi's invasions had interrupted, which led to favorable conditions and an established practice of Korean delegation visits to Japan. When Shō Nei, the King of Chūzan (Ryūkyū), who had been the Satsuma domain's captive, visited Ieyasu in Sunpu in 1610, he was carried in a palanquin as far as the *genkan* entryway, seated on the dais in the reception hall during the meeting, and was received courteously and hospitably as befits a monarch of a foreign country. Ieyasu's treatment of Shō Nei was probably based in part on his accurate understanding of East Asian political dynamics and his strategic conception of the Ryūkyū as well as the Yi dynasty in Korea as being points of contact with the Ming dynasty. Ieyasu, as a leader, had learned in just proportion the saying of Lao-Tse: He who knows he has enough is always content.

Ieyasu left us with the following saying: "The government of the country should use a pestle to clean a *jūbako*." Just as a pestle, a rather thick implement, cannot reach into the square corners of a tiered box for serving meals to clean them, the national government should only address the big picture, not nitpick or get too strictly involved in the details (Higurashi et al. 2011). He apparently was also fond of Ban Chao's biography in the imperial annals section of the history, *Book of Later Han*: "Fish do not live in water that is too clean." The sentiment, suggesting that to use a man, you should take his strengths and set aside his weaknesses, is one that aptly expresses Ieyasu's broad outlook.

In fact, there are few of the sort of politician in history who excelled at employing talented people as much as Ieyasu—wealthy merchants and engravers; lower ranking samurai from subsidiary clans not employed as immediate retainers of the shogun; court nobles separated from Kyoto; descendants of prestigious military families. The surprising thing is he made two foreigners part of his entourage: William Adams (Miura Anjin), a Briton, and Jan Joosten, a Dutchman (the Yaesu area of Tokyo Station is named after him). "Not understanding a man's worth is entirely because one's own intellect is in doubt. Anyone unable to make use of talented and wise men serves no purpose; you must not discuss matters of state with him" (Hotta and Kawakami 1915, vol. 18). There are many lessons to learn from Ieyasu's admonition for the people of Reiwa Japan who will experience the enthronement of a new emperor and the Tokyo Olympics.

A Century After World War I: Japan 2.0 Totters

However, Tokugawa Ieyasu's descendants failed to keep "Japan 1.0" in a good state of repair, and the Edo system he built had to give way to "Japan 2.0," as described by Luttwak, an era of modernization and industrialization under the Meiji Restoration that followed the arrival of the US Commodore Matthew C. Perry's black ships and foreign pressure to open the country to trade and diplomacy. Later, the country entered the "Japan 3.0" phase following its defeat in 1945, the postwar era of high economic growth. As such, it can be said that Japan has managed to maintain and develop its statehood while choosing the most suitable systems and alliances, depending upon the circumstances prevailing in each given period.

As 2018 marks the 100th anniversary of the end of World War I, I think we are in a relevant position to look back at the collapse of the Japan 2.0 phase and the start of the Japan 3.0 phase. Our findings will become good historical grounds for thinking about what kind of new strategy and system should be developed to cope with East Asia's nuclear missile crisis, a situation the Japanese have never encountered before.

During World War I, Japan failed to learn two things of strategic importance—the need to convert from coal to oil as the new mainstay fuel for the military and industrial sectors and the concept of energy security. This failure was greatly responsible for the eventual dysfunction of the Japan 2.0 phase. In 1912, Winston Churchill, who was then the First Lord of the British Admiralty, said the Royal Navy warships that switched to oil fuels were able to sharply improve speed and range of action. The same was true for merchant vessels adopting the innovative fuel conversion. Churchill told the British Parliament in 1913 that ". . .on no one country, on no one route, and on no one field must we be dependent. Safety and certainty in oil lie in variety, and variety alone." This insightful remark points to the essence of a strategy that is applicable to Japan, a country that does not produce oil, especially in terms of ensuring energy supplies from diverse and multiple sources.

In contrast, during World War I, Japan only made the world aware of its weakness: its oil supply and demand characteristics placed it in a vulnerable position compared to the other two major naval powers of the day, the United States and Britain. As many academic experts have already pointed out, as of 1940—the year before Japan went to war with the United States, Britain, and their allies—Japan's annual output of crude oil stood at 330,000 kL, far below its annual consumption of 4.6 million kiloliters. This means that Japan had to rely on imports for about 92% of its oil needs. Further, the country relied on the United States, the largest of its potential enemies, for 81% of its crude oil imports. The decision to go to war with the United States without overcoming the paradoxical energy-related pitfall is the most symbolic of the strategy failures of the Japan 2.0 phase. In related developments, even long after the end of World War II, the country's strategic vulnerability became clear to people in Japan and abroad as the two oil crises of the 1970s shook the foundation of the Japanese economy, then in the Japan 3.0 phase.

During World War I (1914–1918), the Japanese public had only a faint awareness that their country was in a state of war. Therefore, almost no atmosphere of tension permeated the Japanese population—the men in military uniform and the people at large—in a way that would have impressed upon them a life-or-death lesson about energy security. While making few sacrifices, Japan seized Germany's Pacific territories north of the Equator, islands that came under Japanese control after the war as League of Nations mandated territories. In China, Japan had Britain, France, and Russia agree to its temporary takeover of German concessions in the Shandong Peninsula. Thus, Japan succeeded in improving the balance of power against the United States in the Asia-Pacific region for the time being.

Additionally, the Japanese economy began booming in the second half of 1915, the second year of the war, heralding a period of unprecedented economic expansion as Japanese exports dominated the Asian market, where European goods virtually vanished. In particular, Japan's mining, shipbuilding, and trading companies prospered so tremendously that many firms in these three leading industries offered extraordinarily high dividend yields of 50% or even 70% per annum, making many people rich overnight. According to statistician Nakamura Takafusa (1925–2013), who taught at the University of Tokyo, and other scholars, the value of gold reserves held by the Japanese government and the Bank of Japan surged from about 340 million yen to about 1.59 billion yen over an 18-year period from 1914. The accumulation of sovereign wealth transformed Japan from a debtor country before the war, with external debt amounting to as much as about 1.1 billion yen, to a creditor country with external financial assets worth nearly 2.8 billion yen as of 1920 (Nakamura 2012). Japan's development of heavy and chemical industries turned an agricultural country into an industrial one. While Japan enjoyed a feeling of optimism that ignored the realities of the war, there was unexpectedly one personage from abroad who harbored a sense of crisis over the vacillating future of the country: King George V.

Japanese society appeared in the British monarch's eyes to be under the illusion that peace had been restored largely without casualties. Japan's crown prince had set out in March 1921, 5 years before his enthronement as the Emperor Shōwa, on a 6-month tour of Europe, visiting Britain first. So, the king recommended that his Japanese guest make a study tour of World War I battlefields on the European continent filled with the memories of disastrous battles. The crown prince visited Ypres, Belgium and sent a telegram to King George V in June 1921 with his reactions upon seeing the site of one of the war's fiercest battles: "As Your Majesty told me, the scene in front of me acutely reminded me of what Your Majesty mentioned as 'ghastly bloodshed on the battlefield of Ypres' and I was immensely moved and prayed devoutly" (Kunaichō 2015). When he decided 24 years later to accept the Potsdam Declaration, which demanded Japan's unconditional surrender in World War II, it is said that the ghastliness of the European battlefield he visited was present in his mind. His August 1945 strategic decision to make a declaration of surrender on his own should be interpreted to mean his determination to bear the blame alone.

I would like to cite a case of strategic failure within the Imperial Japanese Navy dating back to the latter stage of World War I. In February 1917, Japan, complying with a British request based on the Anglo-Japanese Alliance (1902), dispatched a naval flotilla, the Second Special Squadron, to the Mediterranean to protect Allied shipping from German U-boats. The flotilla, comprising a cruiser and eight destroyers and joined by four vessels later in the mission, carried out anti-submarine escort duties along the Mediterranean sea lanes connecting Malta and Alexandria, Egypt, among other Allied ports. Until its mission was over in 1919, the Japanese squadron escorted a total of 788 Allied vessels and about 700,000 troops and rescued a total of 7075 crew members from Allied vessels torpedoed by enemy U-boats (Hirama 1998). Japan lost 78 members of the squadron, including crew from the destroyer *Sakaki*, all of whom remain buried in Malta.

However, the Imperial Japanese Navy ignored a series of precious lessons the special squadron learned during its Mediterranean escort operations. The naval leadership should have fully realized the importance of destroying merchant shipping with the tactic of unrestricted submarine warfare, as Germany had employed in the Mediterranean. It also should have learned of the need for new technologies to fight enemy submarines trying to disrupt sea lanes or impose blockades and the importance of new tactics in sub-versus-sub clashes. Nonetheless, about a quarter of a century later during the Pacific War, the Imperial Japanese Navy did not have commercial ships to turn into a defensively armed merchant navy nor did it adopt convoy operations—and thus the US Navy easily and catastrophically destroyed Japan's merchant shipping. "If you want to predict the future, you should look at the past." Political philosopher Niccolo Machiavelli's persuasive admonition from his *Discourses* can be applied to Japan's barren personnel system that did not produce an insightful politician, an Ieyasu-like strategist, a failing that is one of the causes of its defeat.

Japan 3.0: After the Empire's Fall and Dissolution

The same is true for Japan's defeat in the war and the dissolution of its empire. There are apparently still people in Japan who feel it intolerable that Japan—after having missed out on opportunities in the era of Great Power expansion, when Britain, France and other Europeans used the Opium War and the Arrow War to colonize China and Asia—is the only one to get criticized for belatedly adopting this Western logic.

That way of thinking is gravely mistaken, however. Those who assess that Japan waged war against Britain and the United States to promote the independence of the West's colonies in Asia do not comprehend the historical postwar trend to dismantle all empires. If anything, the Japanese sense of defeat is linked to the positive significance of having been the first country to experience the collapse of its empire, without any say in the matter. While the British Empire officially came out victorious in the war, it bears the responsibility, in history at least, for the Partition of India and the independence of India and Pakistan (1947) that resulted in 1 million deaths and 11 million displaced, refugees forced to flee their homes and wander the Indian subcontinent. Soon after Egyptian President Gamal Abdel Nasser nationalized the

Suez Canal in 1956, Britain and France started an unjustified war (Suez Crisis) that brought their empires crashing down around themselves as if, to borrow an expression from Jan Morris, "a developing neurosis, erupting into a moment of schizophrenia, had subsided once again, this time for ever, leaving behind some shattered nerve or atrophy" (Morris et al. 2010).

Sadder still is the whole account of how France, lagging Britain in sorting out its imperial legacy, poorly handled the wars of independence in Indochina and Algeria. France suffered roughly 94,000 war fatalities in its 8-year war in Indochina and retreated from its African colonial empire after expending 29,000 lives in Algeria. Even if Japan had kept its empire and held on to its interests in Manchukuo, it is highly likely that, just as the French colonist *Pieds-Noirs* of Algeria called themselves Algerians and depended on the local occupation army yet came to rebel against Paris's authority, there would have been a group of Japanese residents in China calling themselves Manchurians who joined the Kwantung Army and brought the banner of insurrection to Tokyo. It might have led to Tokyo experiencing the intermittent violence and terrorism that happens in London and Paris, both for having induced revolutions of the Chinese and Korean people as well as for the Japanese response to those revolutions and the after-effects of that response. The era of empire and colonial rule had ended.

Starting with the Manchurian Incident in September 1931 (Shōwa 6) and ending in August 1945 (Shōwa 20), Japan's war of aggression and administration on the continent as well as its colonial rule and military governments in other Asian countries spawned a great tragedy that frequently resulted in the deaths of average citizens. We cannot speak as though there were no atrocities committed in China and Southeast Asia during the war. We must not permit "unfacts," to borrow George Orwell's term. MacGregor Knox's point (though inspired by historical revisionist Karel van Wolferen)[9] that "even the immense defeats of 1931–1945 have failed to give the Japanese state the steering and brakes needed to ward off future collisions" (Murray et al. 2019) is nothing but sheer misrepresentation of history.

Examples abound of historical depictions of foreign people and lands that are not only unfavorable or unfair but steeped in malice; they are not limited to how Japan is treated in some parts of East Asia today. In fact, there is a school of thought that regards *The Histories* that Herodotus wrote in ancient Greece in fifth century BCE as a vicious pack of lies. Plutarch, in his essay "On the Malice of Herodotus," lists eight points characterizing how Herodotus portrayed history with ill intent (Plutarch 2013).

First is the willful use of harsh or odious terms and expressions when relating an event. There are many authors today whose forte is employing the sort of characterization that Plutarch reproves, such as "fanatical," "impulsive," and "mad." Second is the method of making excursions and digressions from the main narrative, inserting an out-of-place development into the account, a topic unrelated to the point under discussion, so as to purposefully emphasize a person's foolishness or

---

[9] https://nationalinterest.org/article/no-brakes-no-compass-1239.

insincerity. Third is to omit outstanding accomplishments and laudable deeds. To take pleasure in finding fault not only runs counter to impartiality, in Plutarch's judgment, it is all the more unjust and malicious.

Fourth, when there are two or more possible interpretations of an incident, is to select the worst. A historian must assert such things as he knows to be true and ignore those matters that are uncertain and not worthy of belief. Fifth, when an event's cause and intent is unknown, is to embrace hostility and malice and come up with conjectures that do not merit believing. Many writers have no scruples resorting to insinuations and calumnies to undermine the praise of the achievements and deeds of other people and countries, manifesting in envy and maliciousness of the highest degree. Sixth is to attribute the successful exploits of others to money or Fortune rather than to bravery or ingenuity, a tendency that seeks to diminish the greatness and beauty of the achievements. Seventh is to spread calumnies obliquely, as if shooting slanderous arrows out of corners, and then stop suddenly to profess wonder at why anyone would believe such lies, conduct that is nothing but cowardly and despicable. Eighth is to intermix some praises with reproaches into one's writing.

All of these points are richly suggested in the idiosyncrasies of parts of East Asia concerning Japan's modern history. What is necessary for a proper perception of history in East Asia? Even if realizing an ideal perception of history is impossible, at least it is possible for Japanese, and the points that must be confirmed in principle are not that difficult. First and foremost, as we all have strengths and weaknesses, is to make efforts to praise each other's strengths and be accepting of and magnanimous concerning our weaknesses. Chinese historian and historiographer Liu Zhiji's teachings, spanning 13 centuries of space and time, still ring true in the ears of his readers today:

> Long ago, some lords vied for power and the outcome of their struggle was not clear. The historians of that time always wrote their accounts, commending the good points of the adversary's country while not keeping secret their own country's bad points. In recent times, however, we hardly ever hear of historians who write impartial or objective accounts. Instead, they brag about their own country's outstanding points and find fault with other countries' inferior aspects (Liu and Nishiwaki 1989).

Bibliography: For Further Reading

Rongo (Analects). Kanaya, Osamu (trans). 1999. Iwanami Bunko. [English translation of Analects 3:21 from Muller, Arthur Charles (trans). http://www.acmuller.net/con-dao/analects.html#div-4]

Berlin, Isaiah and Jahanbegloo, Ramin. Kawai, Hidekazu (trans). 1993. *Aru shisoshika no kaiso: Aizaia barin tono taiwa* (Conversations with Isaiah Berlin). Misuzu Shobō.

Higurashi, Masa et al (trans). 2011. *Hon'ami gyōjōki* (Hon'ami Kōetsu: A Biography). Tokyo: Heibonsha.

Hirama, Yōichi. 1998. *Daiichiji sekai taisen to nihon kaigun: gaikō to gunji to no rensetsu* (World War I and the Imperial Japanese Navy: Relations between Military Operations and Diplomacy). Tokyo : Keio University Press.

Hotta, Shōzō and Kawakami, Tasuke (eds). 1915. *Tōshōgū gojitsuki furoku* (History of Tokugawa Ieyasu, Ancillary Documents). Tokyo: Kokushi kenkyūkai.

Keene, Donald. 2000. "Sekai no naka no nihon (Japan in the World)" in Maruyama, Yasunari (eds). *Nagasaki kaidō: sakokuka no ibunka jōhōro* (The Nagasaki Kaidō: the Information Route for Foreign Culture in Japan's Period of National Isolation). Tokyo: NHK Shuppan.

Kimura, Kan. 2014. *Nikkan rekishi ninshiki mondai to wa nani ka: rekishi kyōkasho, "ianfu", popyurizumu* (What the Historical Dispute between Japan and South Korea is: history textbooks, "comfort women," and populism), Kyoto: Minerva Shobo. [Published in English as: Kimura, Kan. Speed, Marie (trans). 2019. *The Burden of the Past: Problems of Historical Perception in Japan-Korea Relations*. Ann Arbor: University of Michigan Press.]

Kunaichō. 2015. *Shōwa ten'nō jitsuroku. 3* (The Annals of Emperor Shōwa [Vol. 3]). Tokyo: Tokyoshoseki.

Le Goff, Jacques. Tachikawa, Kōichi (trans). 2011. *Rekishi to kioku shinsōban* (History and Memory [special edition]). Tokyo: Hōsei University Press. [English translation from preface xx *ad passim* of Le Goff, Jacques. Rendall, Steven and Claman, Elizabeth (trans). 1992. *History and Memory*. New York: Columbia University Press.]

Liu, Zhiji. Nishiwaki, Tsuneki (trans). 1989. *Shitsū naihen maki kyokuhitsu* (*Shitong Neipian: Qubi* [Historiography, Inner Chapters: Distorting facts to hide the truth]). Tokyo: Tōkai University Press.

Luttwak, Edward. Okuyama, Masashi (trans). 2018. *Nihon yontenzero: kokka senryaku no atarashii riaru* (Japan 4.0—The New Reality of National Strategy). Tokyo: Bungei Shinsho.

Morris, Jan. Ike, Hiroaki and Mukuda, Naoko (trans). 2010. *Teikoku no rakujitsu: pakkusu buritanika kanketsuhen. 003.* (Farewell the Trumpets) Tokyo: Kōdansha.

Murray, Williamson; Knox, MacGregor; Bernstein, Alvin H. (eds). Ishizu, Tomoyuki and Nagasue, Satoshi (trans). 2019. *Senryaku no keisei: shihaisha kokka sensō 1* (The Making of Strategy: Rulers, States, and War). Tokyo: Chikuma Shobō. [English from p. 644 of Murray, Williamson; Knox, MacGregor; Bernstein, Alvin H. (eds). 1996. The Making of Strategy: Rulers, States, and War. Cambridge: Cambridge University Press.]

Nakamura, Takafusa. 2012. *Shōwashi jōgekan* (A History of the Shōwa Period, Volumes I and II [1926–1945; 1945–1989]). Tokyo: Tōyō Keizai Shinpōsha.

Ōno, Mizuo. 1996. *Edo Bakufu zaisei shiron* (The Finances of the Edo Shogunate: A Historical Treatise). Tokyo: Yoshikawa Kōbunkan.

Plutarch. Totsuka, Shichirō (trans). 2000. *Moraria dai 6kan* (Moralia [Book 6]). Kyoto: Kyoto University Press. [English translation: Shilleto, Arthur Richard. 1898. "On Curiosity, § VI." in Plutarch's Morals: Ethical Essays. London: George Bell and Sons. Referenced from Project Gutenberg https://www.gutenberg.org/files/2363 9/23639-h/23639-h.htm#Page_238a]

Plutarch. Itō, Teruo (trans). 2013. *Moraria dai 10kan* (Moralia [Book 10]). Kyoto: Kyoto University Press. [English translation informed by "On the Malice of Herodotus" in Essays and Miscellanies, The Complete Works Volume 3. Referenced from Project Gutenberg https://www.gutenberg.org/files/3052/3052-h/3052-h.htm#link2H_4_0163]

Yamauchi, Masayuki. 2018. *"Shōgun no seiki" dai 2kai* (Era of the Shogun) in *Bungei Shunju*, February.

Yonhap News. 2015. As cited by Kyodo News (Seoul Bureau), accessed at https://www.shikoku-np.co.jp/national/international/20150403000493.

Zeami. Ashigari (The Reed Cutter).

Chronology of Key Events

Year	Events
Keio 4 (1868)	Boshin War (through 1869)
	Charter Oath (Oath of Five Articles)
	First year of Meiji
Meiji 4 (1871)	*Han* domains abolished, Prefectures established
	Sino-Japanese Treaty of Amity
	Iwakura Mission dispatched (through 1873)
Meiji 5 (1872)	Ryūkyū domain established (status settled in 1879 establishment of Okinawa Prefecture)
	Japan adopts Gregorian calendar: 3 December 1872 becomes 1 January 1873 (Meiji 6)
1874	Taiwan Expedition
1876	Japan-Korea Treaty of Amity (Treaty of Ganghwa)
	Edict abolishing the wearing of swords in Japan (*Haitōrei*)
1881	Hokkaido Development Commission property sales scandal
	Political Crisis of 1881 (Meiji 14)
	Imperial Rescript calling for national assembly to be established
1882	Imo Incident
1884	Gapsin Coup (ends with Tianjin Convention)
1889	11 February: Constitution of the Empire of Japan (Meiji Constitution) promulgated
1890	Imperial Diet opens
1891	Tsesarevich Nicholas II visits Japan, Ōtsu Incident
1894	First Sino-Japanese War (through 1895)
1895	Treaty of Shimonoseki, Japan begins colonization of Taiwan
	Triple Intervention
1900	Boxer Rebellion (through 1901 Beijing Protocol)
1902	Anglo-Japanese Alliance
1903	Fifth National Industrial Exhibition in Osaka ("Anthropological Pavilion")

(continued)

© The Author(s) 2023

M. Yamauchi, Y. Hosoya (eds.), *Modern Japan's Place in World History*,
https://doi.org/10.1007/978-981-19-9593-4

Year	Events
1904	Russo-Japanese War (through 1905)
	Anglo-French Entente
	(First) Japan–Korea Protocol of August 1904
1905	Treaty of Portsmouth
	Hibiya riots (Hibiya incendiary incident)
	Beijing Treaty of 1905 (Treaty and Additional Agreement between Japan and China relating to Manchuria)
1907	Anglo-Russian Entente, Triple Entente (UK/Russia/France) established
1908	Takahira-Root Agreement
1910	High Treason Incident (through 1911)
	August: Japan's Annexation of Korea
1911	[China] Xinhai Revolution (Republic of China established 1912)
1914	World War I (through 1918)
1915	January: Japan presents China its Twenty-One Demands
	9 May: Yuan Shikai government accepts them (Day of National Humiliation)
1918	Japan joins Siberia intervention (withdraws its troops in 1922)
1919	Paris Peace Conference, Treaty of Versailles (League of Nation Covenant)
	1 March: Manse Demonstration (Korean Sam-il Independence Movement)
	[China] May Fourth Movement
1921	Washington Conference (through 1922: Nine-Power Treaty, Washington Naval Treaty)
1925	[China] 30 May Incident
	[Europe] Locarno Treaties
1927	Shandong Expedition (through 1928)
1928	Sainan Incident
	Zhang Zuolin assassinated (a Certain Important Incident in Manchuria)
	Pact of Paris (Kellogg-Briand Pact)
1929	Great Depression (1930–1932 Shōwa Depression)
1930	Japan lifts gold embargo
	First London Naval Conference
	Prime Minister Hamaguchi Osachi shot by assassin (dies 1931)
1931	Wanpaoshan Incident
	September: Liutiao Lake Incident, Manchurian Incident (through 1933 Tanggu Truce agreement)
	October Incident
1932	Sakuradamon Incident
	(First) Shanghai Incident
	Manchukuo established
	15 May Incident (Prime Minister Inukai assassinated)
1933	[Germany] Hitler regime established
	March: Japan announces its withdrawal from League of Nations
1935	Second London Naval Conference (through 1936)

(continued)

Year	Events
1936	Spanish Civil War
	Japan's Fundamentals of National Policy
	Japanese-German Anti-Comintern Pact
	[China] Xi'an Incident
1937	July: Marco Polo Bridge Incident, Second Sino-Japanese War starts
	August: Second Shanghai Incident (Battle of Shanghai)
	December: Nanjing Incident
1939	August: Soviet-German treaty of non-aggression (Molotov–Ribbentrop Pact)
	September: Invasion of Poland, World War II starts
1940	Tripartite Pact (Japan-Germany-Italy alliance)
1941	April: Japanese-Soviet Neutrality Pact
	July: Japan occupies southern French Indochina; its US assets are frozen
	September: "Guidelines for Implementing the Imperial National Policy"
	November: Hull Note
	December: Pacific War starts (through 1945)
1943	[US/UK/China] Cairo Declaration
1945	August: Japan accepts the Potsdam Declaration
	September: Japan signs instrument of surrender, start of GHQ occupation policies
1946	Tokyo Trials (through 1948)
	3 November: Constitution of Japan promulgated (enters effect May 3, 1947)
1949	People's Republic of China founded
1950	Korea War (through 1953 Armistice Agreement)
1951	(Peace) Treaty of San Francisco and Japan-US Security Treaty signed (effective 1952)
1955	Asian-African Conference (Bandung Conference)
	1955 System established in Japan
1956	Suez Canal Crisis
1964	Vietnam War intensifies (through 1975)
1965	Treaty on Basic Relations Between Japan and the Republic of Korea
1972	Reversion of Okinawa
	Japan-China Joint Communiqué; normalization of Japan-China relations
1973	First oil crisis (through 1974)
1975	First meeting of leaders of advanced industrialized nations (G-6 Summit)
1978	Japan-China Treaty of Peace and Friendship
	[China] Reform and Opening begins
1982	First history textbook issue
1985	Prime Minister Nakasone makes official visit to Yasukuni Shrine
1989	[Germany] Fall of the Berlin Wall
	[US-USSR] leaders meet in Malta, declare end of the Cold War
1991	(First) Gulf War
1992	Emperor Akihito (emperor of the Heisei era) visits China
1995	Murayama Statement
1997	Asian Financial Crisis
2001	9/11 terrorist attacks
2011	Great Eastern Japan Earthquake

Index

© The Author(s) 2023
M. Yamauchi, Y. Hosoya (eds.), *Modern Japan's Place in World History*,
https://doi.org/10.1007/978-981-19-9593-4

Printed in Great Britain
by Amazon

43959509R00130